VOCATIONAL CURRICULUM FOR DEVELOPMENTALLY DISABLED PERSONS

D1197354

VOCATIONAL CURRICULUM FOR DEVELOPMENTALLY DISABLED PERSONS

by

Paul Wehman, Ph.D.
Programs in Mental Retardation
School of Education
Virginia Commonwealth University

and

Phillip J. McLaughlin, Ed.D.
Division for the Education of Exceptional Children
College of Education
The University of Georgia

with contribution by
W. Grant Revell, Jr., M.S.,
Lawrence J. Kriloff, M.S., and
Michelle Donnelly Sarkees, Ed.D.

University Park Press
Baltimore

UNIVERSITY PARK PRESS
International Publishers in Science, Medicine, and Education
233 East Redwood Street
Baltimore, Maryland 21202

Copyright © 1980 by University Park Press

Composed by University Park Press, Typesetting Division.
Manufactured in the United States of America by
The Maple Press Company.

All rights, including that of translation into other languages, reserved.
Photomechanical reproduction (photocopy, microcopy) of this book or
parts thereof without special permission of the publisher is prohibited.

LC4812
W44

Library of Congress Cataloging Data

Wehman, Paul.
Vocational curriculum for developmentally disabled persons.

Bibliography: p.
1. Handicapped—Education—United States.
2. Vocational education—United
States. I. McLaughlin, Phillip J., joint author. II. Title.
LC4812.W44   371.9'28   79-16433
ISBN 0-8391-1512-1

CONTENTS

THE AUTHORS

Paul Wehman, Ph.D.
Programs in Mental
  Retardation
School of Education
Virginia Commonwealth
  University
Richmond, Virginia 23284

Lawrence J. Kriloff, M.S.
Richmond Career Education
  Center
Richmond Public Schools
Richmond, Virginia 23219

Phillip J. McLaughlin, Ed.D.
Division for the Education of
  Exceptional Children
College of Education
The University of Georgia
Athens, Georgia 30602

W. Grant Revell, Jr., M.S.
Department of Rehabilitative
  Services
4901 Fitzhugh Avenue
Richmond, Virginia 23230

Michelle Donnelly Sarkees, Ed.D.
Division of Vocational Education
College of Education
The University of Georgia
Athens, Georgia 30602

FIGURES

TABLES

PREFACE

This book was written as an outgrowth of our work with public school secondary programs in Georgia and adult activity center programs in Virginia. Although based primarily on experiences with moderately, severely, and profoundly developmentally disabled individuals, the curriculum has utility with mildly handicapped clients as well. The text reflects the authors' philosophy that developmentally disabled persons are capable of productive sheltered work or successful competitive employment.

This book has two major purposes. The primary objective is to provide a vocational curriculum for teachers in special education and vocational education, practitioners in adult activity centers, and supervisors in sheltered workshop facilities. The curriculum provides a cross-section of task-analyzed vocational skills and teaching procedures that have been systematically field tested with a population of moderately and severely developmentally disabled students in a public school program. The second purpose of this text is to present information on three important areas in vocational habilitation of developmentally disabled individuals. These include: 1) sheltered workshop training techniques, including illustrative case studies; 2) competitive employment placement, training, and advocacy techniques, including illustrative case studies; and 3) traditional and alternative methods of vocational evaluation.

The first section of this book is an overview of vocational habilitation of developmentally disabled individuals. This information provides an empirical basis for understanding how to implement the curriculum. Following the initial four chapters, the curriculum itself is provided. It is divided into seven subdomains: core skills, domestic skills, food service skills, home industry skills, horticulture skills, janitorial skills, and office / clerical skills.

The text concludes with an annotated bibliography of selected vocational programming references.

ACKNOWLEDGMENTS

There are a number of individuals we would like to thank for their help in the preparation of this text. First, the curriculum portion of the book would not have been written without the support of the Northeast Georgia Cooperative Educational Service Agency (CESA). Ms. Gloria Frankum, Director of Special Education/Georgia Learning Resources System of Northeast Georgia CESA, had the insight to see the need for such a vocational curriculum project. We also used Ms. Frankum's idea of a set of core skills undergirding the various vocational skills in the development of the curriculum. The approval and support that Mr. Lyndol Cain, Director of Northeast Georgia CESA, gave to this project are also acknowledged.

The staff of Bostwick School was instrumental in helping us write the vocational curriculum. The teachers participated in selecting appropriate vocational skills and developed most of the teaching procedures. The teachers were also responsible for field testing the task analyses and teaching procedures. For their contributions we would like to thank Ms. Mary Margaret Bagwell, Ms. Susan Hardee, Ms. Sandra Jolly, Ms. Donna Martin, Ms. Beth Richardson, and Ms. Mary Jean Wilson. Also, we acknowledge the administrative aid of Ms. Martha Stewart, Special Education Coordinator of Bostwick School for Northeast Georgia CESA.

Special thanks go to Mr. Greg Beitzel, Director of Henrico County, Virginia, Adult Activity Center, and Mr. Steve Winner, Director of Chesterfield County, Virginia, Adult Activity Center, for many of the initial task analyses they provided.

The first author would like to gratefully acknowledge the positive influence and stimulation that Adelle Renzaglia of the University of Virginia has provided. Our vocational research and work together have significantly shaped my perspective on vocational training of severely disabled persons.

The chapter on vocational evaluation was written by a rehabilitation counselor, a rehabilitation evaluation specialist, and a special needs vocational educator. These professionals represent the type of experts who daily interact with, plan for, and evaluate and place developmentally disabled clients. Chapter 4 is a valuable addition, and we very much appreciate the contribution of W. Grant Revell, Jr., Lawrence J. Kriloff, and Michelle Donnelly Sarkees.

We are also grateful to Ms. Sheila Myers for her extraordinary typing skills and aid in seeing to a variety of details in preparation of this text.

VOCATIONAL CURRICULUM FOR DEVELOPMENTALLY DISABLED PERSONS

VOCATIONAL PROGRAMMING
State of the Art

State and federal agencies in education, rehabilitation, labor, and mental health continue to devote more and more attention to vocational and occupational education for developmentally disabled persons. This has been demonstrated through the allocation of numerous grants and funds for direct client service programs, model demonstration projects, research, and personnel preparation. In fact, a recent U.S. Department of Health, Education, and Welfare booklet, *Federal Assistance Guide for Vocational and Career Education for the Handicapped* (Bureau of Education for the Handicapped, 1979), lists as many as 24 sources of funds for vocational and career education. Preparing developmentally disabled students for the world of work and rehabilitating disabled adults has clearly become a top priority in the United States.

The development of several positive trends can be attributed to the availability of these funds. First is the increase in the number of professionals trained in vocational programming for developmentally disabled individuals. More colleges and universities are establishing preservice and inservice training programs in this area. Second, as a result of recent legislation (e.g., Vocational Amendment, PL 95-482; Education for All Handicapped Children Act, PL 94-142; and the Comprehensive Developmental Disabilities and Rehabilitation Amendments of 1978) mandating program services for *all* developmentally disabled persons, more disabled clients than ever before are receiving services. Third, research and demonstration projects, too numerous to list here, are providing a wealth of knowledge about the vocational capabilities of developmentally disabled persons. Many of these projects have developed specialized training techniques, evaluation systems that are increasingly sensitive to the needs of severely disabled clients, and job placement programs that demonstrate competitive employment potential of disabled individuals. Admittedly, we have much to learn in each of these three major areas of vocational programming. However, major advances have been made, and replication of selected model programs has begun in many parts of the country.

This chapter summarizes the authors' perception of vocational programming for developmentally disabled individuals as it currently exists. For purposes of organization, the chapter has been divided into two parts: 1) what we already know and what seems to be in common practice, and 2) what we need to know and how we need to improve vocational programming.

VOCATIONAL PROGRAMMING: CURRENT KNOWLEDGE

A review of the available research and demonstration projects offers a means of assessing what we currently know about vocational programming of developmentally disabled individuals. The discussion below focuses on *training techniques, curriculum content and job selection, evaluation techniques,* and *placement.*

Training Techniques

The literature is rich with examples of how developmentally disabled persons can *acquire* complex skills and *perform* them at acceptable rates. As an illustration, the Specialized Training Program (see Bellamy, 1976), based at the University of Oregon, has empirically demonstrated the efficiency and effectiveness of operant stimulus control, shaping, and chaining techniques with profoundly retarded individuals (IQ < 20) on a variety of difficult industrial assembly tasks (e.g., assembly of a cam switcher). This program has clearly established the viability of severely developmentally disabled clients in workshop settings.

Gold (1972, 1974, 1976) has also demonstrated the utility of operant training techniques for severely handicapped persons in assembly of a bicycle brake. Similarly, Karan, Wehman, Renzaglia, and Schutz (1976) have provided empirical support for the improvement of workshop performance of severely developmentally disabled persons, who have never worked before, through specialized instruction.

There are numerous other projects and research reports that have investigated vocational training for the developmentally disabled, but the above-mentioned programs suffice to highlight the following conclusions:

1. The difficulty of the task should not impede the selection of a job for a trainee. Although, as a general rule, it may take longer to train a lower

functioning individual with a high rate of interfering behaviors, there appear to be very few manual assembly jobs that a physically able retarded person cannot do (Gold, 1976; Bellamy, Horner, and Inman, 1979).

2. Detailed breakdown in a task analysis and systematic chaining of components are critical, especially with severely and profoundly retarded persons (Bellamy, Horner, and Inman, 1979).

3. Size discriminations are made more easily by matching a very large item with the standard size item. Reinforcement of correct responses will then facilitate a reduction in the number of errors. Fading the size of the large item until reaching the target discrimination size must be done gradually (Gold and Barclay, 1973; Irvin, 1976).

4. Color coding items will help retarded trainees *orient* to the salient or most critical parts of a task. For example, one step of a ball-point pen assembly task is putting the spring over the top of the metal insert. Coloring the top of this insert will help reduce repeated errors (Gold, 1972).

5. Massed practice (many trials) may increase the rate at which a skill is learned; it may also increase the production rate of workers who are consistently off task (Wehman, Schutz, Renzaglia, and Karan, 1977).

6. Positive reinforcement in the form of verbal praise, trainer proximity, graphs, tokens, pennies, edibles, or adjacent peer attention are positive influences on rate of learning and in accelerating production rates (Karan, Wehman, Renzaglia, and Schutz, 1976). Setting easily obtainable production goals and then gradually increasing the criterion for reinforcement is an effective shaping technique.

Curriculum Content and Job Selection

Developmentally disabled students need to acquire *generalized* work skills; that is, learning only one, two, or three specific tasks can severely limit employment opportunities. First, the type of employment available will depend directly on economic conditions of, as well as type of industry in, the local area. Having skill in more than one job area, e.g., having both domestic and clerical abilities, will make the individual more marketable. Second, if the student learns how to respond in a variety of job situations and, more importantly, that all jobs require certain behaviors, such as being on time and staying on task, the likelihood of long term employment and advancement will be enhanced.

Job selection should be the result of several factors. These include the individual's preference, his or her home living situation and financial situation, and individual physical, social, and intellectual capabilities. The selection process also very much depends on a careful analysis of the requirements of the work environment.

The following points seem indicated by the work to date in the area of vocational curriculum content:

1. A vocational curriculum must be functional and multifaceted. Skills must have utility in more than one area of instruction. For example, teaching horticultural skills, i.e., plant care, will also be functional for leisure skills education and can be functional in language targets such as function of object use ("Show me what you do with the water sprinkler") or verbal labeling ("What is this?" — teacher points to plant).
2. Vocational skills should be taught in each of the different subdomains suggested in the latter part of this book. Although not all skills need be taught, some within each subdomain should be made available for instruction.
3. Students will learn best if presented with skills from the different subdomains that are consistent with their motor and language functioning level. The core skills in the curriculum will facilitate this assessment.
4. A detailed analysis of work environments, similar to the job analysis done by Belmore and Brown (1977) of a dishwasher position, must be part of the basis for job selection.

Vocational Evaluation

Use of traditional psychometric testing measures has characterized the evaluation of developmentally disabled clients by rehabilitation specialists. The merits and limitations of these evaluation systems are discussed in depth in Chapter 4. However, two points, evident in the assessment/evaluation process with developmentally disabled individuals, warrant mention here:

1. There is virtually no test that can demonstrate the work potential of a developmentally disabled client as well as a continuous and direct measurement of performance during training can. Many trainees, especially the severely handicapped, will show their abilities only after initial training under optimal reinforcement conditions.
2. Behavioral assessment measures provide more objective data on rate of learning by recording number of trials to criterion for each step in a task analysis and by tracking performance rate over time. Charting and graphing of work behavior, particularly when data are recorded daily, often reveal trainee improvement, improvement that in some instances might go undetected until a later date.

Placement

Job placement requires the careful attention of the teachers, counselors, and other vocational practitioners who work with the developmentally disabled. Competitive employment placement of moderately and severely mentally retarded and cerebral palsied persons is difficult, and in many communities the service is almost nonexistent. Yet competitive employment placement is an excellent vocational goal toward which to strive because of the potential for greater remuneration and integration with nonhandicapped co-workers.

Unfortunately the amount of research literature relevant to the long term competitive employment of developmentally disabled workers, especially those with moderate and severe retardation and severe cerebral palsy, is sparse. There have been some noteworthy demonstration projects in Washington, Illinois, Nebraska, and Virginia, however, and the following conclusions can be made partly on the basis of results from these projects:

1. Independent living skills and success in competitive employment cannot be separated. The inability to adequately perform the former leads to problems in acquiring and maintaining a job in the community (Schalock and Harper, 1978).
2. Client advocacy plays a critical role in persuading employers to provide administrative support for job-training programs and placement efforts (Wehman and Hill, 1979).
3. Certain vocational subdomains, such as food service, janitorial, and domestic skills, are well suited as initial employment areas for developmentally disabled individuals. As a good work record is developed and maintained, other more advanced jobs may be considered.
4. The initial 2 weeks to 3 months of employment will be the most difficult for developmentally disabled workers. The adjustment process from unemployment to a full 40-hour work week for a retarded adult usually requires special support from employers or from a counselor who is regularly available.
5. There appears to be a substantial number of severely disabled persons who have been excluded from rehabilitative services, yet who, with training and advocacy, could succeed in sheltered and/or competitive employment.

The points listed above are not meant to oversimplify the current state of knowledge in the field of vocational habilitation. Clearly, other information is also important. However, these points are particularly salient in vocational habilitation of the developmentally disabled.

VOCATIONAL PROGRAMMING: WHAT WE NEED TO KNOW

Training Techniques

The most important aspects of training techniques for which knowledge is lacking concern workshop supervision and management strategies. Some of this information involves issues of specific training technology. For example, questions about efficiency of supervisor management strategies and conduciveness of workshop environmental arrangements must be resolved. Consideration needs to be directed to the following:

1. Improving production rates to standard is always a goal of any industrial unit. Although reinforcement is certainly a demonstrated means of increasing work rates, the most efficient way for a supervisor with, for example, 50 disabled workers and 2 aides to maintain a standard performance rate is not yet clear. Pairing high and low rate workers, refining the development of client-administered reinforcement, planning room arrangement, and setting goals are among the strategies that merit closer attention.
2. Many practitioners are unclear as to the efficiency of forward versus backward chaining. The former technique involves repeated practice on the initial step(s) in the task analysis with guidance on the remainder of steps, whereas backward chaining commences with work on the final step(s). Researchers must investigate which of these training techniques is most efficient.
3. Establishing sheltered enclaves within private sector factories and industry is another service delivery model that requires further attention. Training techniques similar to those listed above can be employed, but in a less restrictive setting. This is a laudable goal; yet it can only be attained when point 1, that of increased production rates, becomes a reality for most developmentally disabled workers.

Curriculum Content and Job Selection

Systematic analysis of job environment and of client abilities is critical to making an appropriate match. The need for the generation of increased numbers of vocational skills for instructional purposes is probably not as important as determining which student should be matched with which job and with which employer. The following areas need further attention:

1. Job requirements need to be specified behaviorally across a variety of jobs. All aspects of a job, including unique features of the work environment, must be described. Belmore and Brown (1977) have provided this

type of in-depth inventory for a dishwasher position in a drugstore. This type of analysis needs to be made available for many more jobs.

2. With this information, teachers must be taught to write instructional objectives and to program for skills that are consistent with these inventories of job requirements. One of the most inefficient uses of instructional time is skill development in areas in which no jobs exist in the community.

3. Field testing and empirical validation of vocational skill sequences, in many more job domains than are listed in this text, are required. A careful analysis of the behaviors required in different vocational skills must be undertaken. This will facilitate logical ordering of skills from easy to more difficult.

4. More attention must be given to the development and maintenance of critical nonvocational social behaviors, such as going on a job interview, telling time, using public transportation, using a telephone, operating a vending machine, and so on. Although isolated examples of these programs are available, few have been offered in the community (natural) environments (i.e., outside of a classroom or center). Independent living skill curricula must also be developed.

Vocational Evaluation

The initial assessment and ongoing evaluation of client progress is a continual issue that must be addressed. Service agencies are "under the gun" to demonstrate the value of their work; improving the employability of developmentally disabled individuals is a major step in the appropriate direction. In the earlier section on vocational evaluation it was noted that continuous data collection provides more information on the success of a client. Listed below are areas in need of further investigation:

1. The relationship between vocational rehabilitation counselors, vocational educators, and special educators in conducting vocational evaluation needs to be refined. Systematic ways to establish cooperative and complementary roles need to be investigated. The U.S. Office of Education and the Rehabilitation Services Administration have an interagency agreement to implement such cooperative efforts; however, how to effectively and efficiently get the job done at the local level remains to be determined (Razeghi and Davis, 1979).

2. The validity and reliability of traditional vocational evaluation tests with severely disabled clients need to be determined. For example, most commercial laboratory work samples have not been standardized on this population. This lack of standardization greatly minimizes the usefulness of these evaluation devices with severely disabled clients.

Placement

Job placement and postemployment follow-up of developmentally disabled persons are a current priority in vocational rehabilitation. This is supported in other programs, e.g., the Comprehensive Employment Training Act (CETA), which also stress employment of handicapped individuals as an important goal. There are several milestones, however, toward which we must work. These include:

1. Identifying in more detail, and not only through mail survey, the characteristics of employers willing to hire disabled individuals; this also includes developing strategies to overcome employer reluctance to have "too many" disabled workers even though the client(s) may be doing an excellent job.
2. Identifying which types of businesses and organizations are best suited to employment of disabled persons; this also involves investigating salient co-worker characteristics (e.g., similar or different race, sex, age, and previous disability) to facilitate optimal matching for placement within a supportive work environment. We suspect that this is a *major factor* because of the inclination of positively biased co-workers to "cover" for disabled workers.
3. Identifying which disability groups and family support systems, e.g., group home or single-parent family, require the most postemployment follow-up and counseling.
4. The advancement of disabled workers, currently employed, into more challenging jobs. There are many developmentally disabled individuals who are *underemployed* and should receive greater job opportunities.
5. Development of professional and/or advocacy support systems for disabled workers who initially are placed in competitive employment. The tremendous caseload carried by most rehabilitation counselors would seem to indicate that other agencies will have to help shoulder this burden. However, our experience suggests that without this type of initial support many developmentally disabled individuals will be unable to maintain their job in competitive employment.

CONCLUDING REMARKS

The one issue that has not been addressed throughout this chapter but that potentially places the greatest limitation on our vocational knowledge today involves the lag in information flow to practitioners. We have learned a great deal about training disabled workers in difficult manual assembly tasks; similarly, given the necessary support staff, we know how to accelerate production rates. Less information is available about long term placement. Unfortunately, most of the current knowledge is not in practice in public school secondary programs, sheltered workshops, and adult activity and developmental centers. Making pot holders and stringing beads remain prevalent in many programs. These activities are a result of a philosophy, the advocates of which do not view developmentally disabled individuals as capable of productive sheltered work or successful competitive employment.

This type of protective philosophy is extremely limiting to the lives and potential development of disabled clients. The only way to overcome this problem is to expose practitioners to current information and then provide intensive inservice training and skill building. Short 1-day workshops, journal articles, and textbooks will usually not be adequate; instead, practicum experiences with professionals familiar with behavioral training technology are necessary.

This book provides information helpful in these types of inservice efforts. The next three chapters involve sheltered workshop training, competitive employment job placement, and vocational evaluation. The balance of the text is devoted to vocational curriculum content, which includes objectives, task analyses, materials, and, with selected skills, special teaching procedures. The book concludes with an annotated bibliography of selected vocational programming literature for further reference.

REFERENCES

Bellamy, G. T. (ed.). 1976. Habilitation of Severely and Profoundly Retarded Adults. Center on Human Development, University of Oregon, Eugene.
Bellamy, G. T., Horner, R., and Inman, D. 1979. Vocational Habilitation of Severely Retarded Adults: A Direct Service Technology. University Park Press, Baltimore.
Belmore, K., and Brown, L. A. 1977. A job inventory strategy for severely handicapped students. *In* N. Haring and D. Bricker (eds.), Teaching the Severely Handicapped, Vol. III. Special Press, Columbus, Oh.
Bureau of Education for the Handicapped. 1979. Federal Assistance Guide for Vocational and Career Education for the Handicapped. U.S. Department of Health, Education, and Welfare, Office of Education, Washington, D.C.
Gold, M. W. 1972. Stimulus factors in skill training of the retarded on a complex assembly task: Acquisition, transfer, and retention. Am. J. Ment. Defic. 76:517–526.
Gold, M. W. 1974. Redundant cue removal in skill training for the mildly and moderately retarded. Educ. Train. Ment. Retard. 9:5–8.
Gold, M. W. 1976. Task analysis: A statement and an example using acquisition and production of a complex assembly task by the retarded blind. Except. Child. 43: 78–84.
Gold, M. W., and Barclay, C. 1973. The learning of difficult visual discriminations by the moderately and severely retarded. Ment. Retard. 11:9–11.
Irvin, L. K. 1976. General utility of easy-to-hard discrimination training procedures with the severely retarded. Educ. Train. Ment. Retard. 11:247–250.

Karan, O. C., Wehman, P., Renzaglia, A., and Schutz, R. (eds.). 1976. Habilitation Practices with the Severely Developmentally Disabled. University of Wisconsin Rehabilitation Research and Training Center, Madison.

Razeghi, J. A., and Davis, S. 1979. Federal mandates for the handicapped: Vocational education opportunity and employment. Except. Child. 45:353–359.

Schalock, R., and Harper, R. 1978. Placement from community-based mental retardation programs: How well do clients do? Am. J. Ment. Defic. 83:240–247.

Wehman, P., and Hill, J. W. (eds.). 1979. Vocational Training and Placement: Project Employability. School of Education, Virginia Commonwealth University, Richmond.

Wehman, P., Schutz, R., Renzaglia, A., and Karan, O. C. 1977. The use of positive practice training in work adjustment of two profoundly retarded adolescents. Vocat. Eval. Work Adjust. Bull. 10(3).

2

DEVELOPMENT AND IMPLEMENTATION OF A SHELTERED WORKSHOP PROGRAM

For many disabled individuals sheltered work is a terminal vocational placement. This may constitute a sheltered enclave in industry, a sheltered workshop, or an adult activity center that provides work adjustment services. It has become increasingly clear that most developmentally disabled individuals are capable of acquiring sheltered workshop skills (e.g., Bellamy, Horner, and Inman, 1979).

There is research evidence available to suggest that developmentally disabled clients can be effective workers on complex manual tasks (Gold and Barclay, 1973; Bellamy, Peterson, and Close, 1975). Several researchers have investigated the viability of presenting severely handicapped workers with complex tasks, such as putting together a drill machine (Crosson, 1969) or bicycle brakes (Gold, 1976). In the Crosson (1969) study, a 16-step task analysis was used to teach severely retarded adolescents how to put a drill machine together. With a task analysis approach a behavior is divided into smaller increments and presented in a logical sequential chain. Difficult learning discriminations are made easier as positive reinforcement is delivered for successful responses. Brown and his associates have also used a task analysis approach successfully in studying the effects that different reinforcement contingencies have on rate of production with moderately and severely retarded adolescents (Brown, Bellamy, Perlmutter, Sackowitz, and Sontag, 1972; Brown, Perlmutter, Van Deventer, Jones, and Sontag, 1972).

Much of the work reported in this chapter was completed in conjunction with Adelle Renzaglia, Paul Bates, Dick Schutz, and Orv Karan. The authors are indebted to them for their support.

Gold provided a series of research studies demonstrating the effectiveness of moderately to severely retarded clients on complex work tasks (1973b). Through the use of errorless learning, or easy-to-hard discriminations, moderately to severely retarded adults were trained to put together a 15-piece bicycle brake (Gold, 1972). In the same report, subjects demonstrated successful transfer of training by putting together a 24-piece bicycle brake. A 1-year follow-up study indicated significant retention effects by clients.

Through use of an easy-to-hard method of errorless learning, it was also shown that moderately to severely retarded clients were able to make discriminations between different bolt lengths as fine as 1/8 inch (Gold and Barclay, 1973; Irvin, 1976). Gold (1973a) also has reported the successful performance of 20 moderate to severely retarded clients in putting together a 14-piece coaster brake. An important finding of this study was a nonsignificant statistical relationship between IQ and production rate of clients participating in the program. This is in direct conflict with earlier reports, which supported the notion of higher IQs leading to greater production rates in severely retarded clients (Tobias and Gorelick, 1963).

FACTORS TO CONSIDER IN
SHELTERED WORKSHOP PROGRAM DEVELOPMENT

Physical Setting

Location is a critical factor in the successful implementation of a program. Church basements and YMCAs are not acceptable sites for a sheltered workshop program because they are not normal work sites. This type of setting can lead to serious problems with staff and client morale.

The ideal work location is one based in the community that is well lighted and provides ample space and ventilation. There should be a breakroom, and restrooms should have necessary supports for nonambulatory clients.

Task Selection

Identification of the appropriate tasks in the workshop is also important. The following considerations are necessary:

Is the task *simple* or *complex?*
Does the task require *fine* motor or *gross* motor skills?
Are raw materials expensive or inexpensive?
Is the task arts and crafts, ''make work,'' or contract work?

The issue of "make work," subcontract work, or arts and crafts is one that is a continual problem when initiating a workshop program. Subcontract or contract work, which results in pay, may be ideal for adults in an all-day workshop; on the other hand, some public school programs or developmental centers for retarded adults may find it more advisable to utilize "make work" tasks, which provide some opportunity for work training along with self-care, language, and social skill instruction. The biggest problem with simulated work is that staff and clients frequently find it too artificial and lose interest in the program. The taking apart of a completed job may be time consuming and demoralizing.

Teacher Behaviors

In addition to the physical location and tasks that comprise the workshop curriculum, teacher and trainee behaviors will influence the success of the program. Teacher behaviors include the type of instructions provided, frequency and number of prompts and reinforcers, use of prosthetic devices (jigs), special coding of parts, and task analysis, i.e., the logical breakdown of a skill into small steps. Because teacher behaviors and arrangement of the work environment are so important, training strategies are discussed in more detail in a later section of this chapter entitled "Instructional Techniques."

Trainee Behaviors

Client work behavior may be subdivided into learning a skill (acquisition) and then performing it accurately (production) at a rate high enough to meet competitive employment production standards. These two areas can be analyzed closely through a more specific description of an individual's behavior as it relates to workshop performance.

Acquisition Problem: Discrimination Deficits   A typical problem of many retarded workshop clients is a failure to attend to the salient cues (size, color, form) of a task. Relevant variables are ignored; instead, the person may try to assemble or sort materials without watching what he or she does or while attending to the wrong cue in the task. As Gold (1973b) notes, this is a main obstacle for the mentally retarded in acquiring complex manual skills. Gold (1972) has found that retarded learners can master a difficult job at a rate similar to that of nonretarded peers when they attend to relevant dimensions.

Acquisition can also be impeded through a client's failure to attend to the verbal cues of the supervisor. Characteristic of severely handicapped adults are noncompliant behavior and an inability or unwillingness to follow simple instructions. Even though a worker may attend to the learning task, if he or she does not follow instructions, acquisition rate may be impaired. This is particularly true if job requirements or materials vary, even slightly, from day to day.

Acquisition Problem: Sensorimotor Deficits   Many developmentally disabled persons receiving vocational programming services also display sensorimotor deficits. Cerebral palsy, loss of limb, and spasticity or athetosis may be present, thus requiring prostheses or specially arranged environmental support.

Certain clients may be visually handicapped or suffer a hearing loss, thus prohibiting the use of standard training procedures. The rare combination of both aural and visual handicaps in retarded workers is perhaps the most difficult disability to overcome for the acquisition of complex work skills. Yet some trainers have found that such disabilities need not impede learning progress on difficult tasks, such as bicycle brake assembly (Gold, 1976).

Low Production: Slow Motor Behavior   Once a vocational task is mastered, high rate performance then becomes important. This is a serious problem with many severely and profoundly retarded workers, particularly those with a long history of institutionalization. Slow motor behavior is one characteristic of developmentally disabled workers who have not been required to meet a work criterion for success. Clients may be persistent and stay on task, but their actual motor movements are lethargic and at far too low a rate to enable entrance into competitive employment. Often such clients are unresponsive to many of the commonly used workshop incentives such as praise or money. Without objectively established work criteria, it is difficult for workshop supervisors to determine which clients are performing competitively. Workers who stay on task and do not disrupt workshop routine are viewed as performing adequately. This is based on a popular vocational training model of ''work activity or keep busy'' rather than a model that seeks to expand the work skill repertoire of clients.

Low Production: Interfering Behaviors   Equally problematical in accelerating production rates with the severely and profoundly retarded is the presence of interfering or competing behaviors. High levels of distractibility and hyperactivity, out-of-seat behavior, excessive looking around, bizarre noises, and playing with the task represent competing behaviors that preclude the development of appropriate vocational skills.

Similarly, the work performance of developmentally disabled clients may be highly susceptible to changes in the work environment. Fairly commonplace alterations in the work setting or routine can upset client work behavior, thus making continuity of programming difficult. Many individuals may display criterion level work rates but only for short durations of time.

BEHAVIORAL ASSESSMENT IN SHELTERED WORKSHOPS

The data collected on each client's performance provide the basis for program decision making and modification. Data serve as the means of evaluating both the progress of each client and the effectiveness of instructional techniques. The types of data listed below may be collected:

1. *Number of steps acquired independently in task analysis for each target objective.* This involves keeping a record of the number of steps in a task analysis that a client completes independently. It provides a sensitive evaluation of client progress.
2. *Amount of teacher assistance required.* The number of verbal prompts required in each training situation can also be recorded for a more specific analysis of teacher behaviors.
3. *Number of trials to criterion.* The number of training trials until the skill(s) is acquired is a third source of data that may be used to evaluate client progress.
4. *Number of minutes required to complete task (duration) or number of units completed in selected time period (rate).* These measures provide a valid indication of the client's performance in vocational and independent living instructional situations. Rate assessments are computed by dividing the total number of units completed by the total number of minutes the individual worked.
5. *Pretest-posttest gains in the Prevocational Assessment and Curriculum Guide (Mithaug, Mar, and Stewart, 1978).* This guide offers a standardized index of behavior change in clients, and is, in the authors' opinion, the leading test for developmentally disabled clients being evaluated for work. Table 2.1 provides a copy of this checklist.

INSTRUCTIONAL TECHNIQUES

In this section, training strategies are described according to the type of training problems discussed above. Table 2.2 provides a hierarchy of intervention techniques that may be employed. Case studies are provided in the latter half of this chapter to illustrate these techniques.

Acquisition Problem: Discrimination Deficits

The most frequently employed training method is the use of verbal instruction. Many times a new task will be acquired with only a verbal explanation. This should logically be the initial method used to train a new task. If

Table 2.1. Prevocational Assessment and Curriculum Guide

Rank	Does Your Client:	Yes/No
	I. Worker Behavior	

1. Participate in work environments for 6-hour periods? _____
2. Move safely about shop by:
   a. Walking from place to place? _____
   b. Identifying and avoiding dangerous areas? _____
   c. Wearing safe work clothing? _____
3. Work continuously at a job station for 1–2-hour periods? _____
4. Learn new tasks when supervisor explains by modeling? _____
5. Come to work on an average of 5 times per week? _____
6. Correct work on task after the second correction? _____
7. Leave job station inappropriately no more than 1–2 times per day? _____
8. Want to work for money/sense of accomplishment? _____
9. Display or engage in major disruptive behavior no more than 1–2 times per week? _____
10. Understand work routine by not displaying disruptive behavior during routine program changes? _____
11. Continue to work without disruptions when:
    a. Supervisor is observing? _____
    b. Fellow worker is observing? _____
    c. Stranger is observing? _____
12. Display or engage in minor disruptive behavior no more than 1–2 times per week? _____
13. Adapt to new work environment with normal levels of:
    a. Productivity in 1–5 days? _____
    b. Contacts with supervisors in 30–60 minutes? _____
14. Complete repetitive tasks involving 1 step at 95% accuracy? _____
15. Work alone without disruptions for 15-minute periods with no contacts from supervisor? _____
16. Deviate from shop rules no more than 1–2 times per week? _____
17. Work at job station with no more than 1–2 work disruptions per day? _____
18. Work in a group situation and increase production:
    a. When supervisor asks to work faster? _____
    b. When supervisor asks to produce more than previously? _____
    c. When supervisor asks to complete work by specified time? _____
19. Learn a new 1-step job to minimum proficiency in 0–15 minutes? _____
20. Work alone without disruptions for 30-minute periods with 1–2 contacts from supervisor? _____
21. Work alone and increase production:
    a. When supervisor asks to work faster? _____
    b. When supervisor asks to produce more than previously? _____
    c. When supervisor asks to complete work by specified time? _____

II.   Social/Communication Skills

22. Communicate basic needs such as thirst, hunger, sickness, pain, toileting conditions? _____
23. Communicate basic needs receptively by means of:
    a. Verbal expression? _____

(continued)

Table 2.1. *(continued)*

Rank	Does Your Client:	Yes/No

II. Social/Communication Skills (Cont'd)

    b. Gestures?   _____

24. Communicate basic needs expressively by means of:
    a. Verbal expression?   _____
    b. Gestures?   _____

25. Respond to instruction requiring immediate compliance within 0–30 seconds?   _____

26. Respond appropriately to safety signals given:
    a. Verbally?   _____
    b. Through signs?   _____
    c. Through signals?   _____

27. Initiate contact with supervisor when:
    a. Cannot do job?   _____
    b. Runs out of materials?   _____
    c. Finishes job?   _____
    d. Feels too sick/tired to work?   _____
    e. Needs drink/restroom?   _____
    f. Makes mistake?   _____

28. Initiate contact inappropriately with strangers no more than 1–2 times per day?   _____

29. Respond appropriately to social contacts on one out of two occasions?   _____

III. Self-Help/Grooming Skills

30. Maintain proper grooming by:
    a. Dressing appropriately for work?   _____
    b. Dressing appropriately after using restroom?   _____
    c. Cleaning self before coming to work?   _____
    d. Cleaning self after using the restroom?   _____
    e. Cleaning self after eating lunch?   _____
    f. Eating food appropriately at lunch?   _____
    g. Displaying proper table manners at lunch?   _____

31. Reach place of work by means of:
    a. Company-sponsored vehicle?   _____
    b. Own arrangement?   _____

32. Maintain personal hygiene by:
    a. Shaving regularly?   _____
    b. Keeping teeth clean?   _____
    c. Keeping hair combed?   _____
    d. Keeping nails clean?   _____
    e. Using deodorant?   _____

33. Eat lunch independently with no assistance in:
    a. Getting lunch sack/container?   _____
    b. Getting food out of container?   _____
    c. Pouring liquid into cup/glass?   _____
    d. Putting food back into container?   _____
    e. Putting food container away?   _____

34. Take care of toileting needs independently with no accidents per month?   _____

From Mithaug, Mar, and Stewart, 1978; reprinted by permission.

Table 2.2.   A logically arranged hierarchy of procedures for alleviating work problems

---

I.   Acquisition or Learning Problem: Discrimination Deficits
  1.   Provide verbal instructions.
  2.   Pair modeling with verbal instructions.
  3.   Use verbal and physical guidance.
  4.   Break task down into simpler steps
       (easy-to-hard seqence), and repeat
       steps 1–3.
  5.   Use cue redundancy or stimulus fading,
       depending on task.
  6.   Steps 1–5 are always accompanied
       by positive reinforcement for
       correct responding.

II. Acquisition or Learning Problem: Sensorimotor Deficits (assess handicap
     to be sure there is a physical problem)
   A.   Poor motor coordination
     1.   Provide verbal instructions.
     2.   Pair modeling with verbal instruction.
     3.   Use verbal and physical guidance.
     4.   Break task down into simpler steps
          (easy-to-hard sequence), and repeat
          steps 1–3.
     5.   Provide prosthetic device or physical support.
     6.   Use cue redundancy or stimulus fading.
     7.   Same as step 6, above.
   B.   Visual handicap
     1.   Provide detailed verbal instructions.
     2.   Use physical guidance and verbal instructions.
     3.   Provide tactile cue redundancy, and repeat steps
          1 and 2.
   C.   Aural handicap
     1.   Use gestural instructions.
     2.   Provide physical guidance.
     3.   Break task down into simpler steps
          (easy-to-hard sequence), and repeat
          steps 1 and 2.
     4.   Use cue redundancy or stimulus fading,
          depending on task.
   D.   Deafness-Blindness
     1.   Provide physical guidance.
     2.   Use tactile cue redundancy.

III. Low Production: Slow Motor Behavior
  1.   Provide verbal prompt (e.g., "Work faster").
  2.   Pair modeling with verbal prompts.
  3.   Provide physical prompt (paired with verbal).
  4.   Establish reinforcer proximity.
    a.   Pennies present.
    b.   Back-up also present.

(continued)

Table 2.2. *(continued)*

5. Increase frequency of receiving pennies.
6. Increase number of pennies and/or back-ups given.
7. Increase frequency of redemption of pennies.
8. Use verbal reprimand plus no reinforcement.
9. Use response cost procedure.
10. Use isolation avoidance procedure.
11. Provide positive practice.
12. Present aversive stimuli.

IV. Low Production: Interfering or Excessive Behaviors (representative classes include a) nonfunctional competing behaviors, b) bizarre noises, c) out-of-seat, d) aggression toward objects, e) aggression toward people)

1. Verbally reprimand and prompt.
2. Verbally reprimand and physically prompt.
3. Establish reinforcement proximity (pennies, then back-up).
4. Increase frequency of receiving reinforcement (pennies).
5. Increase number of pennies and/or back-up given.
6. Increase frequency of redemption of pennies.
7. Use response cost procedure.
8. Restrain.
9. Provide overcorrection and positive practice.
10. Use isolation avoidance procedure.
11. Present aversive stimuli.

unsuccessful, a trainer can then attempt to teach a task through the use of alternative methods.

Illustrations of these supplementary measures include verbal instructions paired with modeling of the correct movements (Bellamy, Peterson, and Close, 1975), priming of the response, and physical guidance (Williams, 1967). Breaking down a task into small measurable components (task analysis) is also an effective technique for aiding acquisition (Crosson, 1969; Gold, 1976), as is the method of presenting learning material in an easy-to-hard sequence (Gold and Barclay, 1973). In the case of clients who fail to attend to relevant cues or task dimensions, the use of cue redundancy (e.g., color-coded parts) facilitates acquisition (Gold, 1974).

Acquisition Problem: Sensorimotor Deficits

In meeting the needs of clients with sensorimotor deficits, each client's physical capacity must be the first consideration. In the case of poor motor coordination due to cerebral palsy or loss of limb, the first four suggested strategies in the hierarchy do not differ from those used with clients whose acquisition problems are the result of discrimination deficits. However, if the client's physical limitations are extensive, the arrangement of materials or the use of prosthetic devices, such as specially designed jigs, may be a crucial factor in the acquisition of vocational skills. It may be necessary for a trainer to modify the task so that clients will be able to complete a task with the least effort and most speed.

Low Production: Slow Motor Behavior

As clients become more proficient at performance of a task, increasing the rate of production to competitive employment standards becomes a focal point. The severely developmentally disabled must produce at a competitive level in order to obtain and maintain community workshop employment. The use of a verbal prompt to "work faster" appears to be the least time consuming and most efficient technique, provided that it is effective (Bellamy et al., 1975). Peer modeling (Kliebhahn, 1967; Brown and Pearce, 1970; Kazdin, 1971) and trainer modeling have also facilitated an increase in production rate.

The manipulation of reinforcing events provides another extensive area of possible techniques. Strengthening reinforcer proximity, increasing the frequency or the amount of reinforcement, and increasing the number of redemptions of token reinforcers in a work period have all been demonstrated as viable techniques for improving production rates (e.g., Schroeder, 1972). Furthermore, the use of mixed schedules of reinforcement, such as continuous social reinforcement for each unit completed, and penny or token reinforcement for every 10 units completed, can be extremely effective in altering production rates.

However, if the problem of low production rates still persists, it may be necessary to provide aversive consequences. Once a trainer has established a level of expectancy or a minimum criterion for production rate, the use of aversive consequences may be appropriate. Implementing a verbal reprimand procedure and providing no reinforcement or using a response cost procedure for low production may be effective if used in conjunction with positive consequences for acceptable work rates. With an established minimum criterion for performance, the use of an isolation avoidance procedure may also be used successfully (Zimmerman, Overpeck, Eisenberg, and Garlick, 1969). An isolation avoidance procedure entails the removal of the client from the work area if a designated work criterion is not met.

Because low production is often a result of slow motor behavior, which is characteristic of the severely developmentally disabled, implementing a positive practice overcorrection procedure with the intent of teaching faster motor behavior is also a feasible alternative. This involves guiding the client through a task a number of times (so that the repeated action constitutes an extended duration) at a fast rate, thereby teaching a client to move with speed. If this procedure is implemented, a trainer must take care to make the physical guidance sufficiently unpleasant so that it is not socially reinforcing to a client. Although the efficacy of positive practice in sheltered workshop settings has not as yet been demonstrated in the research literature, this remains a fertile area for future investigation.

Low Production: Interfering or Excessive Behaviors

Low production rate as a result of nonfunctional competing behaviors poses a somewhat different problem. A trainer must not only increase clients' work, but also decrease or preferably eliminate the amount of time a client engages in the interfering behaviors. Manipulating different parameters of reinforcement may also be effective in alleviating this problem; unfortunately, only recently has research been published that describes efforts to overcome excessive distractibility of developmentally disabled clients in vocational settings (Mithaug, 1978).

To decrease many interfering behaviors it may be necessary to implement aversive consequences. The use of response cost (Kazdin, 1973), restraint, and positive practice overcorrection (Azrin, Gottlieb, Hugharts, Wesolowski, and Rahn, 1975) procedures as immediate consequences for engaging in interfering behaviors may successfully decrease stereotypic behavior, aggression, out-of-seat behavior, and bizarre noises. These procedures have been effective with several handicapped populations in different settings and should be seriously considered for use in workshops for severely developmentally disabled persons.

General Strategies for Treatment

To facilitate specific sequences of training and management techniques, a number of general strategies for treatment may be employed. The general intervention strategies discussed in this section include a changing criterion methodology, an intensive treatment program outside of the work area, and self-management strategies.

Changing Criterion Design   A changing criterion design may be used when work behaviors are gradually shaped to a competitive level (Axelrod, Hall, Weis, and Rohrer, 1974; Bates, Wehman, and Karan, 1976). Employing this design, a minimum criterion, or minimum level of expectancy, for production rate must be met for a client to earn reinforcement. As a client's productivity consistently meets the criterion, the criterion is gradually increased or made more stringent. Thus, over time and with the use of effective behavior-shaping methods, productivity level may greatly increase from the initial criterion.

The changing criterion design may be employed with specific operant techniques to alleviate low production attributable to slow motor behavior or competing behaviors. In the case of low production behaviors, a changing time contingency may be introduced. The procedure requires setting a specific time limit for the completion of a task and places the client under a time limit in order to receive reinforcement. A timing device, such as a kitchen timer or sports time clock, may be used as a cue for the client and a subsequent indicator if a time limit is not met. As the client consistently meets the required time limit, the time criterion can be gradually decreased. This procedure has the potential of increasing client work rate while successfully decreasing the amount of time a client engages in competing behaviors.

Intensive Treatment Program   Low production rates, resulting from a client's excessive interfering behaviors, pose a difficult remediation problem. Operant techniques employed within the work environment, such as manipulating different parameters of reinforcement, may not obtain successful results with particularly distractible and/or disruptive clients. With such clients, it may be advantageous to implement a treatment program in a relatively stimulus-free environment. Previously discussed training techniques may be enhanced by reducing the number of environmental cues to which a client might attend. As a client demonstrates increased on-task behavior, the treatment program may be gradually faded back into the work environment.

Self-Management Strategies   The operant techniques and procedures discussed so far pertain to external control on the part of a significant change agent, such as a workshop supervisor. These techniques involve staff-administered contingencies; if relied on entirely, they can present potential disadvantages to self-sufficient vocational behavior (Kazdin, 1971).

One major problem is that an external control approach precludes the development of self-directed choice behaviors on the part of severely developmentally disabled clients. Many rehabilitation professionals recognize this deficit as a primary obstacle in the community transition process for these clients. Second, an external control approach presents a number of inherent drawbacks. Because it is virtually impossible to notice all instances of an appropriate response, a workshop supervisor or counselor usually misses many opportunities to reinforce a client. Furthermore, change agents may become a cue for behaviors to occur rather than natural environmental stimuli conditions (Redd and Birnbrauer, 1969). This drawback relates also to the problem of transfer of training and durability of program progress. Thus, whenever possible, the external control approach must not be viewed as an end itself, but rather as a means to train a client to control his or her own behavior and achieve self-selected goals.

Self-control has been defined in reference to "those behaviors an individual deliberately undertakes to achieve self-selected outcomes" (Kazdin, 1975, p. 192). Self-control, or self-management, training procedures that are applicable to the severely developmentally disabled include self-observation, self-reinforcement, and stimulus control.

Self-observation has been successfully utilized with mentally retarded clients through the use of behavioral graphs (Jens and Shores, 1969) and daily feedback of work performance from videotape (DeRoo and Haralson, 1971). Employing this procedure, a client is trained to become aware of his or her work performance through immediate external feedback and by checking a visual record of his or her work behavior. Gradually, a client's self-observation can be faded to a pictorial representation of improvement in work performance.

Self-reinforcement is another strategy that holds potential, particularly in workshops that use token economies as a motivational system. Two concepts of self-reinforcement are self-administered reinforcement and self-determined reinforcement. An important requirement for both self-administered reinforcement and self-determined reinforcement is that the individuals be free to reward themselves at any time whether or not they perform a particular response (Skinner, 1953).

Self-administered reinforcement refers to a client taking a reinforcer himself or herself, but under an externally determined criterion. Once a client's self-administered reinforcement response is shaped, it becomes possible to move toward self-determined reinforcement. This broader concept of self-reinforcement allows for clients to determine their own work criterion (see

Glynn, 1970). It may be possible for contingency contracts to be set up between clients and workshop supervisors. Within such a contract would be a set rate of work and social skills which a client agrees to perform. In return, he or she would self-select reinforcement preferences for performance of the contract.

Another self-control strategy that may be employed is *stimulus control*. Stimulus control refers to specific behaviors performed in the presence of specific stimuli which serve as cues and increase the probability that the behavior is performed. For example, self-observation may function as a reinforcing consequence initially, but may also function as a discriminative stimulus for subsequent task-related behaviors.

Possible applications of the stimulus control strategy in workshops for the severely developmentally disabled include altering stimuli that consistently lead to frustration/aggression situations, modifying cues that presumably contribute to task failure, and pairing possible stimuli with low preference tasks. Social behaviors, such as eliciting social greetings, being on time, or appropriately using leisure time, might also be developed through stimulus control.

This section has attempted to provide direction in treatment strategies for workshop personnel who work with the developmentally disabled. A handicapped worker presents a unique set of learning and behavior characteristics that can make traditional types of training and management techniques less applicable. It is strongly suggested that the hierarchy of strategies proposed for treatment be systematically examined with different learning/behavior problems in an effort to validate which methods are most effective with which workshop problems.

DEMONSTRATIONS OF VOCATIONAL
POTENTIAL IN DEVELOPMENTALLY DISABLED WORKERS

To assist the practitioner in fully understanding the techniques described in the previous section, five case studies are presented below. These were completed in the University of Wisconsin Rehabilitation Research and Training Program (Karan, Wehman, Renzaglia, and Schutz, 1976) and represent data-based demonstrations of vocational potential of severely developmentally disabled individuals.

Case Study 1:   Use of Positive Reinforcement to Improve Work Performance

Robert[1] was an 18-year-old, Caucasian male who had been classified as profoundly retarded by an institution psychologist, with a measured intelligence

---

[1]All names used in the case studies are fictitious.

of 18. He had been institutionalized most of his life and exhibited spasticity and tremors in his hands and arms as a result of a cerebral palsy condition. He also displayed high rates of stereotypic body rocking, excessive jabbering noises, and consistently noncompliant behavior.

The staff-client ratio in this program was low, as a result of the use of practicum students and paid staff. Therefore, Robert was able to receive 1:1 instruction and training. Robert's job involved the 5-step assembly of a small drapery pulley that was produced by a local manufacturer. Robert could perform the task assembly, but worked at a very low rate and displayed high rates of off-task behavior. He participated in the workshop program daily from 8:15 a.m. to 11:00 a.m. along with eight other severely disabled clients.

Program   Robert was seated at a table facing a wall of the workshop room with a large supply of the necessary work materials in front of him. During baseline phases of the program, he was given instructions to begin work shortly after he first arrived. No further prompting or attention was given unless he attempted to leave his work station.

Treatment was initiated after stable baseline rates of work performance were established. The training setting consisted of the following:

1. A 2" by 15" wooden board with 10 circular indentations in which pennies could be placed
2. An edible reward placed within 1 foot of Robert
3. A trainer seated next to Robert during the work session

Robert was informed that each time he completed a unit he would receive a penny in the board. After the coin board was completely filled, he could exchange the pennies for the edible reward. Edibles included crackers, pretzels, lifesavers, and small portions of candy bars. As a method for reducing possible satiation effects these rewards were frequently rotated.

With the completion of each unit, the trainer praised Robert, patted him on the back, showed him the penny he earned, and then placed it in the board. Therefore, a continuous schedule of reinforcement was used as one means for improving work behavior. Once the 10 units were completed, the second reinforcement contingency of edible payoffs was delivered.

With the beginning of each set of 10 units, the trainer started a stopwatch which ran until the set was completed. Rate data were computed by dividing the total number of units completed by the total number of minutes spent in unit assembly. Time spent in penny exchange for edible reinforcers was not counted in production time.

Results   Examination of Figure 2.1 reveals substantial gains made in production rates by Robert. Reinforcement for completed units resulted in a 250% increase in work output in the first treatment phase over the initial baseline. A brief withdrawal of the treatment contingencies indicated a de-

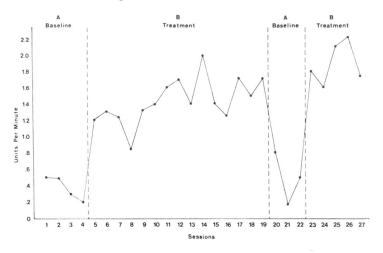

Figure 2.1. Use of reinforcement to improve Robert's work performance.

crease in performance during the second baseline phase. Reinstatement of the reinforcement program, however, led to increased production again.

Case Study 2: Use of a Changing Criterion Strategy

Larry was an 18-year-old Caucasian male diagnosed as autistic whose measured intelligence on the Wechsler Adult Intelligence Scale (WAIS) was 84 with a performance IQ of 73. He was enrolled in a high school special education program and was referred by his rehabilitation counselor for vocational training and evaluation. The counselor seriously questioned the capability of this client to engage in competitive employment, based on a previously unsatisfactory work record in the community. Typical work behavior characteristics included low rates of production, high levels of off-task behavior, and poor interpersonal/social relationships with fellow workers.

The task was a jump rope assembly which required stringing 1" plastic tubing on insulated wire and then affixing wooden handles to the ends by double knotting the wire through each handle end. The completed jump rope was packaged in a zip lock bag along with a 3" by 5" card upon which the word *completed* was printed. This task was selected because it was a real job and one of the most important subcontracts held by a community-based sheltered workshop from which the materials were borrowed.

The work schedule consisted of 2½-hour daily afternoon sessions interspersed with regular 15-minute coffee breaks and 15-minute academic tutoring sessions. The number of clients present ranged from six to eight daily.

There were usually between one to four staff members present. Staff was made up of graduate and undergraduate students, some of whom were research assistants while the others were receiving course credit as a practicum assignment.

Program   Specific verbal instructions and modeling were given to Larry for assembling the jump ropes. A trainer observed Larry assemble the jump rope and, when necessary, assisted him through the various steps until he demonstrated competency. Competency was determined to be the consecutive assembly of two jump ropes without error.

Larry was informed that jump rope assembly was to be his job for a period of time and that he would receive a $2.00 stipend at the end of the week for regularly attending and working on his assigned job. He also received periodic praise for work on the jump rope assembly. Five days of baseline production were recorded, during which the periodic praise and the stipend conditions were in effect.

Production time began as soon as Larry either started unwinding the wire or placed a wooden handle on an assembly board. It ended at the time he left the worktable for scheduled breaks or at the end of the day. The number of ropes completed per minute was recorded daily by dividing the number of completed ropes by the number of minutes worked.

A changing criterion design was utilized for evaluating Larry's production rate. Following the baseline period, an initial criterion performance level was selected. This was arbitrarily determined and based on the assumption that the new criterion was within the capabilities of Larry. Simultaneously with the shift in criterion, an additional contingency was implemented which consisted of a $1.00 bonus per day for meeting the new criterion. The daily bonus plus the $2.00 stipend was paid in a lump sum at the end of the week. Red stars placed at the bottom of a daily check sheet were used to inform Larry that he had reached criterion for that day and had thus earned his bonus. All criterion shifts were discussed thoroughly with Larry before implementation.

A new criterion was established whenever Larry successfully matched the previous criterion for a minimum of 3 consecutive days. The magnitude of each subsequent criterion change was subjectively determined by the trainer. Future programs can correct this limitation by stipulating in advance that a change of 10%, 20%, 30%, and so on, in the new criterion will be made once the standard is met.

As the requirements became more stringent, Larry often voiced reluctance to working at increased rates, yet his production output continued increasing. The terminal criterion rate was established at 0.165/min and was compatible with normal employee (nonhandicapped) competitive work stan-

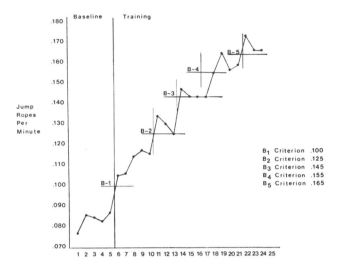

Figure 2.2. Evaluation of Larry's performance through changing criterion design.

dards. This criterion was established by assessing the jump rope assembly performance rates of several of the staff.

Different trainers worked with Larry, but all followed the same procedure. At the beginning of the work day, Larry was informed of the criterion in effect. From that point on he was given feedback on the average of every 10 minutes relative to whether or not he was on schedule.

Results   Examination of Figure 2.2 reveals that, in a period of 24 sessions, Larry's production increased more than 100% through the gradual criterion changes and positive reinforcement. Production rates increased to a competitive employment level of 0.166/min, and there was only 1 day during which a target criterion was not met.

Case Study 3:   Use of a Goal-Setting/Cue Redundancy Strategy

Nick was a 33-year-old Caucasian male who had been institutionalized since the age of 2 years. He had a measured intelligence of 9 and was classified as profoundly retarded by institution psychologists. Salient behavior characteristics included slow motor behavior and a lack of attending skills.

Nick participated in a work program from 8:15 a.m. to 2:30 p.m. Monday through Friday. He was required to assemble an 8-step water softener, which consisted of 23 individual parts. The water softener was being manufactured by a local company. He was able to perform the task with a high rate of accuracy. However, because of slow motor behavior and lack of attending skills, his production rate was very slow.

Program   Nick was seated at a large worktable at which one other client also worked. All of the necessary materials for the task were placed on the table directly in front of him.

During the baseline phase of the program, Nick was instructed to start work at the beginning of each work period. No further prompts or instructions were given unless he left his work station. Daily rate data were taken by dividing the total number of units completed by the total number of minutes of work.

After baseline rates of production had stabilized, training was initiated. The training strategy consisted of the following steps:

1. A target criterion for production rate was set.
2. Nick selected a back-up reinforcer for which he wished to work (e.g., candy bar, potato chips, fresh fruit) and placed it on the work table within his reach.
3. A 1' by 2' sheet of white paper on which circles (2" diameter) were drawn was placed on the worktable directly to the right of Nick's work materials. The circles indicated the number of tasks to be completed for the work period.
4. He was instructed to complete the required number of tasks and place them on the circles before the next break signal.
5. He was told that if all the circles were filled with tasks before the break signal, he would earn one penny for each task.

With the pennies Nick could buy the prechosen back-up reinforcer. No further instructions were given. However, Nick was reminded of the contingencies approximately once every 60 minutes.

At the break signal, the trainer exchanged one penny for each completed work task. Nick placed the pennies on the circles from which the tasks were taken. After the exchange was completed, the trainer pointed to the circles. If they were not all filled with pennies, the empty circles were pointed out and he was told that he had not worked fast enough and could not keep the pennies to buy the back-up reinforcer. Figure 2.3 provides an illustration of the work setting.

A changing criterion design was used in which target criterion rates were initially increased by 0.02 tasks per minute for the first three changes. The remaining target criterion rates were increased in increments of 0.01 tasks per minute. These target criteria had to be met across 3 consecutive days before

Figure 2.3. Illustration of Nick's work setting. A, work materials; B, prechosen back-up reinforcer; C, cue redundancy card.

the required rates were increased. Work criteria for this task were established according to production rates expected of workers in the local community workshop.

Results   Examination of Figure 2.4 reveals steady gains in work production rate. With reinforcement made contingent upon meeting a target criterion, Nick's work rates increased by approximately 80% over the initial baseline phase.

An increase in required work rate by increments of 0.02 tasks per minute was initiated for the first three criterion changes. However, a drop in production rate can be observed upon the third increase. Target criterion increases were then dropped to increments of 0.01 tasks per minute. With smaller increases, work production rates continued to rise.

Case Study 4:   Use of a Positive Practice Strategy

Mickey was a 16-year-old Caucasian male with a measured intelligence of 21. He had been institutionalized since early childhood. Mickey displayed basic self-help skills, was nonverbal, and exhibited a high rate of self-stimulatory behaviors, such as bizarre verbalizations and head banging. He was responsible for assembling a 5-piece drapery pulley. This was a marketable task, obtained from a local manufacturer.

Program   During a brief baseline period the work materials were placed in front of Mickey and a command to "begin work" was given. Training consisted of penny and social reinforcement for appropriate work rates and im-

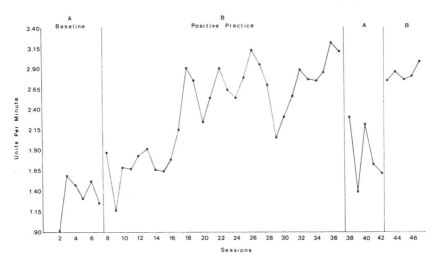

Figure 2.4. Use of cue redundancy to accelerate Nick's production.

plementation of positive practice for failure to meet the target rate. A small container in which 5 units could be placed was located near Mickey. He was praised by an adjacent trainer for completion of each unit and received a penny for each set of 5 units he completed. A time limit of 10 minutes was allowed for the completion of 25 units.

If Mickey failed to complete the necessary units within the 10-minute limit, he was told that he did not finish in time and must practice by completing the remainder of the 25 units. He was then rapidly guided through another set of 25 units. A trainer stood behind Mickey and physically guided him through the completion of each unit. Nothing was said to him during the entire training period.

Training was performed either by research assistants or by practicum students earning credit in a behavior modification class in the School of Education. Rate data were computed by dividing the total number of units completed by the total number of minutes worked. A reversal design was used to evaluate the combined effects of the training program.

Results Because of a brief period of staff shortage, the positive training could not be carried out in several sessions (sessions 10 through 15). Only positive reinforcement was given for appropriately meeting the target rate. This appeared to have little effect on the overall results. Mickey performed at a work rate substantially higher during intervention periods than during baseline. Figure 2.5 indicates that increases of approximately 150% occurred once

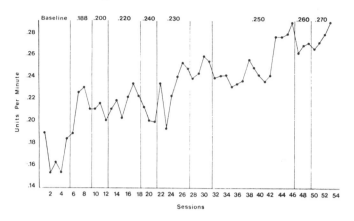

Figure 2.5. Use of positive practice to accelerate Mickey's production rate.

positive practice training was implemented. A return to baseline conditions resulted in a decrease in work rate. The second intervention also led to higher levels of production.

Case Study 5: Use of a Self-Reinforcement Strategy

Henry was a 34-year-old Caucasian male with an IQ of 27, who had been institutionalized for more than 25 years. He demonstrated basic self-help skills and could complete all tasks presented to him in the workshop. However, his production rates on various workshop tasks were far below competitive employment criteria, thereby precluding his placement in a community-based workshop facility.

Program Henry was exposed to a specially designed training sequence through the application of an ABCAD design. The training conditions included: A, baseline; B, externally administered reinforcement; C, self-administered reinforcement; A, baseline; and D, self-determined reinforcement. During the external reinforcement phase, a trainer delivered verbal praise contingent upon Henry's appropriately using a time clock and reinforcing himself with three pennies for each unit completed within a specified time limit. In the second reinforcement phase, self-administered reinforcement, Henry paid himself three pennies for each unit completed within a specified time limit. In the self-determined reinforcement phase, Henry determined his own schedule of reinforcement and the amount of reinforcement he was to receive.

Program Henry performed a jump rope assembly/packaging task at a table at which two other clients also worked. All the components of the task were placed on the table in front of him. Rate data were computed by dividing the total number of units completed by the total number of minutes of work. During the baseline phases of the program, staff members gave Henry instructions to "begin work" before each work period. No further prompting or attention was given except to provide materials when needed.

After an initial baseline rate of production had stabilized, the external reinforcement phase was initiated. This phase served as an instructional period for the development of self-administered reinforcement behaviors. During this phase, a time clock, a dish of pennies, and a three-slot counting board were placed on the worktable adjacent to the components of the jump rope task. A staff member sat across the worktable from Henry in order to instruct him in the use of the time clock and in paying himself three pennies for each unit completed within an 8-minute time limit. Money earned during each work period could be exchanged at scheduled breaks (9:45 a.m., 11:30 a.m., and 1:30 p.m.) for edible back-up reinforcers. Verbal praise was delivered contingent upon Henry's appropriate use of the time clock and for appropriate reinforcement of himself.

Once Henry demonstrated the appropriate use of the time clock and reinforced himself appropriately over a sufficient number of trials, the self-administered reinforcement phase was initiated. During this phase, Henry continued to work under an 8-minute time limit per unit and to administer three pennies to himself if the time limit was met. However, the staff member monitored Henry's work-related behaviors from across the workshop rather than while sitting at his worktable. No verbal praise was administered. It was also found that the three-slot counting board was no longer required for him to administer the correct number of pennies per unit; consequently, it was eliminated midway through this phase.

After a return to baseline period, the self-determined reinforcement phase was initiated. In this condition, Henry determined his own schedule and amount of reinforcement. The time clock was removed for this phase, and "begin to work" was the only instruction given to the client.

Results Examination of Figure 2.6 reveals that a mean production rate of 0.134 units per minute occurred with the implementation of the externally controlled reinforcement condition. Further increases in work production rates, to a mean level of 0.153/min were observed during the second treatment phase. Following a second baseline phase, the self-determined reinforcement condition increased to a mean level of 0.172/min. This increase was not accompanied by a substantial increase in the amount of reinforcement Henry delivered to himself. The schedule of reinforcement was approximately equivalent to that imposed in the previous conditions.

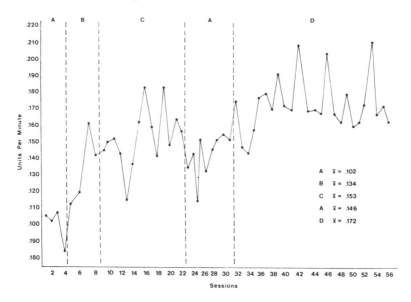

Figure 2.6. Use of self-reinforcement to accelerate Henry's production rate.

SHELTERED EMPLOYMENT FOR
DEVELOPMENTALLY DISABLED PERSONS: CONCLUSIONS

The following conclusions about the sheltered work potential of the developmentally disabled seem warranted:

1. Under appropriately arranged learning conditions, the developmentally disabled worker has the potential to perform reasonably complex (manual) work tasks.
2. Levels of supervision and training are maximal in the initial training stages, which may be at least 3 months depending on task complexity, but as the task is acquired supervision can be substantially reduced.
3. The critical lack of appropriate social behavior poses a significant problem in programming. Inability to cope with frustrating events, the presence of bizarre verbal or motor behaviors, and basic social skill deficits all may contribute to rejection of the severely disabled individual as a successful employee.
4. Few programs are available that demonstrate that the severely disabled are capable of maintaining competitive employment level production rates over long periods of time.

Although the work reported in this chapter demonstrates vocational potential in developmentally disabled individuals, there are several issues that may strongly prohibit their entry into community work forces. An initial problem is the often encountered reluctance of employers to take on severely disabled workers. There have been immense job placement problems with the mildly handicapped; certainly, acceptance of the severely disabled, a population with unique behavior characteristics, will be no easier. Job placement in competitive employment is discussed in depth in Chapter 3.

Two potential avenues are open for overcoming this difficulty. Filing discrimination lawsuits or initiating related litigation may alter employer behavior, if not attitudes. Second, the possibility exists that government subsidies might be granted temporarily to employers who are symphathetic to giving severely handicapped workers a chance to prove themselves. Sheltered work enclaves within factories would still provide *sheltered* work, yet the setting would be less restrictive than that in the traditional workshop.

Another issue that must be addressed by rehabilitation counselors is the preparation of appropriate transitioning experiences from the original training site of the least restrictive work environment to a job placement in which the clients can perform at their optimal levels of independence. Most vocational rehabilitation failures of developmentally disabled individuals revolve around placement without proper preparation for the job. Role playing, similar work environments, behavior rehearsal, and gradual on-the-job training are ways of overcoming such failures. Volunteers and university practicum students can be used to assist rehabilitation counselors in this transitional phase.

A third consideration in the eventual job placement of severely retarded persons is the type of task or skill that they can perform. The complex assembly skill research reported herein, although most impressive, is not always practical. Many communities do not have any industry or need for performance of complex tasks. It may be wisest to train clients to meet the vocational needs of the community. Perusal of local newspaper job openings is one possible method of determining viable skills for instruction.

The long range outlook for developmentally disabled clients is presently at a pivotal point. Rehabilitation professionals, with their broad-based training and service with many disabled populations, are in a position to help severely retarded persons adjust to vocational settings. However, vocational rehabilitation counselors must gain familiarity with behavior management techniques and give acceptance to this training technology. With these added skills, counselors can become even more effective in delivering vocational training and services.

REFERENCES

Axelrod, S., Hall, R. V., Weis, L., and Rohrer, S. 1974. Use of self-imposed contingencies to reduce the frequency of smoking behavior. *In* M. J. Mahoney and C. E.

Thoreson (eds.), Self-Control: Power to the Person, pp. 77–85. Brooks/Cole, Monterey, Cal.

Azrin, N. H., Gottlieb, L., Hugharts, L., Wesolowski, M. D., and Rahn, T. 1975. Eliminating self-injurious behavior by educative procedures. Behav. Res. Ther. 13: 101–111.

Bates, P., Wehman, P., and Karan, O. C. 1976. Evaluation of work performance of a developmentally disabled adolescent: Use of a changing criterion design. In O. C. Karan, P. Wehman, A. Renzaglia, and R. Schutz (eds.), Habilitation Practices with the Severely Developmentally Disabled, Vol. I. University of Wisconsin Rehabilitation Research and Training Center, Madison.

Bellamy, G. T., Horner, R., and Inman, D. 1979. Vocational Habilitation of Severely Retarded Adults: A Direct Service Technology. University Park Press, Baltimore.

Bellamy, G. T., Peterson, L., and Close, D. 1975. Habilitation of the severely and profoundly retarded: Illustrations of competence. Educ. Train. Ment. Retard. 10: 174–186.

Brown, L., Bellamy, T., Perlmutter, L., Sackowitz, P., and Sontag, E. 1972. The development of quality, quantity, and durability in the workshop performance of retarded students in a public school pre-vocational workshop. Train. School Bull. 69:58–69.

Brown, L., and Pearce, E. 1970. Increasing the production rate of trainable retarded students in a public school simulated workshop. Educ. Train. Ment. Retard. 5: 15–22.

Brown, L., Perlmutter, L., Van Deventer, D., Jones, S., and Sontag, E. 1972. Effects of consequence on production rates of trainable retarded and severely emotionally disturbed students in a public school workshop. Educ. Train. Ment. Retard. 7: 74–81.

Crosson, J. 1969. A technique for programming sheltered workshop environments for training severely retarded workers. Am. J. Ment. Defic. 73:814–818.

DeRoo, W., and Haralson, H. 1971. Increasing workshop production through self-visualization on videotape. Ment. Retard. 9:22–25.

Glynn, E. L. 1970. Classroom applications of self-determined reinforcement. J. Appl. Behav. Anal. 3:123–132.

Gold, M. W. 1972. Stimulus factors in skill training of the retarded on a complex assembly task: Acquisition, transfer, and retention. Am. J. Ment. Defic. 76:517–526.

Gold, M. W. 1973a. Factors affecting production by the retarded: Base rate. Ment. Retard. 11:41–45.

Gold, M. W. 1973b. Research on the vocational habilitation of the retarded: The present, the future. In N. R. Ellis (ed.), International Review of Research in Mental Retardation, Vol. 6. Academic Press, New York.

Gold, M. W. 1974. Redundant cue removal in skill training for the mildly and moderately retarded. Educ. Train. Ment. Retard. 9:5–8.

Gold, M. W. 1976. Task analysis: A statement and an example using acquisition and production of a complex assembly task by the retarded blind. Except. Child. 43: 78–84.

Gold, M. W., and Barclay, C. R. 1973. The learning of difficult visual discriminations by the moderately and severely retarded. Ment. Retard. 11:9–11.

Irvin, L. K. 1976. General utility of easy-to-hard discrimination training procedures with the severely retarded. Educ. Train. Ment. Retard. 11:247–250.

Jens, K., and Shores, R. 1969. Behavioral graphs as reinforcers for work behavior of mentally retarded adolescents. Educ. Train. Ment. Retard. 4:21–26.

Karan, O. C., Wehman, P., Renzaglia, A., and Schutz, R. (eds.). 1976. Habilitation Practices with the Severely Developmentally Disabled, Vol. I. University of Wisconsin Rehabilitation Research and Training Center, Madison.

Kazdin, A. E. 1971. Toward a client administered token reinforcement program. Educ. Train. Ment. Retard. 8:4–11.

Kazdin, A. E. 1973. The effect of response cost and aversive stimulation in suppressing punished and nonpunished speech disfluencies. Behav. Ther. 4:73–82.

Kazdin, A. E. 1975. Behavior Modification in Applied Settings. Dorsey Press, Homewood, Ill.

Kliebhahn, J. 1967. Effects of goal setting and modeling on job performances of retarded adolescents. Am. J. Ment. Defic. 72:220–226.

Mithaug, D. 1978. Case studies in the management of inappropriate behaviors during prevocational training. AAESPH Rev. 3:132–144.

Mithaug, D., Mar, D., and Stewart, D. 1978. Prevocational Assessment and Curriculum Guide. Exceptional Education Press, Seattle.

Redd, W. H., and Birnbrauer, J. S. 1969. Adults as discriminative stimuli for different reinforcement contingencies with retarded children. J. Exper. Child Psychol. 7:440–447.

Schroeder, S. 1972. Parametric effects of reinforcement frequency, amount of reinforcement, and required response force on sheltered workshop behavior. J. Appl. Behav. Anal. 5:431–441.

Skinner, B. F. 1953. Science and Human Behavior. Macmillan Publishing Co., New York.

Tobias, J., and Gorelick, J. 1963. Work characteristics of retarded adults in trainable levels. Ment. Retard. 1:338–344.

Walls, R. T., and Werner, T. J. 1977. Vocational behavior checklists. Ment. Retard. 15:30–35.

Williams, P. 1967. Industrial training and renumerative employment of the profoundly retarded. J. Ment. Subnormal. 13:14–23.

Zimmerman, J., Overpeck, C., Eisenberg, H., and Garlick, B. 1969. Operant conditioning in a sheltered workshop. Rehabil. Lit. 30:323–334.

3

TOWARD COMPETITIVE EMPLOYMENT FOR DEVELOPMENTALLY DISABLED PERSONS

As noted in the previous chapter, there have been ample illustrations of the sheltered work potential of developmentally disabled individuals. The results of these studies suggest that developmentally disabled individuals can succeed in a sheltered work environment. Although this is a positive development, job placement for the developmentally disabled still falls considerably short of competitive employment (Usdane, 1976; Mithaug and Haring, 1977). There are several reasons for this. First, most sheltered workshops do not pay the minimum wage but rather compensate on a piece rate basis. Consequently, many workers earn only $80 to $100 a month, if that. Second, sheltered employment is primarily restrictive; that is, it includes only handicapped workers and therefore provides limited opportunities for interaction with nonhandicapped individuals. Sheltered employment unfortunately perpetuates segregated programming. Furthermore, in sheltered workshops there is rarely the full spectrum of fringe benefits (e.g., Blue Cross) that is available in many competitive employment situations. A final limitation of sheltered employment is that it is often a needlessly terminal placement for many individuals. It becomes terminal because the employee is a critical part of the production process and invariably is "carrying" several less productive workers. Therefore, the workshop supervisor may be reluctant to move the capable worker into competitive employment from the shop.

The purpose of this chapter is threefold. First, factors involved in facilitating the entry of developmentally disabled individuals into competitive employment are discussed in depth. Second, specific assessment and intervention strategies unique to on-the-job training programs are described.

Portions of this chapter were supported by an Innovation and Expansion grant to the first author from the Virginia Department of Rehabilitative Services.

Finally, several case studies that demonstrate the process of placing severely disabled individuals in competitive employment situations are presented.

FACILITATING THE ENTRY OF SEVERELY
DISABLED INDIVIDUALS INTO COMPETITIVE EMPLOYMENT

The information in this section concerning the factors involved in helping developmentally disabled individuals enter competitive employment complements the job inventory strategy guidelines presented by Belmore and Brown (1978). Through implementation of Project Employability, a project funded by the Virginia Department of Rehabilitative Services and directed by the first author, the authors have been working with moderately to severely retarded adults who heretofore have been excluded from vocational rehabilitation services because of their lack of demonstrated employment potential. This project uses an on-the-job training model by which a trainee is placed in a potential job opening in the community and supervised on a continual, but gradually decreasing, basis by project staff. The project staff member serves as a means of insurance both to the employer that the job will be completed even during the initial stages of training and to the trainee and his family that the needed skills will be acquired for employment. As the prospective employee's performance reaches acceptable standards, the employer may then exercise his or her option to officially hire the trainee. Extensive follow-up services are continued by the project staff. This chapter is based on experiences that the authors have had in placing severely disabled individuals through Project Employability and is directed to special and vocational education teachers, job coordinators, and rehabilitation counselors.

Factors to Consider in Job Selection

There are numerous client-related variables that must be evaluated before job placement. Because potential job openings for severely disabled individuals are often difficult to locate, program staff are frequently tempted to decide arbitrarily which trainee is most suited for placement in a rare job opening rather than search for job specifications that most suit a given individual. In this regard, Mithaug, Hagmeier, and Haring (1977) have noted:

> We can begin by focusing upon one job at a time, rather than trying to analyze the entire job market at once. Also, we should specify the most probable job placements for our client's immediate career. Finally, we can analyze the job situation of selected placements, noting and listing the work skills and habits necessary for entry.... Unfortunately, information on methods to use in this assessment is not available. All we can suggest is that the focus be on the job supervisor... (p. 91).

We have found that there are several other factors that must be considered. These points, discussed below, are essential to the identification of the most appropriate job for a severely handicapped client.

Client's Previous Work History   Systematic vocational instruction for severely handicapped individuals has been in practice only in recent years (e.g., Bellamy, Horner, and Inman, 1979). Therefore, examination of the previous work record of a severely handicapped adult will frequently yield a history marked by successive failures. In the past, the severely handicapped have been dismissed from public school vocational education programs, sheltered workshops, and even community-based activity centers under the rationale that progress was not possible. However, even a record of failure may provide important information when considering job placement. Through this record, specific breakdowns in programming can be identified. Examples of this might include client preference for certain reinforcers, lack of seizure control, or volatile behavior problems that occur under different conditions.

An investigation of previous work may be done by initially surveying the following sources:

1. Parents and family members
2. School personnel
3. Rehabilitation intake workers and counselors
4. Case managers or social workers assigned to the trainee
5. Written records from schools, activity centers, or workshops

These sources frequently document some aspect of the trainee's previously attained production rates, quality of work, length of work history, and level of independence in a work setting. Information concerning the work attitude of the trainee, as well as the family's attitude toward work and transportation needs, may also be available. An analysis of this material, which is admittedly not always a valid predictor of job success (Gold, 1973), can nevertheless help the job coordinator avoid mistakes that may have been made earlier.

Client's Level of Functioning and Physical Characteristics   Once previous job history information has been gleaned, a careful analysis of the client's functioning level should be undertaken.

Mithaug, Mar, and Stewart's (1978) *Prevocational Assessment and Curriculum Guide* (see Table 2.1) is one assessment tool that might be used. Although this tool was designed for sheltered workshops, it contains numerous items that would be equally appropriate for those entering competitive employment. The interested reader can also consult the vocational behavior checklists identified by Walls and Werner (1977). From this screening, a list of job categories or types of jobs that most suit the trainee's competencies can be generated. The following client characteristics influence the type and length of job placement:

1. Frequency of on-task behavior
2. Degree of independent mobility
3. Communication skills
4. Degree of self-initiated work behavior
5. Appropriateness of social skills
6. Presence of concomitant handicaps (e.g., visual impairment)

Clearly, certain jobs require more of the above-stated abilities than others. For example, picking up trash and bagging it on a college campus will require independent walking and orienting skills, while well developed social skills might not be necessary. On the other hand, in order to operate a utility elevator in a large hospital, ambulatory skills could be impaired but receptive and expressive identification of numbers, fine motor skills, and social skills would need to be well developed.

There are other more subtle variables regarding the characteristics of the trainee that may be critical for the ultimate success of a placement. As with nonhandicapped workers, certain trainee personality and physical characteristics when mixed with certain personality traits of the immediate supervisor are related to job success and ease of adjustment to a new work setting. The easiest way of analyzing the interaction of these factors is to have program staff spend time within the work setting before making the placement. It is usually necessary to examine the group dynamics, the flexibility or rigidity of the supervisor, the age and openness of co-workers, and whether other handicapped personnel are present in order to identify critical behaviors necessary for entry in that job site. If supervisors have had previous experiences with disabled employees, and these experiences have been *positive,* opportunities for making a placement are usually enhanced.

Supplemental Security Income (SSI)   One frequently cited obstacle to job placement of the handicapped is the threat of losing guaranteed financial aid from the government. Although these payments are relatively low ($189.40 per month (as of July, 1978), if there is no other earned income) parents and sometimes clients themselves often prefer the arrival of a guaranteed check each month rather than risk job placement. In addition, if the SSI benefits are reduced to zero dollars per month according to local and federal deduction formulas, Medicaid benefits are also lost. Since Medicaid pays all but $.50 on every prescription, the loss of these benefits can present serious financial difficulties for those individuals who require much medication. However, other than in this area, a good medical insurance plan gained through employment provides medical coverage for the working individual equal to or better than that provided through federal services.

Placement personnel must approach this aspect of the employment process as a serious concern to all involved, and reduction of financial aid as a result of employment must be fully explained to the family. If the client and family understand these procedures, they will find that during the first 12 months of employment there is little risk of losing all forms of monthly income. That is, if the job is terminated, SSI benefits can be readjusted to the preemployment level within 10 to 20 days. If an individual clearly must retain Medicaid benefits, it would be wise to arrange for part-time employment rather than a full-time job. In this way, the part-time employee, depending upon his or her rate of pay, would probably retain some portion of the SSI benefits and, therefore, remain eligible for Medicaid coverage. Table 3.1 provides a written fact sheet which Project Employability provides to the client and family regarding the effects of employment on SSI benefits.

Client's Living Situation and Transportation Needs   The client's living situation is another factor that can play an important role in job selection. For example, the distance of the job from the trainee's home must enter into the decision to seek employment with a given company. Transportation is usually a problem because most severely disabled individuals cannot drive and may not be able to use public transportation. Thus, transportation must be worked out by the job coordinator, rehabilitation counselor, and parents. Listed below are some of the ways to work out this potential obstacle to placement:

1. Consider whether a placement is available within walking distance for the client.
2. Have parents take the trainee to work.
3. Have parents form a car pool with parents of other trainees if possible.
4. Complete bus training if public transportation is available and feasible.
5. Have co-worker pick up trainee and take him or her home; work out equitable pay situation.
6. Investigate whether the locality has a bus or van that is used to help disabled or senior citizens get around the community.

Unquestionably, the transportation problem can be a major stumbling block. A job coordinator must be diligent and initially may have to participate in the actual transporting of the trainee. Once the individual is formally hired and is being paid regularly, parents and other co-workers may view him or her in a more credible light and therefore make a greater commitment toward transportation assistance.

The type of home in which the trainee resides will also influence the job selection process. As Schalock and Harper (1978) have noted, the disabled individual's physical grooming, clothing care, eating and sleeping habits, and financial resources are important variables in the competitive employment

Table 3.1.   The Effects of Employment on Supplemental Security Income (SSI)

When a disabled person who is receiving SSI benefits takes a job, the federal government does not view this person as suddenly rehabilitated or no longer requiring benefits, but rather, the disabled person is viewed as "working regardless of his or her impairment." This is an important statement because it indicates that the government is well aware that this person is still disabled and that, if the current job does not work out, the handicapped individual may again require SSI benefits. In fact, the government automatically sets aside a 9- to 12-month job adjustment period during which the benefits can be quickly reinstated (within 10 to 20 days) if the person's new job is terminated for whatever reasons. This grace period indicates that the government encourages the handicapped individual to try to hold down a job, but it also realizes that a handicapped person is handicapped for life. The government, therefore, understands that if job requirements change and the person loses the job, he or she may again require and fully deserve SSI benefits. However, if the job is lost after a 12-month period, the disabled person must reapply for benefits. Reinstatement of benefits would then require approximately 3 months before a check would be received. It would be wise for the disabled working person to save a small portion of his or her earnings each month in the event that the job would be lost after the 12-month adjustment in order to carry the person through this possible 3-month period of no income.

What must be done regarding SSI when the disabled person is employed?

The local social security office must be notified *immediately* regarding this change in employment status. The easiest way of accomplishing this is to obtain a statement from the employer describing the new employee's hours of work per week and the rate of pay per week. Project Employability staff will arrange for this statement. The statement must be taken to any local social security office in order that the benefits can be reexamined in view of this information. The next monthly check should be reduced. If it is not, notify the social security office immediately to find out why the reduction did not occur. The social security office may have "overpaid" you and, if so, it will request that the overpaid amount be returned later. Therefore, be certain that the first check received after employment is reduced.

Will the handicapped person lose all SSI benefits due to employment?

SSI benefits are reduced according to a person's income. Handicapped persons can earn income without losing all benefits ($65 to $85 in earnings per month are allowed before any reduction); however, if the person holds down a full-time job at minimum wage, the benefits will probably be reduced to zero for as long as the person remains on the job. When the social security office receives the

(continued)

Table 3.1   *(continued)*

statement from the employer regarding earnings, a reviewer will figure the necessary reductions to the current SSI payment. Remember, the check can be increased rapidly if the job is terminated by simply notifying the local social security office.

How does employment affect Medicaid?

As long as the new employee remains eligible for some reduced portion of SSI payments, even if only a few dollars a month, the person will still receive Medicaid benefits. Thus, a person who is working full-time will probably no longer be eligible for SSI or Medicaid while he or she remains on the job. However, again, both benefits can be regained if the person leaves or is terminated from the job. In addition, Project Employability only places disabled persons in jobs where they receive full medical benefits with a full-time position; therefore, the loss of Medicaid benefits while working with insurance should not alter the person's medical coverage. In fact, a good medical insurance plan gained through employment provides equal or better medical coverage for the working individual.

What are the financial benefits of employment vs. the receipt of SSI benefits?

1. If full-time employment is gained, even at minimum wage, the employee's income will increase from the maximum SSI benefit of $189.40 to at least $424.00 per month (gross salary) and full medical insurance coverage is provided.
2. If part-time employment is obtained, some portion of the SSI payment will continue each month and Medicaid benefits will also continue. Therefore, the employee will receive salary and SSI payments.
3. With employment, the disabled person becomes eligible for regular social security income in the future due to his or her contributions from earnings.

process. The individual's competency in these areas may vary depending on whether he or she lives in a real home, a group home, a boarding house, or a residential facility. To take this factor one step further, consider a family of three. The parents are in their late 60s; the father is physically incapacitated and the severely retarded son is in his mid-30s. Assume the son has an opportunity to work as a kitchen laborer at $3.00 per hour at a nearby restaurant for 40 hours a week. However, the only work shift available is 5:30 a.m. to 2:30 p.m. This may pose a real dilemma for the parents in terms of transportation and, equally important, of interruption of the normal life-style in the home. These are real concerns which a job coordinator must face in placing severely disabled adults with limited work histories. These problems are best solved by patience, use of other parents to persuade skeptical families, and, most importantly, assurances of initial supervision and training on the job.

Client's and Parent's Attitudes   As noted above, many developmentally disabled individuals have experienced more than one disappointment as a result of unkept promises made through previous programs. Therefore, the objective of job placement is frequently met with much skepticism on the part of the parent or guardian. Indeed, the client's attitude may also reflect that of the parent. The "I don't want a job" philosophy often stems from the fact that the individual has learned from his or her parents that it is not necessary to work. If this is the case, job placement personnel must provide assurance to the entire family that the objectives and techniques of the program are sound and that the prospective employee deserves the dignity of risk (Perske, 1972). There are several factors that may help persuade reluctant families:

1. Assurance of continual daily on-the-job supervision and "inservicing" of nonhandicapped co-workers in the job setting.
2. Assurance that the trainee's placement spot in his current program will be kept open if the job placement does not work out.
3. Careful explanation of the rules and regulations governing the Supplemental Security Income that most severely disabled persons receive and that will be halted upon full-time employment.
4. Careful explanation of the amount of weekly wages and fringe benefits that will now be available to the individual.

After consent to job placement is gained, client and parents must be involved in the initial planning as to the location of the job, type of work required, and any special employer requirements. The location of the job may be a source of fear, particularly for families of women involved in the program. If no definite assurances can be made regarding the long term safety of the person, then certainly the parents' wishes must be viewed as realistic concerns. The trainee and the parents should be clearly informed as to the type of work and its requirements before placement is made (e.g., crew work versus working alone, hours, and clothing required). Parents should also be made aware of any changes in job responsibilities as they occur.

Frequent communication will help families remain informed and avoid potentially embarrassing incidents with the employer concerning job requirements imposed on the trainee. Even with daily communication, however, some parents may telephone the employer unnecessarily. As with most companies and government organizations, the employer is largely concerned that the employee is performing the job adequately; there is not usually time available to counsel worried or overprotective parents. Furthermore, this tends to cast a negative light on the trainee, who may subsequently be viewed as less independent.

In short, the job coordinator, teacher, or counselor must not only function in a training and placement capacity but must also provide systematic supervision and follow-up once the placement is made. It is critical that the job coordinator serve as a mediator between the employer's needs, the client's capabilities, and the parents' wishes.

Factors Involved in Identification of an Appropriate Employer

Once relevant factors that influence the job selection process have been assessed, the selection of an appropriate employer is necessary. This includes selection of the company or organization to which the job coordinator and client will apply. It also involves how to approach employers initially and overcoming the type of misconceptions and problems that many employers have with retarded workers. Finally, an extended field-training period for purposes of evaluation may be established.

Community Job Assessment   A survey of available community jobs must be initiated as the first step in locating a place of employment for the client. This may be facilitated through screening newspaper want ads for low skilled or nonskilled employment opportunities. "Will train" and "No experience necessary" are descriptions to look for within ads for jobs that will meet the skill criteria. The types of jobs may vary from location to location. However, *food service, grounds keeping,* and *maintenance* are among the categories under which appropriate employment opportunities will be listed. Although these are but a few of the types of jobs disabled individuals can perform, they have proved to be ones in which severely developmentally disabled individuals can excel (Becker, 1976).

There are other means of screening the community for jobs. For example, reviewing the yellow pages in local phone books may yield major contractors in target occupational categories. Personal contacts within companies or organizations that have relevant jobs should also be used if appropriate. The National Alliance of Businessmen usually has a local branch that may prove helpful since they receive many job pledges from business and industry every year. Most states have an employment commission that receives a listing of job vacancies that may be appropriate as well.

Frequently, universities, colleges, hospitals, and other large institutional settings are most fruitful in terms of job placement for developmentally disabled individuals. This type of employer has several positive points. First, they typically have a high turnover in the types of jobs that severely disabled persons can perform. Second, they frequently have a commitment to hire handicapped individuals. Third, the pay and benefits are frequently quite desirable. Finally, it may be most efficient to assign one teacher or job coordinator to the same job site and gradually increase the number of trainees. As a trainee becomes increasingly competent at the job, a second individual can be introduced to the employer. This process can continue until several trainees have been hired.

Once several job leads have been identified, the next step is to follow through by making the initial telephone contact. This can be facilitated by a social contact or someone already working in the company who is willing to talk to the employer before the phone call. The director of personnel is the logical contact person in most cases. In the authors' experience, an honest, yet optimistic, approach is best received. A brief explanation of the program in general terms should be followed by asking if the company would consider allowing a mentally retarded person to train for the advertised position or a similar one. At times, employers may have unadvertised jobs that would be more appropriate for the client.

Through the telephone contact the prospective employer's general reaction to hiring a developmentally disabled person should be assessed. This reaction may be positive, cautiously positive, or negative. In most cases it is best to eliminate the negative employers and concentrate on the positive employers. To a certain degree, this preliminary selection will be influenced by the type and number of appropriate job vacancies that an employer has. With the employer who appears to be receptive, an interview date should be set as soon as possible.

Approaching the Employer   The initial personal contact is critical in terms of making a placement. It is during this stage that a full description of the program, clients' abilities, and staff's training capabilities, as well as the generally positive aspects of hiring mentally retarded workers, is related. This contact will also give the job coordinator an opportunity to find out what other job possibilities are available and what the prevailing sentiment is toward hiring disabled clients.

Some employers, unfortunately, have had disappointments in attempting to work with other programs for the handicapped. These disappointments may be expressed in terms of "The counselor only came the first day," or "No one else was here to teach us how to work or communicate with him," or "They came the first day with the teacher and we never heard from them again." During the initial contact, it is important to dispel these concerns and point out the differences between the present training program and others. *The sincerity demonstrated during this time must be kept to establish a good future working relationship with the company or organization.* It is necessary to keep in mind that interacting with businessmen is not the same as interacting with special education and rehabilitation personnel. Mentally retarded clients' capabilities must be presented in general, descriptive terms. Their potential benefit to the company must be presented in business terms, such as the predominantly positive track record that retarded workers have after initial supervision. If the attitude toward the program and future placements seems positive, then a trial training period may be negotiated.

Establishing a Training Period   Arrangements for a training period may be made during the initial personal contact or during future contacts. It is not unlikely that several more contacts will precede the conclusion of an agreement on the training period. This becomes more likely with larger businesses with extensive personnel division hierarchies. Approval needs to be given from the director of personnel down through the immediate foreman or supervisor. The length of the training period should be based on the client's abilities, his or her previous training, the job surroundings, and the skills involved. The training period may be viewed as extended training from the classroom or workshop and hence may be nonpaid for a short period of time. On the other hand, National Association for Retarded Citizens funds may be used for on-the-job training, or rehabilitation counselors may provide funds to reimburse employers. For rehabilitation funds to be used, however, the counselor must be convinced of the trainee's employment potential. This is usually quite difficult with severely disabled individuals who have been previously excluded in most cases. The training period should be presented to the potential employer and parents as a predictor of the client's ability to perform the job accurately and within the specified time frame.

Ideally, the immediate supervisor will agree to directly observe the trainee at certain periods throughout training. In this way the company will be aware of the progress that the trainee is making. Furthermore, the supervisor can advise the job coordinator of ways in which the job may be completed more efficiently. The job coordinator must keep careful, objective records of the trainee's progress. These may include:

1. Observations at different intervals of the day of on-task versus off-task behavior

2. Recording at different intervals of the day of frequency and type of trainer prompts required
3. Recording at the end of each day of the client's general work behaviors (these include absenteeism, tardiness, appearance, and social behavior with the supervisor and co-workers)

These data should also be collected after the hiring at selected follow-up intervals. This will document to the employer the success of the trainee and pave the way for other clients. This system is described in more detail in the next section.

The training period is a time when the job coordinator and supervisor can work together in helping the client (Cooper, 1977). To a large extent, the rapport established between the supervisor and trainee will facilitate his or her hiring as well as the hiring of future trainees. The job coordinator's role in this process is twofold. One, there may be a demonstration of how to most effectively work with the trainee. The caution here is to not work with the client to the exclusion of the real supervisor; if this occurs, there may be difficulties in maintaining work performance once the job coordinator leaves. The second function of the job coordinator is to be an effective advocate for the trainee with other individuals in the environment. This may include getting media support, explaining the client's role in the work force to others in the work environment who are not informed, or simply helping the trainee get adjusted to unfamiliar work surroundings.

The Job Interview   After the training period is established, a time for an interview between supervisor, trainee, and staff member must be set. The interview should take place after formal interview training has occurred. The job coordinator should only enter the interview if the trainee's interview abilities break down, as may be the case with some nonverbal individuals. The following job interview skills should be stressed in preplacement training:

1. Eye contact upon introductions
2. Good body posture when standing and sitting
3. Firm handshake and release after appropriate time span
4. Ability to respond to small talk characteristic of an interview (e.g., "How are you?" "Have you worked before?")

Although lack of proficiency in each of these skills will not necessarily preclude placement, the trainee's chances of being hired will be considerably enhanced if there is evidence of good interview behavior and neat appearance.

BEHAVIORAL ASSESSMENT IN COMPETITIVE EMPLOYMENT

In order to document the effectiveness and impact of training and placement efforts, an observation and recording system must be established. The ideal assessment system relies on direct observation of client's job performance. Observations may be recorded immediately and graphed. When this type of data collection system is used in conjunction with more traditional survey and test forms, a true picture of client vocational abilities emerges.

There are several characteristics of an optimal recording system that should be noted. First, target behaviors for observation must be defined carefully so that two or more observers can agree on the occurrence or nonoccurrence of the behavior. On-task versus off-task behavior must be defined according to the specific parameters of the job. For example, the on-task behaviors of a groundsman will be different from those of an elevator operator. Second, because in some situations there will be many clients and few staff, it may be impossible to record each client's behavior continuously. Therefore, sampling work behavior by observing and recording several 5-, 10-, or 15-minute intervals each day may be performed. Third, an effort can be made to periodically involve a second independent observer to collect data simultaneously. Data sheets can then be compared and checked interval by interval for agreement. This provides an index of reliability and thereby ensures the accuracy for the performance recording system. As a fourth characteristic of efficient and effective recording, behavior should be observed and recorded daily.

The use of an ongoing system of job performance assessment provides the advantage of empirically verifying the successful work adjustment made by previously excluded clients in competitive employment situations. Furthermore, in many situations trainees will be placed in extended (field) training situations; objective data will help determine the trainees' work potential.

Three primary types of records may be used in job performance assessment in the field. These include:

1. Sample of work regularity
2. Levels of assistance required for job completion
3. Supervisor evaluation form filled out by employer

Work Regularity

The assessment of work regularity involves defining the on-task versus off-task job behavior, observing and recording the client through several 5- to 10-minute intervals daily, and graphing the results. This information may be recorded on a data sheet such as that illustrated in Table 3.2. By recording nonhandicapped workers' performance rates as well, a job coordinator can also make helpful comparisons between the work of severely disabled trainees and that of "normal" workers.

Table 3.2.   Sample of work regularity: Percentage of time on task

Trainee: _____   Job site: _____

Evaluator: _____   Job title: _____

	Observation period	Time: Start	Time: End	Percentage of time (in sec) on task Total time	Percentage of time on task	Job(s) or activity(ies)
Monday Date:	I.					
	II.					
	III.					
	IV.					
				Daily total:	Daily avg.:	
Tuesday Date:	I.					
	II.					
	III.					
	IV.					
				Daily total:	Daily avg.:	
Wednesday Date:	I.					
	II.					
	III.					
	IV.					
				Daily total:	Daily avg.:	
Thursday Date:	I.					
	II.					
	III.					
	IV.					
				Daily total:	Daily avg.:	
Friday Date:	I.					
	II.					
	III.					
	IV.					
				Daily total:	Daily avg.:	
Weekend				Weekly totals:	Weekly average:	

Definitions:

On task: _____

Off task: _____

Momentary time sampling is the measurement technique used. As an example, this form of assessment requires the observer to look at the trainee's behavior every 10th second within a selected interval. If the trainee is on task, a plus (+) is recorded; if not, a minus (–) is recorded. A percentage of pluses and minuses is then computed.

Although this index is of value for recording work rate over time, it fails to evaluate the *amount* and *degree* of intervention required to develop and maintain consistent work performance. Therefore, an observation and recording system should also allow for the coding of which forms of assistance are necessary to help the trainee complete a job. These levels of assistance include:

1. *Verbal cue only*   Example: "John, don't forget to clean the ashtray, too."
2. *Verbal cue plus gesture*   Example: "John, don't forget to clean the ashtray over there." — Trainer gestures to ashtray.
3. *Verbal cue plus model*   Example: "John, clean the ashtray like this." — Trainer demonstrates how to clean ashtray.
4. *Verbal cue plus physical prompt*   Example: "John, clean the ashtray." — Trainer physically assists John through task.

Since this hierarchy also provides the sequence of instruction that may be used in training, these data provide feedback as to the effectiveness of trainer intervention. Typically, when a client is initially placed, a higher amount and greater degree of trainer assistance are required to facilitate the adjustment. These prompts can generally be diminished as the trainer is able to gradually reduce his or her physical proximity and subsequent cueing.

Table 3.3 illustrates a data sheet that can be used to record and assess the level of assistance necessary.

Supervisor Evaluation

The supervisor evaluation presented in Table 3.4 is a routine yet surprisingly sensitive predictor of client performance and job future. This form of evaluation also provides feedback as to the employer's perception of and receptiveness toward project staff and the program. This is a particularly good indicator for evaluating when the employer feels a client is ready to leave the extended training phase and be officially hired.

Related Types of Evaluation

Although the above assessments are useful in evaluation of client job performance, there are also two other modes of data collection that may be used. These involve 1) assessment of the level and function of social interaction between severely disabled workers who have been placed and nondisabled workers in the same work area, and 2) a cumulative record of wages earned and rate of absenteeism. These forms are shown in Tables 3.5 and 3.6, respectively.

DEMONSTRATIONS OF COMPETITIVE EMPLOYMENT POTENTIAL: THREE CASE STUDIES

The information above provides a framework for setting up a competitive employment training program. It also describes relevant assessment

Table 3.3.   Levels of assistance required for job completion and proficiency

Trainee: _____   Job site: _____

Trainer: _____   Job title: _____

Indicate the number of *prompts* used and your *physical proximity* from the trainee by placing the appropriate distance code under the correct prompt column *each time* a prompt is used.

Distance codes:
A = Trainer within 3 feet (arms' reach)
B = Trainer 4 to 10 feet away
C = Trainer more than 10 feet away

Observation period	Date	Time: Start/ End	Verbal cue only	Verbal cue plus gesture	Verbal cue plus model	Verbal cue plus physical prompt	No prompt given
Day: I							
Specific problem area(s)--→							
II							
Specific problem area(s)--→							
III							
Specific problem area(s)--→							
IV							
Specific problem area(s)--→							
Day: I							
Specific problem area(s)--→							
II							
Specific problem area(s)--→							
III							
Specific problem area(s)--→							
IV							
Specific problem area(s)--→							
Day: I							
Specific problem area(s)--→							
II							
Specific problem area(s)--→							
III							
Specific problem area(s)--→							
IV							
Specific problem area(s)--→							
Daily totals:							

Table 3.4. Supervisor's evaluation form—Bimonthly

Trainee/employee's name: _____ Date of placement: _____
Job title: _____ Date hired: _____
Job site: _____ Current date: _____
Job coordinator: _____

Please circle all items that apply to the trainee/employee:

1. The employee   (a) generally arrives and leaves on time.
                        (b) maintains good atttendance.
                        (c) takes meals and breaks appropriately.
                        (d) maintains a good appearance.
    Comments on uncircled items: _____

2. The employee has (a) mastered all aspects of present job.
                        (b) mastered many but not all aspects of job to date.
                        (c) not mastered essential aspects of job to date.

3. In order for the employee to follow directions regarding the job, the
    supervisor   (a) can just give *verbal* instructions.
                        (b) has to give many *gestures* as well as verbal
                            instructions.
                        (c) has to show the employee exactly what to do
                            before he or she knows what to do.

4. A project staff member is present
                        (a) too often.
                        (b) too little according to the employee's need.
                        (c) an appropriate amount of time.

5. This employee   (a) frequently stops work and needs to be reminded to
                            return to work.
                        (b) stops working occasionally but no more than other
                            employees.
                        (c) works at a constant rate without reminders.

6. The employee is   (a) a good worker.
                        (b) an average worker.
                        (c) a below average worker.

7. Does the project staff member in any way interfere with your supervision or
    plans for the employee? (a) no   (b) yes   (*If yes, please briefly describe.*)
    _____
    _____

Other comments: _____
_____

                            Supervisor _____

Table 3.5. Interactions between handicapped workers and nonhandicapped persons in competitive employment

Name: _____

Blacken circles as appropriate by referring to the code below.

Interaction initiated by:	*Emphasis of interaction:*	*Proximity:*	*Type of interaction:*
A = Handicapped worker	A = Instruction	A = Physical contact	A = Verbal
B = Nonhandicapped co-worker	B = Social (Work-related)	B = Within 4 feet	B = Gesture
C = Other nonhandicapped individual	C = Social (Non-work-related)	C = 4–10 feet	C = Model
D = Supervisor	D = Harrassment	D = More than 10 feet	D = Physical

		Date:													
		Time:													
Interaction initiated by	A	0	0	0	0	0	0	0	0	0	0	0	0	0
	B	0	0	0	0	0	0	0	0	0	0	0	0	0
(Tally number of	C	0	0	0	0	0	0	0	0	0	0	0	0	0
interactions here:____)	D	0	0	0	0	0	0	0	0	0	0	0	0	0
Emphasis of interaction	A	0	0	0	0	0	0	0	0	0	0	0	0	0
	B	0	0	0	0	0	0	0	0	0	0	0	0	0
	C	0	0	0	0	0	0	0	0	0	0	0	0	0
	D	0	0	0	0	0	0	0	0	0	0	0	0	0
Proximity	A	0	0	0	0	0	0	0	0	0	0	0	0	0
	B	0	0	0	0	0	0	0	0	0	0	0	0	0
	C	0	0	0	0	0	0	0	0	0	0	0	0	0
	D	0	0	0	0	0	0	0	0	0	0	0	0	0
Type of interaction	A	0	0	0	0	0	0	0	0	0	0	0	0	0
	B	0	0	0	0	0	0	0	0	0	0	0	0	0
	C	0	0	0	0	0	0	0	0	0	0	0	0	0
	D	0	0	0	0	0	0	0	0	0	0	0	0	0
		Date:													
		Time:													
Interaction initiated by	A	0	0	0	0	0	0	0	0	0	0	0	0	0
	B	0	0	0	0	0	0	0	0	0	0	0	0	0
(Tally number of	C	0	0	0	0	0	0	0	0	0	0	0	0	0
interactions here:____)	D	0	0	0	0	0	0	0	0	0	0	0	0	0
Emphasis of interaction	A	0	0	0	0	0	0	0	0	0	0	0	0	0
	B	0	0	0	0	0	0	0	0	0	0	0	0	0
	C	0	0	0	0	0	0	0	0	0	0	0	0	0
	D	0	0	0	0	0	0	0	0	0	0	0	0	0
Proximity	A	0	0	0	0	0	0	0	0	0	0	0	0	0
	B	0	0	0	0	0	0	0	0	0	0	0	0	0
	C	0	0	0	0	0	0	0	0	0	0	0	0	0
	D	0	0	0	0	0	0	0	0	0	0	0	0	0
Type of interaction	A	0	0	0	0	0	0	0	0	0	0	0	0	0
	B	0	0	0	0	0	0	0	0	0	0	0	0	0
	C	0	0	0	0	0	0	0	0	0	0	0	0	0
	D	0	0	0	0	0	0	0	0	0	0	0	0	0

techniques. However, data-based case studies from Project Employability, provided below, highlight the training and placement techniques utilized. Figure 3.1 presents the sequence of activities required to train and place a severely disabled client. The three case studies described next are representative of the placements made by Project Employability. Clients have been selected for case study presentation with varying behavioral and physical characteristics.

Table 3.6. Monthly financial summary

Job coordinator: _____   Job site: _____

Name	Month	Absences	Days worked	Monthly earnings	Previous financial aid monthly payments	Increase in monthly income through employment	Present monthly financial aid	Taxpayers' savings per month
Monthly combined totals:								
Monthly combined totals:								
Monthly combined totals:								

Case Study 1:   Food Service Placement

Behavioral Characteristics   Chuck[1] is a 22-year-old male with a measured intelligence quotient of 27. He has been classified as severely mentally retarded. Chuck is nonverbal yet follows 1-step instructions and exhibits most self-care skills independently. His social behavior is outgoing and friendly, but he has no reading or computational skills. Chuck is free of any physical or sensory impairments and lives with his family. The excerpt below is taken from a recent rehabilitation evaluation of his work potential. This evaluation was completed by a licensed psychologist.

---

[1] All names used in the case are fictitious.

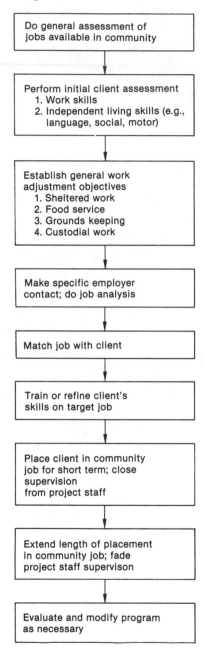

Figure 3.1. Training and placement model for severely disabled individuals.

Chuck is a small mongoloid white man, who looks much younger than 21. He is mostly without speech though it is possible to understand an occasional word in his usual monosyllabic utterances. He is pleasant, smiling and cooperative, a little given to perseverative and ritualistic behavior.

Measure of intellectual function derived from the FRPV forms A and B yields IQ scores of 27 and 30, respectively. This is in complete accord with the findings of the school psychologist in 1973. He is in the lower end of the trainable MR range — severely retarded.

Chuck is good natured, friendly and willing, but realistically unemployable. He can under close supervision do things like simple household chores, leaf raking and he will enjoy it but he is not really employable. Under sheltered workshop conditions he may be able to sweep or do some other repetitive perseverative operation.

Test results discover a great deal of organic difficulty, one of the prime results of which is his perseveration. He will, once he starts doing a thing, do it over and over and over until stopped.

I am sorry I cannot give a more optimistic report. Chuck is a very likeable fellow.

Previous Vocational Training   Chuck was attending an adult activity center when Project Employability staff began to work with him. His previous vocational training involved a limited amount of domestic skill instruction when he attended public school. Chuck had never worked for wages, in either sheltered or competitive employment.

Job Requirements and Setting   The job identified for Chuck was a kitchen utility position in the student union at a small university near Chuck's home. Requirements for this job included clearing tables, sanitizing trays, emptying ashtrays, and doing other related clean-up work. The hours were from 9:00 a.m. to 3:30 p.m. Monday through Friday. Chuck was expected to function independently since his supervisor was in and out of the area all day.

The student union was most crowded during lunch hours. There were a number of college students and professors who regularly visited the student union.

Job Training   Chuck was hired for the job after an initial round of discussions between Project Employability staff and supervisors of food service at the university. Before his interview he had undergone a food service training program at the activity center. This program indicated he could perform the skills required for the job designated for him. The role of project staff was that of *advocacy* and *training*. The basic training model that was used involved a verbal prompt to Chuck if he was off task or performing a job incorrectly. For example, a verbal cue like the following would be used: "Chuck, you forgot to empty the ashtray." If this was not effective, the verbal cue was repeated and a gesture provided. If this was still ineffective, then the trainer

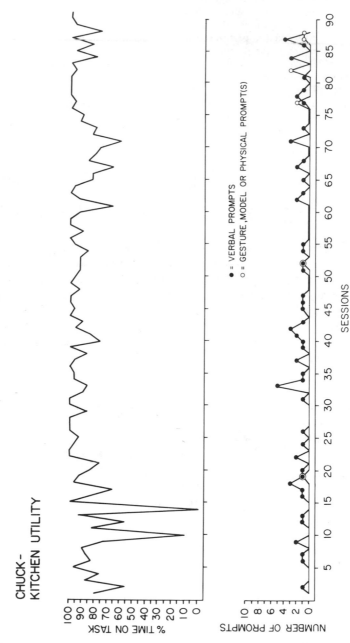

Figure 3.2. Percentage of time on task and number of prompts required on kitchen utility job for Chuck.

60

physically prompted Chuck. As Chuck became increasingly independent, the trainer moved farther away and eventually out of his line of vision. Efforts were made to involve the real supervisor in working with Chuck, although project staff were readily available to help Chuck interact with nonhandicapped individuals initially. This advocacy proved to be a positive factor in Chuck's success.

Client Evaluation Data   Several sources of data were collected to evaluate Chuck's progress on the job:

1. *Absences and tardiness.* Chuck has missed 0 days and has not been late in a total of 90 possible days of work.
2. *Percentage of work time on task.* By collecting daily four 5-minute observations (i.e., momentary time sampling) of Chuck's work behavior, we were able to document his overall work rate as being consistently over 85% of the observations. Figure 3.2 depicts his work rate. This rate was computed by looking at Chuck's work behavior every 10th second in 5-minute intervals and recording his on-task or off-task behavior. On task was defined as: "Clearing tables, returning trays to dishroom, walking to dirty tables, and cleaning counter area." Off task was defined as: "Looking out windows, standing still behind columns, and walking away from work area."
3. *Frequency of trainer prompts.* Figure 3.2 also indicates the level of verbal, gestural, and physical prompts that project staff had to provide Chuck. These data were collected in four 10-minute observations and indicate that, on the average, less than three prompts per day were required. Unfortunately, this data system was implemented after Chuck had been working for several weeks. Hence, his initial need for trainer assistance is not accurately portrayed. Reliability for this was computed by dividing the total number of agreements by the total number of observations. Total reliability was 0.92%.
4. *Supervisor evaluations.* The most recent supervisor evaluation is reported in Table 3.7. Supervisor evaluations were collected biweekly.
5. *Total wages earned.* Since beginning work, Chuck has earned a total of $1,498.00 over 90 days of paid full-time work. (This is computed at a wage of $2.90/hr.) He is also receiving full fringe benefits.

Case Study 2:   Elevator Operator Placement

Behavioral Characteristics   Eric is an 18-year-old male with cerebral palsy (spastic quadriplegia). He has a good vocabulary but a severe speech impairment. He is classified as a borderline slow learner; however, because of motor and speech impairments, Eric is viewed as severely disabled by state re-

Table 3.7. Supervisor's evaluation form—Bimonthly

Trainee/employee's name: _"Chuck"_   Date of placement: 9-25-78
Job title: _Kitchen Utility_   Date hired: 10-23-78
Job site: _____   Current date: _____
Job coordinator: _____

Please circle all items that apply to the trainee/employee:

1. The employee   (a) generally arrives and leaves on time.
            (b) maintains good atttendance.
            (c) takes meals and breaks appropriately.
            (d) maintains a good appearance.
   Comments on uncircled items: _____

2. The employee has   (a) mastered all aspects of present job.
             (b) mastered many but not all aspects of job to date.
             (c) not mastered essential aspects of job to date.
          ✱ *filling of spray bottle*

3. In order for the employee to follow directions regarding the job, the
   supervisor   (a) can just give *verbal* instructions.
             (b) has to give many *gestures* as well as verbal
                 instructions.
             (c) has to show the employee exactly what to do
                 before he or she knows what to do.

4. A project staff member is present
             (a) too often.
             (b) too little according to the employee's need.
             (c) an appropriate amount of time.

5. This employee   (a) frequently stops work and needs to be reminded to
                 return to work.
             (b) stops working occasionally but no more than other
                 employees.
             (c) works at a constant rate without reminders.

6. The employee is   (a) a good worker.
             (b) an average worker.
             (c) a below average worker.

7. Does the project staff member in any way interfere with your supervision or
   plans for the employee? (a) no   (b) yes   (*If yes, please briefly describe.*)
_____
_____
_____

Other comments: _Chuck's appearance has improved with_
       keeping his shirt on.
                   Supervisor _B. D._ _____

habilitation standards. Other pertinent evaluation data from the state Department of Rehabilitative Services are provided in the excerpts below.
Unlike Chuck, Eric was already on a rehabilitation counselor caseload but was
about to be closed out because of the difficulty in finding a job for him. He
was referred to Project Employability.

Reason for referral:
    Eric was originally referred for Rehabilitation services through the resources
of the Cerebral Palsy Center. An analysis of his health indicates that Eric is a CP
victim and that this has caused spastic quadriplegia and speech impairment. It
has been suggested that Eric could benefit from Rehabilitation services and with
this in mind he was referred for vocational evaluation in March of 1976. At that
time the examiner felt that competitive employment was not likely but recommended further evaluation in approximately one year to determine the extent of
any improvement. Current evaluation is being undertaken to ascertain whether
or not that improvement occurred.

Discussion:
    At the time of Eric's last evaluation, he was characterized as being out of
reach of competitive employment. At that time, it was suggested that he be reevaluated because of his age and the possibility of further improvement.

Eric is an attractive young man who expressed the desire to work with
people in a service-related job rather than in a production type job. Although
Eric is ambulatory, his physician had previously recommended a sit-down
type job because Eric's gait is unsteady and mobility is limited by permanent
contractures in the knee and ankle joints.

Previous Vocational Training   Eric had received no formal vocational
training in the past, and the state rehabilitation evaluator had recommended
sheltered work adjustment. Eric had previously volunteered at a camp for
handicapped people and at his school for the children's swimming period.
Upon referral, Eric was enrolled at the local cerebral palsy center in an
ungraded program of functional academics. He had received his certifica-
tion of completion a year before; however, because of his age and the lack of
an advanced placement site, he intended to continue in the program until
age 21.

Eric's teacher expressed concern for his future in that, like so many other
graduates, job placements are few for a person with two or more handicaps.
As many special programmers across the country are realizing, "...it is not
that public schools cease caring once students reach 18 or so; rather most
school counseling programs are neither staffed nor structured to help those
with severe and multiple handicaps" (Cooper, 1977, p. 66).

Job Requirements and Setting   The employer indicated during initial
contacts that he had previous experience with cerebral palsied people but expressed some apprehension in the placement of a mentally retarded person.

Therefore, although it has been shown that employers tend to view CP as a more severe disability than mental retardation, it was apparent that in this particular placement a person with cerebral palsy could be selected.

The job match for Eric was a freight and passenger elevator operator in a large downtown hospital. A part-time position was offered on the evening shift. This was to be extended to full-time work later if Eric proved himself a good employee.

An elevator operator must push reverse (i.e., *up* or *down*) buttons as well as the start button and correct floor buttons for each transport. Eric had to develop clear elevator language, such as "going up," at the appropriate time. He had to refuse to permit passengers on the vehicle when freight was aboard or when he was waiting for a freight transport. Perhaps, most importantly, he had to learn what to do when the elevator was stuck between floors or when medical personnel stated that a patient emergency existed. In addition, he had to occupy his time during slack periods and be ready to perform on call.

Job Training   A major part of our job training included advocacy for Eric. Because of speech and physical impairments he appeared far more handicapped than he functioned. The presence of project staff on a regular basis helped to foster an understanding of Eric's abilities and liabilities with the hospital personnel who used the elevator regularly. Soon, Eric was on a friendly basis with many hospital staff, and they began advocating for Eric in the presence of strangers on the elevator.

The basic training model included providing verbal prompts during operation of the elevator. Few more-intrusive prompts were required during training, with the exception of the first occasion when the elevator became stuck between floors. Practice on the procedures for this emergency and the use of clear elevator language were then provided during slow business periods. The trainer gradually faded herself to the back of the elevator and began riding the vehicle on a gradually decreasing schedule.

Client Evaluation Data   Eric's progress may be examined through the following sources:

1. *Absences and tardiness.* After 110 days of work to date, Eric has been absent or late four times.
2. *Percentage of work time on task.* Using the observation techniques discussed above, Eric's overall rate of work regularity can be established. Figure 3.3 illustrates that Eric averaged an on-task work rate of more than 95%. From general observations made of other elevator operators, including Eric's supervisor, he exhibited a higher rate of on-task behavior. On-task behavior was defined as: "Pushing elevator buttons, looking for

passengers and freight from seat, and standing, speaking, or nodding to passengers on elevator or in front of elevator.''

3. *Frequency of trainer prompts.* Figure 3.3 also indicates a somewhat erratic need for prompts initially, probably because the requirements of the job changed from day to day. However, a reduction in the number of prompts necessary can be seen as training progressed.

4. *Supervisor evaluations.* The most recent supervisor evaluation is given in Table 3.8 and indicates a favorable assessment of Eric's progress.

5. *Total wages earned.* Eric's total earnings to date are $1,750.00 for 105 days of work on a 20-hour week at $2.83 per hour. Eric was offered a full-time position to begin in the near future.

Case Study 3:   Food Service Placement

Behavioral Characteristics   Len is a 22-year-old Caucasian male with a measured intelligence quotient of 51. He is ambulatory and verbal although lacking appropriate social skills, i.e., he engages in inappropriate verbalizations. Len was referred to Project Employability for special help in placement because of his difficulty in getting along with peers and his constant seeking of approval and attention. An excerpt from the counselor referral letter is provided below. Len currently lives in a very difficult home situation.

> Len is a very hard worker and an excellent producer in the areas of dishwashing, cleaning, and working with tray carts. His major problem is a need for attention, primarily from his work supervisor. He will demand frequent verbal reinforcement that his work is acceptable. However, when given strong supervision that does not encourage this attention seeking, he can work effectively. His participation in the employability project would allow your instructor to assist him without demanding so much time and energy from the university work supervisor. I am expecting that at the end of a 30 day trial placement period, Len will be well enough adjusted to the work site.

Previous Vocational Training   Len had received formal food service training from the Woodrow Wilson Rehabilitation Center in Virginia. Although he did not have prior employment experience he had favorable evaluations on his work adjustment performance. Project Employability staff felt that with appropriate advocacy and supervision Len could succeed in a food service position. He had also received less intensive training in a public school program for trainable level mentally retarded students.

Job Requirements and Setting   A kitchen utility placement was made at the same university at which Chuck worked; Len's position, however, was in a much more hectic cafeteria setting. This cafeteria prepared a large num-

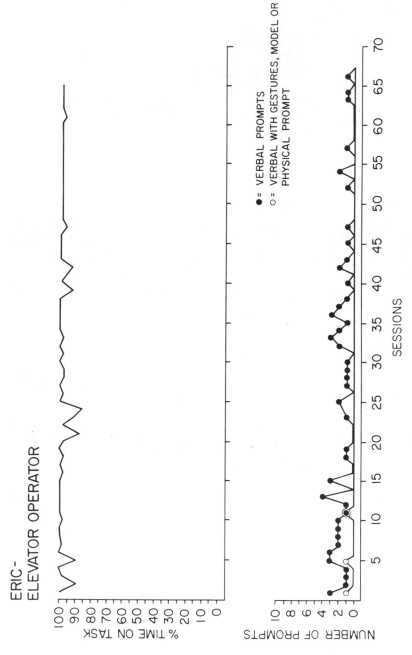

Figure 3.3. Percentage of time on task and number of prompts required on elevator operator job for Eric.

66

Table 3.8.   Supervisor's evaluation form—Bimonthly

Trainee/employee's name: _Eric_   Date of placement: _11-20-78_
Job title: _Elevator Operator_   Date hired: _12-1-78_
Job site: _____   Current date: _____
Job coordinator: _____

Please circle all items that apply to the trainee/employee:

1. The employee   (a) generally arrives and leaves on time.
                               (b) maintains good atttendance.
                               (c) takes meals and breaks appropriately.
                               (d) maintains a good appearance.
     Comments on uncircled items: _____

2. The employee has   (a) mastered all aspects of present job.
                               (b) mastered many but not all aspects of job to date.
                               (c) not mastered essential aspects of job to date.

3. In order for the employee to follow directions regarding the job, the
     supervisor   (a) can just give *verbal* instructions.
                               (b) has to give many *gestures* as well as verbal
                                   instructions.
                               (c) has to show the employee exactly what to do
                                   before he or she knows what to do.

4. A project staff member is present
                               (a) too often.
                               (b) too little according to the employee's need.
                               (c) an appropriate amount of time.

5. This employee   (a) frequently stops work and needs to be reminded to
                                 return to work.
                               (b) stops working occasionally but no more than other
                                 employees.
                               (c) works at a constant rate without reminders.

6. The employee is   (a) a good worker.
                               (b) an average worker.
                               (c) a below average worker.

7. Does the project staff member in any way interfere with your supervision or
     plans for the employee? (a) no   (b) yes   (*If yes, please briefly describe.*)
     _____
     _____
     _____

Other comments: _____

                           Supervisor _C. F._

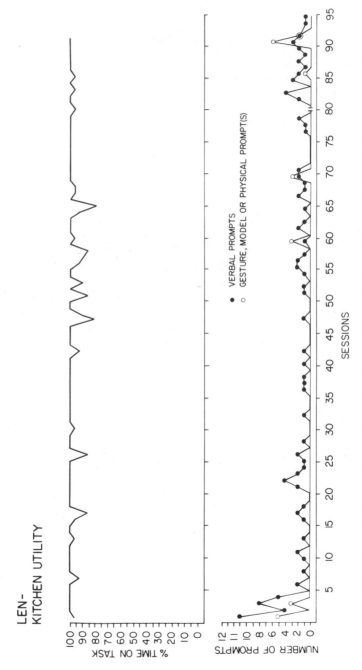

Figure 3.4. Percentage of time on task and number of prompts required on kitchen utility job for Len.

68

ber of servings per day, and had a staff of more than 75 food service employees. The job entailed busing tables, mopping, sweeping, operating heavy equipment, emptying trash, and cleaning trays. It also required that workers perform with minimal supervision. We felt that Len could succeed in this job, provided he had initial support from project staff.

Job Training   Since Len already could perform the jobs competently, our role was one of working out transportation, stabilizing Len's work hours, and helping orient nonhandicapped co-workers to Len. It was evident after several days that Len moved faster than many of his co-workers. Ironically, this was also a problem that had to be considered in establishing co-worker rapport. The major training problem that was presented in Len's case was helping him readjust to work after the 3-week Christmas holiday. It was necessary for staff to resume a closer 1:1 relationship with him until he got back in the work routine.

Client Evaluation Data   The following sources of data provide information about Len's adjustment:

1. *Absences and tardiness.* Len has missed 0 days and has not been late out of a total of 100 days worked.
2. *Percentage of work time on task.* Figure 3.4 indicates that Len was on task during more than 90% of the observations made.
3. *Frequency of trainer prompts.* As might be expected, in the initial week there was a higher frequency of trainer prompts. Verbal assistance has been required to date, although it has steadily decreased from four or five prompts to less than three. After the 3-week vacation during the holidays, Len's work habits needed retraining. Figure 3.4 depicts the frequency of prompting required.
4. *Supervisor evaluations.* Table 3.9, showing the most recent evaluation by Len's supervisor, indicates a generally favorable assessment. Although Len continually arrives at work too early, this problem will be alleviated when he moves into the group home.
5. *Wages earned.* Len has earned a total of $2,320.00 for 100 work days. He receives full fringe benefits.

SUMMARY

The purpose of these case studies has been to identify and describe the critical factors involved in the training and placement process for developmentally disabled individuals. Although these case studies are only demonstrations, they are remarkable with regard to what each of these individuals' previous earning power had been. None of these individuals had ever worked competitively before. They are now drawing a weekly paycheck, which is comparable

Table 3.9.   Supervisor's evaluation form—Bimonthly

Trainee/employee's name: _Len_   Date of placement: _11-13-78_

Job title: _Kitchen Utility_   Date hired: _11-13-78_

Job site: _____   Current date: _____

Job coordinator: _____

Please circle all items that apply to the trainee/employee:

1. The employee
   (a) generally arrives and leaves on time.
   (b) maintains good atttendance.
   (c) takes meals and breaks appropriately.
   (d) maintains a good appearance.
   Comments on uncircled items: _Arrives up to two hours early; needs to be told to break._

2. The employee has
   (a) mastered all aspects of present job.
   (b) mastered many but not all aspects of job to date.
   (c) not mastered essential aspects of job to date.

3. In order for the employee to follow directions regarding the job, the supervisor
   (a) can just give *verbal* instructions.
   (b) has to give many *gestures* as well as verbal instructions.
   (c) has to show the employee exactly what to do before he or she knows what to do.

4. A project staff member is present
   (a) too often.
   (b) too little according to the employee's need.
   (c) an appropriate amount of time.

5. This employee
   (a) frequently stops work and needs to be reminded to return to work.
   (b) stops working occasionally but no more than other employees.
   (c) works at a constant rate without reminders.

6. The employee is
   (a) a good worker.
   (b) an average worker.
   (c) a below average worker.

7. Does the project staff member in any way interfere with your supervision or plans for the employee? (a) no   (b) yes   (*If yes, please briefly describe.*)

_____
_____

Other comments: _Most of Len's problems are related to his inability to tell time._

            Supervisor _S.D._

to what their nonhandicapped peers are making in the same setting. These individuals were selected for presentation because they provide an accurate picture of the planning requirements, observation and intervention difficulties, and follow-up needs that are involved in competitive employment job placement.

An analysis of Chuck, Eric, and Len provides several possible reasons for their success to date. One, they are each young (Chuck, 22; Eric, 18; Len, 22). Second, they are social and outgoing; although Chuck cannot talk and Eric's speech is very difficult to understand, they exhibit positive affect regularly. Third, they each had the benefit of public school training programs. Although only Len received intensive skill instruction for the job on which he was eventually placed, it is evident that some training occurred in social, language, domestic, and self-care training programs for each individual. Fourth, in Eric's and Chuck's cases, the family commitment was less protective and more responsive to professional help. Fifth, all three individuals followed instructions of the project staff and, eventually, the permanent supervisor, with little resistance. Finally, and perhaps most importantly, each client had the good fortune of an immediate supervisor who very much wanted him to succeed.

Placement of developmentally disabled individuals in nonrestrictive competitive employment is a difficult process. There are many avenues along which breakdowns may occur. Without a trainer / advocate available regularly for several weeks initially, the probability of sustained employment would appear to be dubious in the majority of cases. Although the relative newness of Project Employability precludes any definitive conclusions about the key factors in successful employment for this population, it is safe to say that, without important support systems, such as positive parent attitude and transportation, no amount of skill development or wage reimbursement for employers will suffice to bring about successful employment.

The data presented herein reflect the information needed to evaluate the job performance of severely developmentally disabled clients. Multiple sources of data provide staff with the capability of objectively evaluating and tracking an individual's progress. Daily observations yield a steady index of feedback to the employer and project staff. Unfortunately, these case studies were not evaluated in rigorous within-subject designs; the authors hope, in future work, to provide this type of design. However, it must be noted that implementing these types of designs, e.g., multiple baselines or reversals, is at times quite difficult in the high pressure atmosphere of a college cafeteria.

REFERENCES

Becker, R. 1976. Job training placement for retarded youth: A survey. Ment. Retard. 14:7–11.

Bellamy, G. T., Horner, R., and Inman, D. 1979. Vocational Habilitation of Severely Retarded Adults: A Direct Service Technology. University Park Press, Baltimore.

Belmore, K., and Brown, L. A. 1977. Job skill inventory strategy for use in a public school vocational training program for severely handicapped potential workers. *In* N. Haring and D. Bricker (eds.), Teaching the Severely Handicapped, Vol. III. Special Press, Columbus, Oh.

Cooper, B. 1977. Occupational help for the severely disabled: A public school model. Rehabil. Lit. 38:66–74.

Gold, M. W. 1973. Research on the vocational habilitation of the retarded: The present, the future. *In* N. R. Ellis (ed.), International Review of Research in Mental Retardation, Vol. 6. Academic Press, New York.

Mithaug, D., and Haring, N. 1977. Community vocational and workshop placement. *In* N. Haring and L. Brown (eds.), Teaching the Severely Handicapped, Vol. 2. Grune & Stratton, New York.

Mithaug, D., Hagmeier, L., and Haring, N. 1977. The relationship between training activities and job placement in vocational education of the severely and profoundly handicapped. AAESPH Rev. 2:89–109.

Mithaug, D., Mar, D., and Stewart, D. 1978. Prevocational Assessment and Curriculum Guide. Exceptional Education Press, Seattle.

Perske, R. 1972. The dignity of risk and the mentally retarded. Ment. Retard. 10: 24–26.

Schalock, R., and Harper, R. 1978. Placement from community-based mental retardation programs: How well do clients do? Am. J. Ment. Defic. 83:240–247.

Usdane, W. 1976. The placement process in the rehabilitation of the severely handicapped. Rehabil. Lit. 37:162–165.

Walls, R. T., and Werner, T. J. 1977. Vocational behavior checklists. Ment. Retard. 15:30–35.

4

VOCATIONAL EVALUATION

W. Grant Revell, Lawrence J. Kriloff,
and Michelle Donnelly Sarkees

Vocational evaluation, as an assessment of inherent potential, identifies an individual's assets and liabilities. It is not proposed that this evaluation mechanism supplant traditional assessment programs developed for developmentally disabled individuals; rather, data resulting from this process should be used to complement, and subsequently expand, the direction of existing information so that realistic vocational training plans can be developed for this population. The primary objective of vocational evaluation is to provide an assessment technique that will identify vocational potential.

Evaluating the vocational needs of developmentally disabled individuals is a critical part of vocational preparation. Accurate evaluation information provides an opportunity to develop individualized vocational plans within the vocational program. Evaluation information further serves to assist teachers in expanding their vocational curriculum to meet individual client needs and potential. Effective vocational preparation of developmentally disabled individuals is dependent on teachers having functional knowledge of vocational evaluation techniques and tools.

Vocational evaluation is defined as a process designed to assess and predict work behavior and vocational potential, primarily through the application of a variety of practical techniques and procedures. This definition implies that information gained through vocational evaluation is useful both for short term and long term planning.

Specifically, vocational potential may relate to factors and characteristics like the following:

> . . . specific and general skills and abilities, aptitudes and interests, personality and temperament, values and attitudes, motivation and needs, physical capacity and work tolerance, educability and trainability, social skills and work habits, work adjustment and employability, placeability and rehabilitation/habilitation potential (Pruitt, 1977, p. 4).

Vocational evaluation, in relation to developmentally disabled individuals, must entail more than examination of psychometric data. It has become increasingly apparent that this testing alone is an ineffective premise upon which to base a decision regarding the vocational potential of an individual. Nadolsky (1969) states that, although psychological data comprise an important contribution to the evaluation techniques, this information is definitely limiting when attempting to ascertain an individual's vocational attributes and strengths. In short, psychometric data, in isolation, provide a poor predictor of employability potential. Therefore, in order to relate to the nature and degree of vocational potential that an individual possesses, an alternative approach must be used.

Vocational programs for the developmentally disabled that emphasize longitudinal planning are most effective in preparing clients to reach their work potential. Longitudinal planning emphasizes a long term step-by-step approach to vocational preparation. Short term activities and goals are established to assist students in reaching long range objectives.

For example, a moderately retarded adolescent who is nearing the completion of the public school program may have a desire to become competitively employed in the food service area. The teacher of this individual has an opportunity to place a student as a volunteer helper in the school cafeteria. Information gained from a vocational evaluation would be most helpful to the teacher in answering the following questions:

1. Is the long range goal of competitive employment as a food service worker realistic for this student?
2. Should this student be given the cafeteria training slot as a short term activity leading toward the long term goal?
3. If placed in the cafeteria, at what level of activity should the student be started?

Effective use of vocational evaluation procedures enables teachers of the developmentally disabled to assess current performance levels, to set long range expectations, and to develop the needed activities and short term goals that will allow students to reach their vocational potential.

The vocational evaluation can consist of four general categories of activities. These activities, discussed in detail later in this chapter, are as follows:

Clinical Assessment
↓
Laboratory Work Samples
↓
Work Experience Evaluation
↓
Work Tryouts

It is important that vocational evaluation be an ongoing process. The initial evaluation serves only to establish a baseline of information and a working plan to be used by teachers and students in setting up individualized vocational programs with flexible short term and long term goals. These goals can be changed, based on performance and need. Vocational evaluation activities can be used effectively at any point in the developmentally disabled student's vocational preparation.

The vocational evaluation is most effective when training is incorporated into the evaluation activities. Many developmentally disabled individuals enter vocational preparation with very limited vocational exposure. Their entry level behaviors are frequently deficient in terms of the attitudes, skills, and learning abilities needed to readily demonstrate, without special considerations, their full vocational preparation. Societal expectations that the developmentally disabled as a group have limited vocational potential have isolated these individuals from activities that would enhance their early vocational preparation. Although developmentally disabled individuals vary greatly in their vocational needs and potentials, it is important that teachers understand the following general learning principles:

1. Nonmotor abilities are only important during the early stages of learning; once learned, differences in nonmotor abilities do not affect the production of a task (Gold, 1975).
2. The speed at which a retarded individual learns a task cannot be used to predict the speed at which a task will be completed once learned (Gold, 1975).
3. The learning cujve of the retarded differs from the normal learning curve only in that the retarded individual takes longer to learn a task.

In summary, developmentally disabled students need the opportunity to acquire, during their vocational evaluation, the basic skills upon which production ability and potential are being measured.

Thus, vocational evaluation serves one primary purpose: to significantly enhance the opportunities developmentally disabled individuals have to become employed at their full potential level of performance. This purpose is accomplished through providing ongoing information on the vocational development, needs, and potentials of the individual student. This chapter provides special education teachers and other vocational practitioners with the information they need to effectively set up short term and long term vocational goals through use of the vocational evaluation.

CLINICAL ASSESSMENT

Evaluating the vocational needs of developmentally disabled individuals is a multistep procedure. It is important that students receive a full evaluation at the time they initially enter the vocational phase of their program. A comprehensive vocational evaluation can provide information on training methods, curriculum needs, supportive services (such as speech or physical therapy) needed as part of the vocational preparation of an individual student, attitudes and behaviors, and predicted vocational potential and limits. Vocational evaluation tools can also be used selectively and individually at critical points in a developmentally disabled individual's vocational preparation even at the time of job placement. It must be emphasized that vocational evaluation tools should be used both individually and collectively, as appropriate, for the individual student.

As a total predictive process, vocational evaluation involves the four previously mentioned categories of activities. Clinical assessment usually precedes all other testing because it provides information to help narrow the subsequent range of testing. Since testing must be limited to appropriate instruments that will provide essential information, clinical assessment usually covers the following categories:

1. Intelligence
2. Academic achievement
3. Character and personality
4. Aptitude
5. Interests
6. Motor functioning and manual dexterity

In order to fully understand the individual, his or her disability(ies), and his or her performance capabilities, the information gained from clinical assessment is essential. A brief look at each category may be helpful.

Intelligence

Intelligence quotients from the Stanford-Binet or the Wechsler Adult Intelligence Scales (WAIS) are preferred, but, if a psychologist is unavailable to administer these, there are alternatives. The Peabody Picture Vocabulary Test (PPVT) is a good estimate of verbal intelligence, as is the Slosson Intelligence Test. The Revised Beta Examination is a test that claims to estimate intelligence accurately, with emphasis on performance skills. The Culture-Fair Intelligence Test claims to be relatively independent of school achievement and environmental influences.

Intelligence testing assists those working with the developmentally disabled to anticipate the level of nonmotor ability at which someone can perform.

Academic Achievement

A well rounded test that measures a student's current level of knowledge in a variety of areas is preferred. The Wide Range Achievement Test (WRAT) measures reading (work attack and recognition), mathematics, and spelling. The Adult Basic Learning Examination is appropriate for grades 1–9 and measures vocabulary, reading, spelling, arithmetic computation, and problem solving. The Peabody Individual Achievement Test is appropriate for grades 1–12 and can be used with people who cannot write. It measures reading comprehension, reading recognition, spelling, general information, and mathematics.

Information from achievement tests provides the examiner with a basis for future test selection because it signals whether or not the student is capable of handling tests designed for specific educational levels. Also, it provides a basis for remediation, if needed.

Character and Personality

These tests are usually administered by a psychologist but are mentioned briefly here for the reader's reference. Personality tests are usually of the paper and pencil variety or are projective in nature. Paper and pencil tests frequently call for students reading test items at the sixth-grade level or above and responding with choices on an answer sheet. Edwards Personal Preference Schedule, the Minnesota Multiphasic Personality Inventory (MMPI), and the California Psychological Inventory are examples.

Projective tests call for a verbal or performance-oriented response from the student to a variety of stimuli in the belief that the individual ''projects'' his or her personality into his or her responses. The Thematic Apperception Test, the Rorschach Psychodiagnostic Test, the House, Tree, Person Test, and an adaptation of the Bender Visual-Motor Gestalt are examples of this variety.

The result here is to provide information about an individual's personality that may be helpful in guiding him or her into vocational tests that parallel occupations appropriate to his or her temperament.

Aptitude

Since aptitude describes an individual's potential for success in the future, results of aptitude testing can predict whether or not training is likely to have positive effects in specific areas.

Paramount in this category is the General Aptitude Test Battery (GATB), which is owned by the United States Department of Labor. This test describes nine aptitudes and is closely related to the *Dictionary of Occupa-*

tional Titles (DOT) (U.S. Department of Labor, Manpower Division, 1965).
There are paper and pencil sections as well as performance parts, which cannot be taken by those with upper extremity disabilities. A sixth-grade reading knowledge is recommended. A nonreading form is available, and the test is administered by the State Employment Service at no charge.

The Differential Aptitudes Test differs from the GATB in that it has no performance sections. It also calls for a sixth-grade reading level and is normed on grades 8–12. Nine verbally oriented aptitudes are measured, and it can be administered at the student's school.

There are a variety of aptitude tests that measure specific vocational areas including clerical, mechanical, and manual functions.

Interests

Tests measuring interests are essential to the establishment of a basis for further testing. Here the range is narrowed so that examiner and subject have the benefit of knowing where they are going and can set goals for the future.

Interest tests that require a sixth-grade or higher reading level usually involve paper and pencil responses to written vocational stimuli and compare a person's interests with those of the public in general or with those of employees in various occupations. Positive and negative responses identify an individual's interest patterns with those of people already happily situated in these occupations and, therefore, predict a student's compatibility with various vocations. There is no prediction of success, however. The Kuder Occupational Interest Survey, the Strong-Campbell Interest Blank, and the Minnesota Vocational Interest Inventory are examples.

Other interest tests available for nonreaders are based on picture choices and include the Wide Range Interest and Opinion Test and the Picture Interest Inventory.

Motor Functioning and Manual Dexterity

This category of testing usually precedes actual trials with work samples because these tests can identify problems in fine and gross motor responses as well as the level of psychomotor speed and eye-hand coordination at which a person works or is capable of working.

The most comprehensive test for this purpose is the Oseretsky Tests of Motor Proficiency, which measure six separate varieties of motor responses and report a motor age. This age is compared to the student's chronological age, and the difference or similarity is noted as normal, deficient, or above average. The Bender Visual-Motor Gestalt is a good indicator of the existence of brain damage and ultimate level of eye-hand coordination. Because of their clinical implications, these tests are usually administered by a psychologist or trained technician.

The manual dexterity tests are less technical and can reveal the rate at which a person learns a motor response and, ultimately, his or her level of competence. Fine and gross motor responses of the upper extremities are frequently measured.

Tests like the Purdue Pegboard, Pennsylvania Bi-Manual Work Sample, the Crawford Small Parts Dexterity Test, the Stronberg Dexterity Test, and the Hand-Tool Dexterity Test are examples of this category and measure with some accuracy the level at which a person can work with his or her hands and fingers in close and confined space under timed conditions.

Conclusion

Essentially, the clinical assessment of the developmentally disabled individual provides the examiner with a variety of information that precedes the actual sampling of work performance. Measurement of learning capacities, interests, and potential growth, as well as an assessment of physical, mental, emotional, or environmental factors, must be made before work performance is examined or a vocational objective is established. Once these factors are determined, the examiner is ready for the evaluation of work potential in a laboratory setting (e.g., through administration of a commercially available work samples evaluation system). Here, the student is able to sample varieties of work, and both the examiner and the client can explore the possibilities for future employment.

LABORATORY WORK SAMPLES

Work samples represent an important component of the vocational evaluation process. As a close simulation of the tasks required in business, industry, or a specific vocational area, work samples can be useful in assessing vocational strengths, aptitudes, interests, and limitations by lending a realistic perspective to the vocational guidance process.

Work samples can produce useful evaluation data for predicting vocational potential because they emphasize psychomotor skills rather than verbal abilities, can produce feedback relative to the practically based hands-on activities in a short period of time, and provide direct information about the individual's performance level and enthusiasm.

Vocational laboratory evaluation usually employs work samples that have been designed to measure student interest, proficiency, and capacity for sustained concentration in performing set exercises that parallel actual competitive and sheltered employment. Ideally, these exercises should be standardized against a population similar to that for which the tests will be used. The lack of this standardization is one of the several factors that minimize the validity of laboratory evaluations with severely disabled clients.

Objectively scored work samples ensure impartiality and uniform application. In addition, scores may be compared to the standards of a population different from the test subject to determine the quality of his or her performance in a competitive situation. An example of this would involve a comparison between the performance of a retarded individual and that of a normal population to ascertain whether or not the test subject has the skills necessary to compete with those of average intelligence.

A variety of commercially prepared work samples are available. They are based on cluster-trait samples and single-trait samples. Cluster-trait samples use one activity to measure a variety of vocational factors essential to many occupations. Single-traits samples are based on one vocational activity and measure all the qualities necessary for successful performance in that vocation.

Selection of the proper commercial system should take into consideration:

1. Range of jobs available in the community and scope of jobs represented in the work sample
2. Validity and reliability for the client population to be served
3. Purpose of the evaluation
   a. Occupational information through a hands-on experience
   b. Assessment of present skills and aptitudes without relating information to career functions
   c. A thorough evaluation of student aptitudes and work behaviors
   d. Occupational information and dissemination
   e. Occupational exploration

It must be remembered that no one system will meet all needs — and they are expensive. A brief look at selected commercial systems follows.

VIEWS — Vocational Information and Evaluation Work Samples

The Jewish Employment and Vocational Service of Philadelphia has developed the VIEWS system specifically to evaluate moderately to severely handicapped populations. It is a battery of hands-on, job-related work samples that simulate a work environment. One important feature as an evaluation tool is that VIEWS distinguishes between acquisition of learned material and production. Research indicates that nonmotor abilities are important during the early stages of learning but that, once learned, differences in nonmotor abilities do not affect the production of a task (Gold, 1975). Therefore, this system, with its 16 work samples from four basic work areas, seeks to locate the highest level of production at which a handicapped student is capable of functioning.

The work samples are grouped into four categories: 1) elemental work area, 2) machine area, 3) clerical area, and 4) crafts area. The work samples relate to the worker trait groups identified in the *Dictionary of Occupational Titles*.

The work samples are administered from least complex tasks to more complex tasks. Directions are given orally, and demonstrations are also used in order to be certain that the trainee fully comprehends the work sample instructions; therefore, no reading is required.

The trainee is timed from the moment the work sample exercise begins until the task has been completed. Scoring is based on a 3-point scale relating to time and quality standards. A period of 20 to 30 hours is generally needed to administer the entire series of work samples.

The norm base used for this battery was a population consisting of 104 developmentally disabled individuals (median IQ of 50), who ranged in age from 16 to 61 (Botterbusch, 1977). No reliability or validity data are available.

The Tower System

Sponsored by the Vocational Rehabilitation Administration and the Institute for the Crippled and Disabled Rehabilitation and Research Center (ICD) in New York City, the Tower System is designed for physically and emotionally disabled persons. By analyzing various jobs, work samples are grouped into 14 major areas of training.

As the oldest vocational evaluation system for use with handicapped populations, this battery categorizes 93 work samples into the following training areas: 1) clerical, 2) drafting, 3) drawing, 4) electronics assembly, 5) jewelry manufacturing, 6) leather goods, 7) machine shop, 8) lettering, 9) mail clerk, 10) optical mechanics, 11) pantograph engraving, 12) sewing machine operating, 13) welding, and 14) workshop assembly.

The trainee, upon completion of a preliminary screening procedure to document pertinent medical, psychological, and intellectual information, is placed in one of the 14 job-training areas according to interest and/or a planning session with the evaluator. Advancement of job tasks within a specific job-training area is progressive; however, trainees generally do not complete all the work samples in the battery.

The trainee begins the job task after receiving procedural instructions from the evaluator, although no specific timing procedure is used. Evaluators weight the scores in terms of time and quality. Ratings, awarded according to the number of errors, are based on a 5-point scale.

Before a system is purchased by a facility, potential evaluators must attend a 3-week training course. This workshop provides information relative to establishing the evaluation unit and conducting the evaluation sessions.

The population for norming this battery consisted of ICD clients, although no information is provided regarding sample size, specific characteristics of the sample, industrial norms, or reliability data.

The validity of this system was the focus of a study conducted by Rosenberg in 1967. The results of this study did not positively lend themselves to establishing criterion reliability (Halpern, 1978).

The Singer Vocational Evaluation System

The Singer Vocational Evaluation System is a series of hands-on work samples developed by the Singer Corporation to measure performance on job-related tasks. Instructions are provided through earphones and slides. Physically disabled and mildly retarded students can handle some work samples that relate to specific jobs. It is a useful system of job exploration techniques.

This system consists of 20 independent work samples: 1) sample making, 2) bench assembly, 3) drafting, 4) electrical wiring, 5) plumbing and pipe fitting, 6) carpentry, 7) refrigeration, heating, and air conditioning, 8) soldering and welding, 9) office and sales clerk, 10) needle trades, 11) masonry, 12) sheet metal, 13) cooking and baking, 14) engine service, 15) medical service, 16) cosmetology, 17) data calculation and recording, 18) soil testing, 19) photolab technician, and 20) production machine operator.

There are no rigid time limitations imposed by this battery. The usual time allotment for evaluation is approximately 7 days, although as much as 3 weeks may be necessary if all 20 work samples are to be used.

The evaluator rates the trainee on a 5-point scale relative to time and quality norms. Twenty-nine work factors are incorporated into the system. Specified factors are observed in various work samples, and the results can be related to more than 1,000 job areas described in the *Dictionary of Occupational Titles*.

Inadequate information is available about the norm base for this system. The evaluator is not provided with any data relating to industrial norms, reliability, or validity.

The Hester System

Developed by Goodwill Industries of Chicago, the Hester System is designed to measure vocational potential of physically and mentally handicapped rehabilitation clients. It is based on the *Dictionary of Occupational Titles* and is a battery of psychological tests designed to relate student scores to the *DOT*. Twenty-eight pure factor performance and paper and pencil scores are grouped into the following seven categories on a computer printout: 1) unilateral motor ability, 2) intelligence, 3) perceptual-motor coordination, 4) perceptual ability, 5) bilateral motor ability, 6) physical strength, and 7) reading and mathematics achievement levels.

This evaluation system can be administered in approximately 5 hours. Instructions are given to the trainee orally, and demonstrations are used to make certain that individuals comprehend the directions for the tests.

The administrator times the trainee. The score is assigned by computer according to the time required to complete the task and/or the number of correct responses completed during a specific time period.

There are no data available concerning the population used as a norm group for this evaluation system. Data regarding reliability and validity are available.

The McCarron-Dial Work Evaluation System

The McCarron-Dial Work Evaluation System is comprised of 17 instruments that collect data, grouped into the following areas: 1) verbal-cognitive, 2) emotional, 3) motor abilities (fine motor and gross motor assessment), 4) sensory, and 5) integration-coping.

This evaluation system was specifically developed for use with mentally retarded and mentally ill populations. The work samples are administered during a 2-week period of time if all five factors are to be assessed.

All instructions are given to the trainee orally, and demonstrations are also allowed in order to ensure that the examinee fully understands the task directions. Few of the work samples are timed; no time norms are available.

Scoring is assigned according to the quality of work performance on each task. Scores are documented on a client profile after the scores have been converted into percentile scores.

The data resulting from this system provide information about the trainee's aptitudes in the following program areas: 1) extended sheltered employment, 2) work activity experiences, 3) transitional sheltered employment, 4) community placement and employment, and 5) day care experiences (Botterbusch, 1976).

Data pertinent to work sample norms were based on a population of 200 developmentally disabled adults. Norms were determined in sheltered workshop and supervised community employment environments. There are no data available concerning the reliability of this system. Positive results are reported regarding the validity of the battery.

Valpar Component Work Sample Series

While the Valpar Component Work Sample series was designed more for the industrially injured than for the developmentally disabled, it is a well executed series of work samples based on a trait and factor approach. Developed by the Valpar Corporation in Tucson, Arizona, this system consists of the following work samples: 1) small tools (mechanical), 2) size discrimination, 3) numerical sorting, 4) upper extremity range of motion, 5) clerical comprehension and aptitude, 6) independent problem solving, 7) eye-hand-foot coordination, 8) simulated assembly, 9) multilevel sorting, 10) whole body range of motion, 11) trilevel measurement, and 12) soldering.

If all of the components are used as a total vocational evaluation system, 12 to 15 hours are usually necessary. However, each work sample is self-contained, and components can be used independent of each other.

All instructions regarding work sample performance are oral, and demonstrations are included. Reading is not a general requirement, except in cases in which written words are implicit in the work task.

Clients are timed from the point of initial instructions to the point at which the task is completed. A total score for the client represents a combination of time and error scores, which reflect performance, quality, and quantity.

Norms are available for sheltered workshop clients. Most work samples in this system have been tested for reliability; the results have reportedly been good. No validity data are available.

WORK EXPERIENCE EVALUATION

The clinical assessment and laboratory work samples phases of the vocational evaluation provide a significant base of information for use in determining the vocational needs and potential of the developmentally disabled. It is important, however, that performance in simulated and actual work settings be viewed as an integral part of the total vocational evaluation. The use of work experience as an evaluation tool is especially important to the classroom teacher whose access to many of the testing procedures reviewed in the discussion of clinical assessment and laboratory work samples might be limited by time, funding, personnel, or procedural problems. The inclusion of work experience in the vocational evaluation also serves a very useful purpose in terms of the students' attitudes toward testing. Developmentally disabled students experience frequent testing by clinical personnel for a variety of reasons including diagnostic, health, personal development, educational placement, and legal requirements of the school system. The attitude of the frequently overtested student toward further testing can have significant limiting effects on performance. Although attitude problems can be dealt with effectively by an understanding evaluator, including work experience in the evaluation can serve as a concrete motivator for the person undergoing evaluation.

Job Sampling

Two primary parts of the work experience evaluation are job sampling and situational assessment. Job samples differ from the previously discussed work samples in that job samples are replications of actual job tasks available in the community. For example, a local industry has an ongoing assembly task that has job potential for severely retarded individuals. Replicating that assembly task within the classroom for purposes of evaluation and training would serve as a job sample. Job samples that are based on a formal job analysis have the most evaluation potential because of their significantly greater potential for being valid approximations of what occurs in the community. Formal job samples are developed through the following steps:

1. Community job survey
2. Job analysis
3. Completion of job sample
4. Norming the job sample
5. Completion of manual for job sample
6. Administration and evaluation of information gained from job sample (Brolin, 1976, p. 107)

Job sampling has numerous applications in the classroom. Job stations can be set up by replicating jobs in the community potentially available to developmentally disabled students. For example, a job sample for custodial work could be developed by making use of cleaning equipment such as floor buffers, vacuums, and mops. Tasks can be defined that replicate commercial use of this equipment, and the evaluation procedure would include training the student in the required task to a criterion level of performance. Job samples can be developed from general trade areas and also from specific tasks that are performed in the community. Job samples have face validity to the student, and the information gained through their use can be readily applied to both short and long range programing.

The *Dictionary of Occupational Titles,* a useful reference in the process of job analysis and developing work samples, can be a great help in developing job samples. Many of the worker-trait groups identified in commercially prepared vocational evaluation systems are directly related to jobs in the *DOT.* The *DOT* is the most comprehensive source of occupational information available. This dictionary alphabetically identifies and describes jobs found in the work force. Organized in three volumes, the first book lists 35,550 job titles which represent 21,741 occupations.

This reference can be helpful in the process of developing and implementing job sampling activities because it provides information on the type of work being done within a specific job title, how this work is done, and why the work is necessary. In addition, a detailed profile of the occupation can be developed through the supplied information concerning aptitudes and interests necessary for the job, required levels of functioning ability, physical demands, and working conditions relevant to the job. As an illustration, Table 4.1 presents the *DOT* entry for the job of kitchen helper.

Table 4.1. Sample entry from the *Dictionary of Occupational Titles*

KITCHEN HELPER (hotel & rest.) 318.887. cookee; cook helper; kitchen hand; kitchen man; kitchen porter; kitchen runner. Performs any combination of the following duties to maintain kitchen work areas and restaurant equipment and utensils in clean and orderly condition: Sweeps and mops floors. Washes worktables, walls, refrigerators, and meat blocks. Segregates and removes trash and garbage and places it in designated containers. Steam-cleans or hoses-out garbage cans. Sorts bottles and breaks disposable ones in bottle-crushing machine. Washes pots, pans and trays by hand. Scrapes food from dirty dishes and washes them by hand or places them in racks or on conveyor to dishwashing machine. Places silver in revolving burnishing-machine tumbler, dips it in chemical solutions, holds it against buffing wheel, and rubs it with cloth to remove tarnish and restore luster. Holds inverted glasses over revolving brushes to clean inside surfaces. Transfers supplies and equipment between storage and work areas by hand or by use of handtruck. Sets up banquet tables. Washes and peels vegetables, using knife or peeling machine. May be known according to task performed as DISHWASHER, HAND; DISHWASHER, MACHINE; GARBAGEMAN; POTWASHER; SILVERMAN.

Source: U.S. Department of Labor, Manpower Division. 1965. Dictionary of Occupational Titles, p. 399. 3rd Ed. U.S. Department of Labor, Washington, D.C.

Situational Assessment

Within the realm of identifying an individual's aptitudes, the situational assessment technique is perhaps the most common approach. This method of evaluation consists of observing individuals performing real or simulated work tasks in a group situation. In some cases, situational assessment is used to observe specific aptitudes or work habits; in other cases, this method is used to assess overall vocational aptitude (Pruitt, 1977). The information gained from this source should be used in conjunction with other pertinent data to develop realistic vocational training plans.

One advantage of situational assessment is that this approach allows for the observation of a larger number of appropriate worker traits and behaviors than can be seen with the use of job samples. These behaviors are also demonstrated in an environment that is more natural and relaxed than that of a timed work sample or a formal standardized testing situation (Brolin, 1976).

For example, a cerebral palsied handicapped student might want to be a receptionist. A situational assessment activity could be set up in the school office or possibly in a neighboring business or industry office. The student would be placed in the office for a specified length of time in defined job areas. In this example, information would be gained on the student's work attitude toward this task and setting, modifications that might be needed to facilitate performance, additional training or specialization that would be required to reach a more competitive level of performance, and the reaction of the employed office workers to the student. The evaluator would primarily observe the student's performance. Intervention could take place when needed to assist in performance in areas such as training, mobility, and physical modifications of the work area. However, the primary purpose of situational assessment is to provide the evaluator with the opportunity to observe performance in an actual work setting.

As in the case of job samples, situational assessment provides the trainee with activities whose relationship to vocational concerns can be readily experienced. The readily seen meaningfulness of these activities provides important motivational influences. A student can be placed in varied settings for situational assessments with limited costs for equipment and materials. The world of work and the importance of the evaluation are directly experienced, and, as information is gained about the student's work behaviors and skills, situations that meet individual needs can be established. The situational assessment provides both learning experiences for the trainee and indications of further evaluation and training needs.

One of the positive aspects of this approach is that situational assessment can take place in a variety of situations. Sites for assessment can be selected according to the type of work environment of the specific job being considered. Opportunities to establish situational assessment activities can be found in institutional facilities or schools. They may also be based in the community.

During the process of situational assessment, several factors concerning a client's work performance are observed. These factors include specific work skills, work personality, perseverance, and work tolerance. Inferences are also made regarding worker attitudes and values (Pruitt, 1977).

More time can be allowed for situational assessment activities than is normally allowed for commercial work sample batteries. Therefore, a more precise profile of client abilities can be developed so that a *realistic* vocational plan can be formulated.

WORK TRYOUTS

The final phase of vocational evaluation is work tryouts. Work tryouts are placements in the community under the conditions normally associated with a specific job. Work tryouts include formal follow-along activities to ensure that the trainee is given an accurate performance assessment and a fair opportunity to perform. The motivating features of job tryouts for developmentally disabled students can be readily seen in terms of both the relevancy of the evaluation experience and the opportunity to demonstrate skills in an actual work setting. Another very positive feature of work tryouts is the effect high levels of performance by developmentally disabled students can have on attitudes of employers toward disability groups. For example, individuals with epilepsy are frequently excluded from the job market because of societal attitudes toward seizures. This exclusion is particularly relevant to individuals whose seizures cannot be brought under perfect control. A student with epilepsy can be placed in a work tryout with a potential employer. The student would have the opportunity to demonstrate that the job can be completed at a competitive level and that seizure activity can be compensated for without injury or liability. Work tryouts also provide information on a student's current interest level in a particular job area, production level, work attitude, and need for further preparation.

CONTRIBUTIONS OF THE VOCATIONAL EVALUATION PROCESS

Vocational evaluation is the comprehensive process of using real or simulated job samples to gather pertinent data about an individual's vocational aptitudes and interests. This information is necessary to enable the development of realistic vocational training plans for handicapped individuals.

A functional knowledge of the procedures and tools involved in evaluating vocational needs and potential is an important asset for teachers of the developmentally disabled. Positive evaluation results can greatly enhance both the vocational opportunities available to students and the attitude and expectations of trainers. When applied to the evaluation of the developmentally disabled, especially the mentally retarded, there are a number of factors that will facilitate student performance. Revell and Wehman (1978) have listed the following principles:

1. It should be understood by teachers that the job samples phase of an evaluation is made up of tasks that usually must be *learned* by many developmentally disabled students before evaluation of performance can be accurately completed.
2. Because of the limited vocational exposure of many developmentally disabled students, many necessary prerequisite behaviors might not be a part of the student's behavior repertoire, e.g., tool usage, attending behavior, or positioning at the work bench.
3. The completion of the task might not be, in itself, reinforcing to the student; reinforcers should be identified that are shown to be effective, i.e., that their usage results in an increase in desired behavior.
4. Precision teaching techniques are frequently needed to teach a student how to perform the job sample task.
5. Statements on productivity and resulting decisions on employability cannot be accurately attempted until the student demonstrates learning through

reaching a criterion level of performance as measured by a data-based information-gathering system.

6. When a student fails to learn an assigned evaluation task, the teacher should identify the external variables, including environmental distractions, ineffective teaching methods, and lack of appropriate reinforcement contingencies which might be adversely affecting performance. It should not be decided that failure is a result of internal limitations until manipulation of external variables has been exhausted (p. 228).

The implication of these statements is that the evaluation period should be used as a time of exploration and training. Careful attention to these principles during the vocational evaluation will give significantly greater credibility to predictive statements on vocational potential and will help ensure the development of appropriate and effective training assignments based on perceived vocational needs.

CASE STUDIES

The techniques of vocational evaluation can be applied at many different stages in the vocational preparation of developmentally disabled students, and the evaluations should be structured to meet the individual needs and abilities of each student. The following two case studies are examples of vocational evaluations completed for substantially handicapped, developmentally disabled students with very different needs and for different purposes. These case studies underscore the importance of vocational evaluation for the developmentally disabled.

Case Study 1: Striving for Vocational Independence

Glen[1] is a male cerebral palsy victim who, by virtue of his disability, had been receiving special academic instruction through an urban school system in a center for such individuals. After many years of special academic preparation, the time came for graduation and the consideration of the feasibility of vocational independence.

Glen showed good motivation toward rehabilitative services, and he was therefore vocationally evaluated just before graduation from his special academic program.

Glen manifested spastic quadriplegia and walked with the aid of crutches. Only his right hand exhibited normal functioning and all other extremities showed involvement from cerebral palsy. No specific interests were indicated. The usual sequence of testing was conducted in order to explore

---

[1]All names used in the case studies are fictitious.

interests, aptitudes, intellectual functioning, educational achievement, motor functioning, and vocational potential.

Exploration of interests revealed clusters in literature, sales, office work, computational activity, and personal service. Because of his disability, he preferred and needed sedentary vocational activity. Although he was motivated, he was somewhat fearful of attempting a very challenging training program.

Aptitude testing was fairly consistent with the results of intelligence testing and placed him near average with regard to most verbal functions. Of course, motor functions were slow and in some cases blocked, which accounted for reduced efficiency in handling operations. Speech, hearing, and sight were without dysfunction, and communication was adequate. Glen's educational achievement had risen substantially and placed him in an average category of the general population.

Glen was tried on a number of job-related samples in the evaluation laboratory. Clerical trades emerged as the one category for which he showed the greatest potential. He was tried on clerical sorting tasks, use of the adding machine, collating, payroll computation, and visual discrimination exercises. All trials proved that he could perform the tasks and complete the work within competitive time limits.

Evaluation recommended training in clerical trades at the state rehabilitation center with further remediation in mathematics and reading. Low demand, high interest tasks were recommended at first, with slow transition to more complicated activities. Training was recommended in terms of individual instruction with repetition and demonstrations and increasing diversification to allow for individual judgments. Job tryouts were suggested.

Case Study 2:
Enhancing Vocational Potential through Work Adjustment

Mark is a moderately mentally retarded young man of 17 who functions intellectually in the trainable range with virtually no educational skills. He was a student in an urban special education program connected with a school system and was fast approaching the time when his chronological age would prevent his remaining in school. He was thought to be totally unemployable, and his parents had resigned themselves to caring for him indefinitely.

The school system had invested many years of preparation in Mark to bring him to a point at which he was ready to be tested vocationally. The usual exploration was made, and it was confirmed that intellectually this adolescent was functioning in the trainable range with no appreciable skills in reading and arithmetic. Low social maturity also was identified, with verbal skills and ability to communicate as the primary assets.

Testing produced little information about specific aptitudes but did identify interests in manually oriented work in a socially compatible setting.

Motor functioning emerged as somewhat impaired; this, coupled with low social maturity, indicated an unproductive individual. Separation of nonmotor ability from production during testing was attempted. The acquisition of skills was very slow but production suffered in the laboratory because of distractibility and lack of work skills.

With these facts in evidence, recommendations were made for Mark to be placed in work adjustment where attention could be given to improving social skills, activities of daily living, social maturity, and concentration on a given task.

In the work adjustment setting, Mark improved considerably, and a higher degree of independence was achieved. Motor skills were improved by assigning him simulated and real tasks that measured accuracy against rate of production. Appropriate rewards were introduced.

Tasks assigned were simple at first and became slightly more complicated as the levels of concentration, social skills, and ability to engage in sustained work improved.

Mark was reevaluated, this time for the purpose of vocational training and/or job tryouts. Because of improvement in social orientation, manual skills, vocational attitudes, and behaviors, as well as increased ability to handle his own self-image as a worker, he was recommended for work in a laundry, where he is now employed on a trial basis.

SUMMARY

The purpose of this chapter has been to assist teachers of the developmentally disabled in recognizing the important role of vocational evaluation in preparing their students for employment. The two case studies demonstrate that considerable useful information can be obtained through evaluation. The studies also demonstrate that the evaluation process, when properly completed, can give important direction to vocational programming and job placement. Many evaluation procedures and tools can be applied directly by teachers in the classroom and, whenever possible, in the community. Developmentally disabled persons have significant vocational potential. Well planned and executed vocational evaluations can provide the opportunity many developmentally disabled students need to demonstrate their untapped capabilities.

Evaluation, as a continuous process, must focus on the individual's progress and problem areas during the vocational training program and, ultimately, on the job. Only then will the bits and pieces of aptitude, ability, and interest fall into place to reveal the total vocational picture of an individual.

The process of vocational evaluation includes a variety of components. One valuable source of vocational aptitude data is the use of work samples. This method of evaluation emphasizes psychomotor skills rather than verbal abilities. Feedback from this reality-based technique yields information about the trainee's level of performance and interest in the work sample area.

Advantages of other components of the vocational evaluation process have also been discussed. Situational assessment, the practice of observing individuals performing real or simulated work tasks in a group situation, is perhaps one of the most common and effective approaches to vocational evaluation. This method can be used to observe specific aptitudes or work habits and, in conjunction with other pertinent data, can lend itself to the development of a realistic, individualized vocational training plan.

Other evaluation techniques that are useful in assessing the vocational interests and aptitudes of developmentally disabled individuals include job sampling and work tryouts.

Because of the increased emphasis on rehabilitation services for the severely disabled, several types of technical assistance that could be provided to public schools are outlined below:

1. Making available employment information concerning the community, in general, and the severely disabled, in particular
2. Assisting the schools in coordinating their prevocational and vocational programs with the training and employment opportunities that will be available to severely disabled students upon their completion of school
3. Providing consultation or direct evaluation services to assist the schools in setting realistic objectives and effective longitudinal plans for their students
4. Initiating and following through on efforts to identify and train service delivery and administrative staff who are willing to expand their professional competence to enable them to effectively serve the severely disabled

State agency vocational rehabilitation services are needed if severely disabled persons are to develop to their full vocational potential. For example, even with the increasing amount of vocational research literature that has accrued in recent years demonstrating the work capacities of severely retarded persons, a very small fraction of the severely and profoundly retarded are actually employed in the nation's labor force. It is imperative that greater efforts now be directed toward *placing* the severely disabled in community employment and industrial workshops. Applied research efforts are also required to evaluate the efficacy and long term impact of on-the-job training programs. Vocational evaluation must continue to develop new ways to assess the employment potential of developmentally disabled clients.

REFERENCES

Bellamy, G. T., and Snyder, S. 1976. The trainee performance sample: Toward the prediction of habilitation costs for severely handicapped adults. AAESPH Rev. 1:17–36.

Botterbusch, K. 1973. Tests and Measurements for Vocational Evaluators. Materials Development Center, Stout Vocational Rehabilitation Institute, University of Wisconsin-Stout, Menomonie, Wis.

Botterbusch, K. 1976. A Comparison of Seven Vocational Evaluation Systems. Materials Development Center, Stout Vocational Rehabilitation Institute, University of Wisconsin-Stout, Menomonie, Wis.

Botterbusch, K. 1977. A Comparison of Four Vocational Evaluation Systems. Materials Development Center, Stout Vocational Rehabilitation Institute, University of Wisconsin-Stout, Menomonie, Wis.

Brolin, D. E. 1976. Vocational Preparation of Retarded Citizens. Charles E. Merrill Publishing Co., Columbus, Oh.

Esser, T. 1974. Effective Report Writing in Vocational Evaluation and Work Adjustment Programs. Materials Development Center, Stout Vocational Rehabilitation Institute, University of Wisconsin-Stout, Menomomic, Wis.

Gold, M. W. 1975. Vocational training. In J. Wortis (ed.), Mental Retardation and Developmental Disabilities: An Annual Review, Vol. 7, pp. 254–264. Bruner/ Mazel, New York.

Halpern, A. 1978. Principles and practices of measurement in career education for handicapped students. Career Dev. Except. Individ. 1:13–24.

Hoffman, P. R. 1971. History of the vocational evaluation and work adjustment association. Vocat. Eval. Work Adjust. Bull. 4:6–16.

Junkins, J. 1977. S.A.V.E. System: Systematic Approach to Vocational Evaluation. S.A.V.E. Enterprises, Rome, Ga.

Krantz, G. 1971. Critical vocational behaviors. J. Rehabil. July-August.

Kulman, J. et al. 1975. The tools of vocational evaluation. Vocat. Eval. Work Adjust. Bull. 8:49–64.

McClelland, D. 1973. Testing for competence rather than for "intelligence." Am. Psychologist 28:1–14.

Morley, R. (ed.). 1973. Vocational Assessment Systems. State of Iowa, Department of Public Instruction, Des Moines.

Nadolsky, J. 1969. The existential in vocational evaluation. J. Rehabil. 35:22–23.

Neff, W. 1970. Vocational assessment — Theory and models. J. Rehabil. 36:27–29.

Pruitt, W. A. 1970. Basic assumptions underlying work sample theory. J. Rehabil. 36:24–26.

Pruitt, W. A. 1977. Vocational (Work) Evaluation. Walt Pruitt Associates, Menomonie, Wis.

Revell, G., and Wehman, P. 1978. Vocational evaluation of severely and profoundly retarded clients. Rehabil. Lit. 39:226–231.

U.S. Department of Labor, Manpower Division. 1965. Dictionary of Occupational Titles, 3rd Ed. U.S. Department of Labor, Washington, D.C.

5

CORE SKILLS SUBDOMAIN

The initial subdomain in this vocational curriculum describes core skills that are usually prerequisite behaviors for learning the manual skills described in the following vocational subdomains (Chapters 6–11). These skills are elementary, yet many severely, profoundly, and multihandicapped students are unable to perform them. The tasks that follow involve fine motor skills and instruction following.

Whether or not it will be necessary to train core skills in isolation from vocational skills will usually depend on the functioning level of the student. For example, with older learners it may be advisable to find simple vocational activities that correspond to the appropriate motor functioning level. On the other hand, it may be easier for younger children to attain optimal fine motor performance using toys.

The organization of this subdomain should be noted. A developmental sequence of fine motor behaviors is outlined, beginning with very low level skills. For each motor skill an *instructional objective, prerequisite skills,* and recommended *activities* are provided. A brief *task analysis* of student behaviors and *teaching procedures* are also provided.

This fine motor sequence can be used by the teacher to *assess* the student's motor skill level, to provide relevant manual tasks at the appropriate level, and to *evaluate* the progress the student makes in the sequence. The following fine motor skills have been analyzed:

1. Reaching, Grasping, and Retaining
2. Picking Up Object
3. Squeezing
4. Pats, Slaps, Pushes Against
5. Bilateral Reach
6. Voluntary Release

7. Transfer from Hand-to-Hand
8. Scissors Grasp
9. Pincer Grasp
10. Manipulating Small Objects with Purpose

The second aspect of this subdomain involves an instruction-following skill sequence. The five sample instructions are representative of those that might be required in a vocational situation. As with the motor development sequence, instruction following need not be trained separately from vocational skill development; clearly, if the student is learning to comply with the instructor on a given task, some degree of instruction following is taking place. This program might also be further developed by using 2- and 3-step instructions (e.g., "Go to the window and bring me the pencil," or "Take this note to the office, pick up the absentee slips, and come back here"). An instructional objective and teaching procedures for the following instructions are presented:

1. Sit Down
2. Stand Up
3. Come to Me
4. Raise Your Hand
5. Bring Me the Pencil

FINE MOTOR DEVELOPMENTAL SEQUENCE

REACHING, GRASPING, AND RETAINING

Instructional Objective: Given an appropriate cue, S will reach purposefully with either dominant or nondominant hand for object 12 inches from body, grasp it, and retain it with a palmar grasp for 10 seconds, with 100% accuracy for 3 consecutive training days.
Prerequisite Skills: Ability to open hand and ability to maintain eye contact with object.
Activity Ia: Cue: "Hold the pulley." (dominant hand)

Task Analysis	*Teaching Procedures*
1. S reaches for object next to and nearly touching hand.	a) Show S pulley, demonstrate use, place pulley next to S's hand.
	b) Give verbal cue and wait 5 seconds; if S responds correctly, reinforce.

Task Analysis	*Teaching Procedures*

<table>
<tr><td></td><td>c) Repeat verbal cue; if S responds correctly, reinforce.</td></tr>
<tr><td></td><td>d) Model behavior.</td></tr>
<tr><td></td><td>e) Repeat verbal cue; if S responds correctly, reinforce. (Gain S's eye contact by holding reinforcer in front of his or her eyes, then move reinforcer next to pulley).</td></tr>
<tr><td></td><td>f) Physically prompt by taking S's hand and moving it to touch pulley; reinforce.</td></tr>
</table>

2. *S* grasps object next to and nearly touching hand.
    a. Touches object
    b. Opens hand
    c. Closes hand around object
    d. Maintains grasp for:
         2 seconds
         4 seconds
         5 seconds
         10 seconds

a) Place bell directly next to *S's* hand.
b) Give verbal cue and wait 5 seconds; if *S* responds correctly, reinforce.
c) Repeat verbal cue; if *S* responds correctly, reinforce.
d) Model behavior.
e) Repeat verbal cue; if *S* responds correctly, reinforce.
f) Physically prompt by:
    1) Placing slight pressure with one finger on *S's* elbow
    2) Moving *S's* hand to pulley
    3) Opening *S's* hand
    4) Placing pulley in *S's* hand
    5) Closing hand over *S's* to ensure grasp
    6) Reinforcing

3. *S* repeats 1 and 2 with object moved successively to:
    2 inches from *S*
    4 inches from *S*
    6 inches from *S*
    8 inches from *S*
    10 inches from *S*
    12 inches from *S*

Activity Ib: Cue: "Hold the pulley." (nondominant hand)
Task Analysis: Same as that for Activity Ia.
Teaching Procedures: Same as those for Activity Ia. In addition, *T* should pair primary and social reinforcement. As *S's* response becomes fairly consistent after teaching procedures b) and c), gradually reduce primary reinforcement to every third trial, but maintain social reinforcement. Using a weight to immobilize hand not being used may prove helpful.
Activity II: Cue: "Hold the towel."
Task Analysis: Same as that for Activity Ia.
Teaching Procedures: Same as those for Activity Ia. In addition, to promote grasp maintenance, *T* can hold opposite end of towel and gently pull while repeating cue, "Hold the towel." Made into a game situation, this may motivate student. Modeling with another student may be helpful. Exaggerated facial expression and tone of voice in game situation may be helpful variables.

PICKING UP OBJECT

Instructional Objective: Given an appropriate cue, *S* will lift hand and arm completely off any supporting surface while maintaining grasp on object and will maintain this lift with either dominant or nondominant hand for 10 seconds, with 100% accuracy for 3 consecutive training days.
Prerequisite Skills: Ability to open hand and ability to maintain eye contact with object.
Activity Ia: Cue: "Pick up the saw." (dominant hand)

Task Analysis	Teaching Procedures
1. *S* touches object.	a) Show *S* saw; demonstrate action of picking up saw while pairing verbal cue, "Pick up the saw."
2. *S* grasps object (palmar grasp).	
3. *S* picks up object, lifting hand off surface.	
4. *S* picks up object, lifting hand and arm off surface.	b) Place saw by *S's* hand.
5. *S* completes step 4, maintaining lift and grasp for:	c) Give verbal cue and wait 5 seconds; if *S* responds correctly, reinforce.
2 seconds	d) Repeat verbal cue; if *S* responds correctly, reinforce.
4 seconds	
6 seconds	e) Model behavior.
10 seconds	f) Repeat verbal cue; if *S* responds correctly, reinforce.

Task Analysis   *Teaching Procedures*

    g) Physically prompt by:
       1) Moving *S's* hand to touch saw
       2) Placing saw in *S's* hand
       3) Applying slight pressure with one finger on *S's* elbow
       4) Applying slight pressure under *S's* hand
       5) Lifting *S's* hand off supporting surface
       6) Lifting *S's* arm off supporting surface
       7) Reinforcing

Activity Ib: Cue: "Pick up the saw." (nondominant hand)
Task Analysis: Same as that for Activity Ia.
Teaching Procedures: Same as those for Activity Ia. In addition, *T* should pair primary and social reinforcement. As *S's* response becomes fairly consistent after teaching procedures c) and d), gradually reduce primary reinforcer to every third trial, but maintain social reinforcement.

Activity II: Cue: "Pick up the sieve."
Task Analysis: Same as that for Activity Ia.
Teaching Procedures: Same as those for Activity Ia. In addition, the container with sand should be large enough in area to permit free movement of sieve, and the container's sides should be only 3–4 inches high so *S* can easily see over sides and have easy access to the sand and sieve. Sieve should ideally have a handle and large enough holes to allow easy flow of sand so *S* is not required to shake sieve to cause the sand to fall. Primary reinforcement may be faded as the activity of watching the sand becomes reinforcing by itself. Interaction of *T* and *S* using a second sieve and modeling techniques can be used effectively to promote motivation and mastery. Instructional setting should vary from classroom to playground sandbox, and *S* should be placed in different positions (sitting in chair, standing by table, sitting on floor, and so on).

SQUEEZING

Instructional Objective: Given a soft substance (e.g., bread dough), *S* will squeeze it by alternately opening and closing fingers 5 times in 10 seconds (either dominant or nondominant hand) for 3 consecutive training days.
Prerequisite Skills: Ability to open hand and ability to maintain eye contact with object.
Activity Ia: Cue: "Squeeze it." (dominant hand)

Task Analysis	Teaching Procedures
1. *S* grasps dough when handed to him or her.	a) Demonstrate squeezing dough.
2. *S* squeezes dough by closing and opening fingers: once in 10 seconds twice in 10 seconds 3 times in 10 seconds 4 times in 10 seconds 5 times in 10 seconds	b) Put dough in *S's* hand and let him or her feel it; squeeze *S's* fingers into dough a few times. c) Hand dough to *S*. d) Give verbal cue and wait 5 seconds; if *S* responds correctly, reinforce. e) Repeat verbal cue; if *S* responds correctly, reinforce. f) Model behavior with another ball of dough. g) Repeat verbal cue; if *S* responds correctly, reinforce. h) Physically prompt by: 1) Rubbing inside of *S's* wrist 2) Rubbing back of hand 2) Placing *T's* hand over *S's* and squeezing fingers in required manipulation. 4) Reinforcing

Activity Ib: Cue: "Squeeze it." (nondominant hand)
Task Analysis: Same as that for Activity Ia.
Teaching Procedures: Same as those for Activity Ia. In addition, pair primary and social reinforcement. As *S's* response becomes fairly consistent after teaching procedures d) and e), gradually reduce primary reinforcement to every third trial, but maintain social reinforcement. If *S* completes 1 or 2 open-close squeezes, but fails to perform the criterion of 5 in 10 seconds, repeating the verbal cue after each squeeze may be necessary along with rein-

forcing first after 1 squeeze, then only after 2 squeezes, then after 3, and so on, until criterion has been reached.

Other Activities: Instructional settings should change as appropriate. Use activities in as natural a setting as possible.

PATS, SLAPS, PUSHES AGAINST

Instructional Objective: Given an appropriate cue and having made hand contact with an object 10 inches in front of *S*, *S* will exert opposing force on object with hand (either dominant or nondominant) to effect movement of object away from body, with 100% accuracy for 3 consecutive training days.

Prerequisite Skills: Ability to open hand and ability to maintain eye contact with object.

Activity Ia: Cue: "Hit the bolt." (dominant hand)   *S* should be standing or sitting behind table.

Task Analysis	*Teaching Procedures*
1. *S* reaches for bolt.	a) Demonstrate movement of bolt by hitting it.
2. *S* opens hand.	
3. *S* touches bolt with palm of hand.	b) Give verbal cue and wait 5 seconds; if *S* responds correctly, reinforce.
4. *S* pushes against bolt.	
5. *S* withdraws hand.	c) Repeat verbal cue; if *S* responds correctly, reinforce.
	d) Model behavior.
	e) Repeat verbal cue; if *S* responds correctly, reinforce.
	f) Physically prompt by:
	1) Placing slight pressure with one finger on *S's* elbow
	2) Moving *S's* hand to bolt
	3) Opening *S's* hand
	4) Pushing *S's* palm against toy
	5) Withdrawing *S's* hand
	6) Reinforcing

Activity Ib: Cue: "Hit the bolt." (nondominant hand)
Task Analysis: Same as that for Activity Ia.

Teaching Procedures: Same as those for Activity Ia. In addition, pair primary and social reinforcement. As *S's* response becomes fairly consistent after teaching procedures b) and c), gradually reduce primary reinforcement to every third trial, but maintain social reinforcement. Difficulty may be encountered in task analysis step 5. In this case, having someone behind *S* to immediately apply physical prompting to facilitate *S's* arm withdrawal after the hitting motion may be required to hasten mastery of the step.

Activity II: Cue: "Splash the water." (dominant and nondominant hands) *S* should be sitting or standing 10 inches behind a tray partially filled with lukewarm water.

Task Analysis	*Teaching Procedures*
1. *S* extends arm so that hand is directly over water.	a) Demonstrate splashing the water.
2. *S* opens hand.	b) Continue as for Activity Ia.
3. *S* slaps water with palm of hand.	After *S* learns to slap the water, the activity can develop into learning to splash the water in a purposeful direction away from *S*. Some object can be placed at opposite end of water tray and *S* can be taught to directly splash water onto the object.
4. *S* withdraws hand from water.	
Slapping the water should be a quick motion, such that the movements of the hand into and out of the water cannot be differentiated.	
	Reinforce as in Activity Ia. Instructional setting should be varied to outdoors (when possible), to art room, swimming pool, and so on.

Activity III: Cue: "Push the ball." (dominant and nondominant hands) This activity can be started by using a large balloon since it is lighter in weight and requires less muscle strength. As skill is developed, change to a large ball about 12 inches in diameter.

Task Analysis: Same as that for Activity Ia.

Teaching Procedures: Same as those for Activity Ia. In addition, it is helpful to have a third person involved to receive and return the ball. Another person also adds motivation as game atmosphere evolves. Emphasis should not be placed at this time on catching the ball. *S* should be sitting, if physically possible, on floor with legs extended and apart in front of himself or herself. Otherwise, place *S* at the end of table so ball can be rolled along table top. S should not be permitted to pick up ball and throw it, but should be reinforced only when pushing ball on a supporting surface. Instructional setting should be varied to gym, playground, and so on. Reinforce according to Activity Ia. Gradually fade physical and verbal prompting as S learns to push ball to opposite person.

BILATERAL REACH

Instructional Objective: Upon making eye contact with an object 12 inches in front of S, S will move both hands toward object, resulting in S grasping object in hands, with 100% accuracy for 3 consecutive training days.

Prerequisite Skills: Ability to open hands and ability to maintain eye contact with object.

Activity I: Cue: "Pick up the cup."

Task Analysis: Same as that for Activity Ia of Reaching, Grasping, and Retaining, except using *both* hands.

Teaching Procedures: Same as those for Activity Ia of Reaching, Grasping, and Retaining, except using both of S's hands. In addition, primary reinforcement can consist of liquid in the cup, which S is helped to drink after performing behavior of picking up cup. (Junior cup with top is recommended.) This will reinforce the picking up behavior as well as initiate self-feeding responses.

Activity II: Cue: "Pick up the board."

Task Analysis: Same as that for Activity Ia of Reaching, Grasping, and Retaining, except using *both* hands.

Teaching Procedures: Same as those for activity Ia of Reaching, Grasping, and Retaining, except using both of S's hands. A large board is used in this activity.

VOLUNTARY RELEASE

Instructional Objective: With object retained in palmar grasp in one hand (or both hands), S will release object so that hand contact is no longer maintained (either dominant or nondominant hand, or bilateral with large objects), with 100% accuracy for 3 consecutive training days. Initially, release will be on to tabletop or floor or into T's hand. Gradually work into purposeful placement of released object, i.e., placement of object into container or specified spot on table.

Prerequisite Skills: Palmar grasp.

Activity I: Cue: "Drop the envelope." (dominant or nondominant hand)

Task Analysis	*Teaching Procedures*

1. *S* retains object in hand.
2. *S* opens hand to release object.

a) Hand object to *S,* or let *S* reach for and pick up object.
b) Give verbal cue and wait 5 seconds; if *S* responds correctly, reinforce.
c) Repeat verbal cue; if *S* responds correctly, reinforce.
d) Model behavior.
e) Repeat verbal cue; if *S* responds correctly, reinforce.
f) Physically prompt by:
    1) Rubbing hand
    2) Partially opening *S's* fingers
    3) Completely opening *S's* fingers
    4) Reinforcing
    5) Directing *S's* attention to dropped object

Importance should be placed on directing *S's* attention to the dropped object. *S* should be made keenly aware of the fact that the object is no longer in *S's* hand and that his or her voluntary action caused this to change. Ways to thus direct *S's* attention could include attaching a string to the object and tying the other end around *S's* wrist. When the object is released and falls, *S* will be able to feel weight and more readily draw his or her attention to the object. Reinforcement may be held in proximity to dropped object to draw attention in that direction.

Activity II: Cue: "Give me the envelope." (dominant or nondominant hand)

Task Analysis	Teaching Procedures
1. *S* retains object in hand. 2. *S* extends hand toward *T's* hand. 3. *S* places object in *T's* hand. 4. *S* opens his or her hand to release object. 5. *S* withdraws hand.	a) Hold hand out to *S* and give verbal cue; if *S* responds correctly, reinforce. b) If correct response is not made, place hand directly under object held by *S* and repeat cue; reinforce if correct response is made. c) Physically prompt if necessary by gradually removing object from *S's* hand; reinforce. d) As *S* learns to release object, *T* should move his or her hand back gradually to 12 inches from *S's* and require *S* to move his or her arm to meet *T's* hand.

To teach *S* to withdraw hand, it might be necessary to have a third person prompt from behind *S*.

Activity III: Cue: "Bounce the ball." (bilateral release)

Task Analysis	Teaching Procedures
1. *S* retains ball in both hands (one hand on each side of ball). 2. *S* extends arms away from body. 3. *S* releases hands from ball simultaneously.	a) Demonstrate letting ball bounce. b) Give verbal cue; if *S* responds correctly, reinforce. c) Model. d) Repeat verbal cue; if *S* responds correctly, reinforce. e) Physically prompt; reinforce. f) Direct attention to ball as in Activity I.

Instructional setting should vary to outdoors; use various colors, textures, and sizes of balls as learning progresses.

Activity IV: Cue: "Drop the paper in the basket." (dominant or nondominant hand)

Task Analysis	*Teaching Procedures*
1. *S* squeezes paper to crumple it. 2. *S* retains paper in hand. 3. *S* moves to basket. 4. *S* extends hand over basket. 5. *S* releases paper so that it falls into basket.	a) Basket should be immediately beside *S* to begin instruction; if *S* is mobile, basket can gradually be moved farther away so that *S* must move to basket before depositing paper. b) The act of voluntarily releasing object should be mastered by *S* by this time; purposeful placement should be object of this activity, and reinforcement should follow only proper placement of released object. c) Manual gestures should be initially used by *T* to show required placement while giving verbal cue. Fade out gestures.

TRANSFER FROM HAND-TO-HAND

Instructional Objective: Given an appropriate cue, *S* will move grasped object from one hand to the other (L-R and R-L) and retain object for more than 2 seconds, for 3 consecutive training days.

Prerequisite Skills: Ability to grasp object.

Activity I: Cue: "Put it in the other hand."

Task Analysis	*Teaching Procedures*
1. *S* reaches for and picks up object with one hand. 2. *S* brings hands together at midline. 3. *S* opens free hand. 4. *S* grasps object with free hand. 5. *S* releases object from first hand. 6. *S* maintains grasp with second hand for 2 seconds or more.	a) Demonstrate behavior. b) Give verbal cue to pick up object. c) Give verbal cue to put object in the other hand. d) Model behavior from point at which *S's* response breaks down, and reward steps in successive approximation to end behavior.

Task Analysis	*Teaching Procedures*
	e) Physically prompt
	f) Have *S* transfer L-R and R-L.

Task may need to be modified for students with one incapacitated arm and / or hand. Reaching for object may be substituted with *T* placing object in *S's* nondominant hand and then requiring transfer. *S* may be unable to bring hands together at midline. Dominant hand will then need to reach across body to grasp object held in nondominant hand.

Behavior can be strengthened by using all opportunities to teach. Example: Hand an eating utensil at mealtime to *S* and request him to put it in the other hand before beginning to eat.

Activity II: Cue: "Pass the ball." May be done with two teachers and student or teacher and several students. Instructional setting is sitting on floor or chairs in a tight circle.

Task Analysis	*Teaching Procedures*
1. *S* grasps ball with L hand from person on his or her L.	a) *T* may stand in center of circle and physically prompt each *S* through correct behavior.
2. *S* brings ball to midline of body.	b) As ball comes to each person, call his or her name before giving verbal cue to direct *S's* attention to ball.
3. *S* transfers ball to R hand.	
4. *S* extends R hand to person seated on his or her R.	
Reverse order so that *S* grasps with R hand and passes with L hand.	c) Gradually fade all prompts so passing behavior becomes spontaneous.
	d) Avoid the tendency to make irrelevant comments during activity.
	e) Persistent throwing or dropping of ball should be ignored as much as possible. Focus on reinforcing appropriate passing.

Edible reinforcers may be a hindrance in such a group activity and should be used only as necessary. Praise and *T* attention should be relied upon heavily; it is hoped the

Task Analysis	*Teaching Procedures*
	natural reinforcement of the game will be effective enough to maintain behavior.

SCISSORS GRASP

Instructional Objective: Given an appropriate cue, *S* will grasp object with partial opposition of thumb to pads of one or two fingers and object not touching palm of hand, with 100% accuracy for 3 consecutive training days.
Prerequisite Skills: Palmar grasp; ability to maintain eye contact with object.
Activity I: Cue: "Pick up the screw."

Task Analysis	*Teaching Procedures*
1. *S* picks up screw and grips it.	*S* may tend to revert to palmar grasp in holding a screw. Make sure the screw is jumbo size and place *S's* fingers in proper position. *T* may need to place one or two of his or her fingers between screw and *S's* palm to condition *S* to hold screw away from palm. Modeling may be of limited value, because *S* will need to feel the correct position of fingers. Physical prompting and manipulation are important. Reinforce each step, and use successive approximation to proper grasp as outlined in task analysis steps.
2. *S* picks up screw with point of screw at tip of little finger and turns palm toward body.	
3. *S* picks up screw about 1 to 2 inches from point with tips of fingers (thumb on one side and fingers on other side of screw) and palm turned toward body.	
4. *S* picks up screw about 1 to 2 inches from point with thumb, first, and middle fingers and palm turned toward body.	

Activity II: Cue: "Pull the string."

Task Analysis	*Teaching Procedures*
1. *S* reaches for ring on end of string.	a) Demonstrate function of object by pulling string.
2. *S* grasps ring between thumb and one or two fingers with palm facing down or toward body.	b) Tell *S* to pick up ring (ring should be large and painted a bright color initially; gradually fade).

Task Analysis	*Teaching Procedures*
3. *S* maintains grasp while pulling ring.	c) Physically manipulate proper grasp.
	d) Give verbal cue to pull string; if *S* responds correctly, reinforce.
	e) It may be necessary to hold *S's* fingers in place several times while leading him through the pulling motion; reinforce each time.
	f) Major emphasis should be placed on proper grasp, not on the ability to pull the string.
	g) Primary reinforcement should be faded as pulling is mastered; reinforcement provided by the object's action, paired with social reinforcement from *T*, should be sufficient at this point.
	h) Instructional setting should vary.

For higher functioning students, using scissors is a good activity to further develop this basic grasp.

PINCER GRASP

Instructional Objective: Given an appropriate cue, *S* will pick up object between pad of thumb and pad of index finger and / or middle finger (dominant or nondominant hand) and maintain pincer grasp for 10 seconds, for 3 consecutive training days.

Prerequisite Skills: Ability to maintain eye contact with object.

Activity Ia: Cue: "Pick up the ____ (a large item, e.g., eraser, tennis ball)."

Task Analysis	*Teaching Procedures*
1. *S* reaches for object.	Same as those for Activity I of Scissors Grasp.
2. *S* touches object with fingers.	

Task Analysis	*Teaching Procedures*

3. S picks up object using all fingers.
4. S holds object with finger tips.
5. S maintains grasp for:
2 seconds
4 seconds
6 seconds
10 seconds

Activity Ib: Cue: "Pick up the ____ (a small item, e.g., pencil, paper clip, button)."

Task Analysis	*Teaching Procedures*

1. S reaches for object.
2 . S touches object with fingers.
3. S picks up object using thumb and tip of index finger and/or middle finger.
4 . S holds object in pincer grasp.
5. S maintains pincer grasp for:
2 seconds
4 seconds
6 seconds
10 seconds

Same as those for Activity I of Scissors Grasp.

Task Analysis	*Teaching Procedures*

1. S picks up medicine dropper.
2. S holds dropper by bulb end between thumb and tip of index finger (and/or middle finger).
3. S puts tip of dropper in water.
4. S pinches bulb of dropper.
5. S lifts tip of dropper out of water.
6. S pinches bulb of dropper.

a)   Give verbal cue and demonstrate.
b)   Repeat verbal cue; if S responds correctly, reinforce.
c)   Model and repeat verbal cue; if S responds correctly, reinforce.
d)   Physically prompt by:
1)   Taking S's hand that is holding medicine dropper and putting tip of dropper in the water

Task Analysis	*Teaching Procedures*
	2) Squeezing *S's* fingers to draw up water; reinforcing
	3) Moving *S's* hand so dropper comes out of water
	4) Squeezing *S's* fingers so water is released from dropper; reinforcing
	e) Water should have food coloring added for attention-holding purposes.

Other Activities:

Picking up small bits of food
Zipping up coat
Turning on light switch
Using finger cymbals

MANIPULATING SMALL OBJECTS WITH PURPOSE

Instructional Objective: Given the task, *S* will manipulate some small objects with a specific purpose, with 100% accuracy for 3 consecutive training days.
Prerequisite Skills: Pincer grasp.
Activity I: Picking up coins and putting in slot.

Task Analysis	*Teaching Procedures*
1. *S* picks up 1¹/₂-inch coin.	a) Demonstrate.
2. *S* holds in pincer grasp.	b) Give instructions, "Put the coin in the hole"; if *S* responds correctly, reinforce.
3. *S* locates slot.	
4. *S* puts coin ¹/₃ way through.	
5. *S* puts coin ¹/₂ way through.	c) Model behavior.
6. *S* puts coin ³/₄ way through.	d) Repeat verbal cue; if *S* responds correctly, reinforce.
7. *S* releases coin from grasp.	
8. *S* pushes coin completely through slot using tips of thumb, index, and/or middle finger.	e) Verbally prompt; if *S* approximates behavior, but has coin turned crosswise to slot, say, "Turn it around," or "Try another way."

Task Analysis	*Teaching Procedures*

Follows above sequence using coins:
  1 inch in diameter
  3/4 inch in diameter
  1/2 inch in diameter
	f) Physically prompt; reinforce.
	g) Slot should be blatantly outlined in a bright color, then faded.
	h) Pair primary and social reinforcement and fade primary.

Activity II: Stringing beads.

Task Analysis	*Teaching Procedures*
1. *S* pulls end of lace. 2. *S* holds bead with one hand and pulls lace. 3. *S* holds bead, pushes lace tip halfway through bead and pulls lace. 4. *S* holds bead, pushes lace tip 3/4 of way through bead and pulls lace. 5. *S* holds bead, inserts lace into hole, and pushes through bead to end of lace. 6. *S* picks up bead in one hand and tip of lace in other hand; *S* inserts lace into hole and pushes through bead to end of lace. 7. *S* strings 2 beads. 8. *S* strings 3 beads. 9. *S* strings 4 beads. 10. *S* strings 5 beads. Repeat with small beads.	a) Knot one end of lace so beads cannot fall off. b) Other end of lace should be maintained in a point by means of dried glue, etc. This end should initially be painted a bright color, then faded. c) Hold bead and lace and push lace through bead until end is through far enough to be easily grasped. d) Instruct *S* to pull end of lace; if *S* responds correctly, reinforce. e) Physically prompt if necessary; reinforce. f) Hand bead to *S;* push lace through bead and instruct *S* to pull lace with free hand. Prompt and reinforce as above. g) Give *S* the pointed end of lace to hold and a bead; then instruct *S* to push the lace through the bead. h) Complete pushing lace through bead when *S* has pushed it through halfway. i) Instruct *S* to pull end of lace; prompt and reinforce as above.

Task Analysis

Teaching Procedures

j) Follow procedures g), h), and i), with *S* pushing ¾ of way and completely through, then to end of lace without assistance.

k) Lay lace and bead on table in front of *S* and instruct *S* to string the bead.

Activity III: Unscrewing containers.

Task Analysis

1. *S* secures container between knees.
2. *S* grasps lid with palms, one hand on each side.
3. *S* twists lid to R (counterclockwise).
4. *S* lifts lid off.
5. *S* places lid on floor or table beside container.

Teaching Procedures

a) Code lid by using colored paint or magic marker. Set lid on container but do not screw. Paint a line that extends from top of lid to about 2 inches down container. A see-through container would be preferable.

b) Show reinforcer to *S* and place the reinforcer in container.

c) Screw lid to closed position, but not tight.

d) *T* can hold container so that paint mark on container (not lid) is facing *S*.

e) Physically lead *S* through behavior several times, using the reinforcer in the container at the completion of the behavior.

f) Lining up the paint marks can be a visual and verbal cue for *S* if *S* is capable of matching.

g) Fade physical prompts.

h) When *S* has learned to unscrew top while *T* holds container, put container between *S's* knees and teach behavior from this position.

Activity IV: Turning doorknob (opens and closes door).

Task Analysis	*Teaching Procedures*
1. *S* grasps doorknob and closes door ¼ of way.	a) Give verbal cue, ''Close the door.'' Model behavior and
2. *S* grasps doorknob and closes door halfway.	physically prompt; reinforce.
	b) Same as a).
3. *S* grasps doorknob and closes door ¾ of way.	c) Same as a).
	d) Same as a).
4. *S* grasps doorknob and closes door.	e) Give verbal cue, ''Open the door.'' Model behavior of turn-
5. *S* stands to side of door, grasps doorknob, and turns knob.	ing knob and physically prompt. *S* may need to use both hands at first. Reinforce.
6. *S* stands to side of door, grasps doorknob, turns knob, and pulls door toward self.	f) Same as e).
	g) Same as e).
	h) Same as e).
7. *S* stands to side of door, grasps knob, turns knob, and pulls door open ¼ of way.	i) Same as e).
	j) Give verbal cue, ''Open the door.'' Wait for *S* to complete behavior; then give verbal cue,
8. *S* stands to side of door, grasps knob, turns knob, and pulls door open halfway.	''Close the door.'' Model, prompt, and reinforce as above.
9. *S* stands to side of door, grasps knob, turns knob, and pulls door open ¾ of way.	
10. *S* stands to side of door, grasps and turns knob, pulls door open, and then closes door.	

Activity V: Picture puzzle (requires discrimination).

Task Analysis	*Teaching Procedures*
1. *S* removes 1 puzzle piece.	a) Give verbal cue, ''Take this piece out,'' and indicate one
2. *S* replaces same piece.	piece. Model, physically
3. *S* removes 2 puzzle pieces.	prompt, and reinforce.
4. *S* replaces these 2 pieces.	
5. *S* removes 3 puzzle pieces.	b) Give verbal cue, ''Put this piece in the puzzle.'' Indicate
6. *S* replaces 3 pieces.	

Task Analysis   *Teaching Procedures*

piece to be replaced; place in correct form. Verbally prompt by using phrases like ''Turn it around,'' ''Try another way.'' Physically prompt, and reinforce.

c) Give verbal cue, ''Take these pieces out,'' and indicate pieces. Model, physically prompt, and reinforce.

d) Same as b).

e) Same as c).

f) Same as b).

g) Fade prompting, and increase number of pieces in puzzles.

Activity VI: Multiple shape box (requires discrimination).

Task Analysis	*Teaching Procedures*

1. *S* puts 1 shape in corresponding hole (only 1 hole showing).

2. *S* puts 1 shape in corresponding hole (2 holes showing).

3. *S* puts 2 shapes in corresponding holes (2 holes showing).

4. *S* puts 2 shapes in corresponding holes (3 holes showing).

5. *S* puts 3 shapes in corresponding holes (3 holes showing).

6. *S* puts 3 shapes in corresponding holes (4 holes showing).

7. *S* puts 4 shapes in corresponding holes (4 holes showing).

8. *S* puts 4 shapes in corresponding holes (5 holes showing).

9. *S* puts 5 shapes in corresponding holes (5 holes showing).

a) Place shape on table in front of *S*. Give verbal cue, ''Put it in the box.'' Model, prompt, and reinforce.

b) Same as a). Rotate box so holes are in different positions.

c) Repeat these behaviors for remainder of shapes.

INSTRUCTION-FOLLOWING SEQUENCE

SIT DOWN

Instructional Objective: Given the command "Sit down" (by 3 different teachers in 3 different environments), *S* will comply, with 100% accuracy for 3 consecutive training days.

Teaching Procedures: *T* says to *S*, "(Michael), sit down." Be sure to use specific student's name. If *S* does so within 10 seconds, *T* gives verbal praise: "Good boy, (Michael). You are sitting down just the way I told you to!"

If *S* does not comply within 10 seconds, the command is repeated. If *S* does so, he or she is given verbal praise and also given a hug. If *S* does not comply, *T* points to the chair and says, "(Michael) sit down in that chair."

If *S* still does not comply, *T* will physically lead child to chair and say, "I want you to sit down in this chair." After aiding the child to his or her seat, *T* says, "That is what I want you to do when I tell you to sit down."

This procedure is to be followed until the child will comply with 3 different teachers in 3 different environments. (There may need to be some altering of procedure to fit the specific needs of the children.)

STAND UP

Instructional Objective: Given the command "Stand up" (by 3 different teachers in 3 different environments), *S* will comply, with 100% accuracy for 3 consecutive training days.

Teaching Procedures: *T* says to *S*, "(Susan), stand up." If child stands up within 10 seconds, *T* gives verbal praise to the child: "That's really great that you stood up," or "I'm so happy you listened to me," or the like. If child does not stand up, *T* repeats the verbal command: "(Susan), stand up." If *S* does so, *T* hugs child or gives some type of physical reinforcement. If *S* still does not comply, *T* says, "(Susan), I am standing up" (*T* stands up), and then says, "Okay (Susan), now you stand up." If *S* does so, *S* gets a pat on the back and verbal praise. If *S* still does not comply with the verbal command, *T* takes *S* and physically stands child up saying, "This is what I want you to do when I tell you to stand up."

COME TO ME

Instructional Objective: Given the command "Come to me" (by 3 different teachers in 3 different environments), *S* will stop what he or she is doing and walk to the teacher within 10 seconds, on 10 out of 10 trials for 3 consecutive training days.

Teaching Procedures: T says to S, "(Michael), come to me." If child complies within 10 seconds, T gives verbal praise: "Very good, (Michael), you came right to me when I called you!" T also pats child on back or gives other physical reinforcement. If S does not comply, T walks to child and takes S by the hand. T leads S back to T's original seat at the desk and says, "(Michael), when I tell you to come to me, I want you to walk right over to me." T leads S back to S's seat and returns to his or hers. T says, "(Michael), come to me." If S does so, T gives S a big hug and makes a fuss over S. Continue this procedure until child complies to criteria with 3 different teachers in 3 different environments.

RAISE YOUR HAND

Instructional Objective: Given the verbal instruction "Raise your hand" (by 3 different teachers in 3 different environments), S will do so within 10 seconds, on 10 out of 10 trials for 3 consecutive training days.
Teaching Procedures: T says to S, "(Susan), raise your hand." If S complies, T gives verbal praise. If S does not comply, T repeats verbal command: "Raise your hand, (Susan)." If S does so, T says, "Good, (Susan). I am really pleased with you," and so on, and also provides physical reinforcement. If S does not comply, T raises his or her hand and says, "(Susan), I am raising my hand. Now you raise your hand." If S does so, T gives verbal and physical praise. If S fails to comply, T goes over to S and physically raises S's hand and says, "This is what I want you to do when I tell you to raise your hand."

BRING ME THE PENCIL

Instructional Objective: Given a pencil and the verbal cue "Bring me the pencil" (by 3 different teachers in 3 different environments), S will walk straight to T and hand T the pencil. S will do this on 10 out of 10 trials for 3 consecutive training days.
Teaching Procedures: S is given a pencil by T or another student in the room. Let some time elapse before giving the verbal command. T then says to S, "(Michael), bring me the pencil." If S brings the pencil to T, T takes the pencil and gives S verbal praise. If S does not comply, T repeats the command: "(Michael), bring me the pencil." If S complies, T takes the pencil and gives S verbal praise. If S still does not comply, T goes to S and puts pencil in S's hand and leads S to T's desk and says, "When I say to bring me the pencil, this is what I want you to do." At the desk, T takes the pencil. Continue until S follows command from 3 different teachers in 3 different environments.

6

DOMESTIC SKILLS SUBDOMAIN

The domestic skills subdomain involves vocational skills that are required for light housework and clean-up. Domestic skills emphasize clothes cleaning and laundering and room cleaning. The work skills included in this subdomain are typically performed by maids in motels, hotels, convalescent centers, and hospitals. They are also necessary for independent living in group homes or boarding houses. The skills listed below make up the domestic subdomain:

1. Dusting a Table
2. Disposing of Trash
3. Emptying Wastebasket into Trash Can
4. Washing Dishes
5. Drying Dishes
6. Cleaning a Refrigerator
7. Setting a Table
8. Making a Bed
9. Sorting Clothes
10. Washing Clothes by Hand
11. Washing Clothes by Machine
12. Hanging Clothes on Line
13. Drying Clothes by Machine
14. Folding Towels
15. Folding a Sheet

DUSTING A TABLE

Instructional Objective: Given a dust cloth, table, objects on table, and trash can, *S* will dust the table, cleaning the entire surface in 10 minutes, with 100% accuracy for 3 consecutive training days.

Prerequisite Skills: Palmar grasp and extension of one arm.
Task Analysis:
1.   S removes objects from table or moves objects to side.
2.   S picks up dust cloth.
3.   S folds dust cloth to hand size.
4.   S holds dust cloth with fingers spread apart.
5.   S begins at one end of table and sweeps with cloth across table surface.
6.   S continues covering entire table surface with cloth.
7.   S moves objects to other side of table.
8.   S continues to dust table until entire surface is dusted.
9.   S puts dust cloth to side of table.
10.   S puts objects back on table.
11.   S puts dust cloth in proper storage location.

Teaching Suggestions: If S experiences difficulty, sprinkle talcum powder on surface so that S can see dust particles. Have S dust talcum powder off table by sweeping it to one side of table. Fade cue as learning begins to take place.

DISPOSING OF TRASH

Instructional Objective: Given one trash can filled with trash, plastic trash liner, and tie string, S will place trash in appropriate trash receptacle in 15 minutes, with 100% accuracy for 3 consecutive training days.
Prerequisite Skills: Recognition of trash, palmar and pincer grasps, and full extension of upper extremities.
Task Analysis:
1.   S removes lid of trash can.
2.   S twists top of plastic trash liner to close.
3.   S ties top of plastic trash liner with tie string.
4.   S removes full trash liner from trash can.
5.   S takes filled trash liner and places it in dumpster.
6.   S unfolds new trash liner.
7.   S lines trash can with new plastic trash can liner.
Pretest:
1.   Do not provide consequences or physical assistance during the pretest.
2.   Place S in the training area with a trash can filled with trash; a trash can liner should be holding the trash. A tie string for the liner should be made available.
3.   Say to S, ''Empty the trash out of the trash can.'' Give no further verbal cues.

4. Watch *S* to determine which steps he or she completes correctly.
5. Record a plus (+) for each step *S* does correctly. Record a minus (−) for each step *S* does incorrectly or omits.
6. *S* may be able to do some of the steps of the program before training begins. If this occurs, *do not* eliminate these steps from the training sequence.

Teaching Procedures:

1. Say to *S*, "I will show you how to dispose of the trash bag." Explain each step as it is modeled. Proceed through task analysis steps 1–7.
2. When *T* finishes modeling steps 1–7, *S* begins with step 1 with *T* guiding until *S* reaches step 7.
3. For task analysis step 2, if necessary, have *S* first practice twisting a top on a jar to get the idea and feel of twisting in one direction. Then present trash bag and instruct *S* to twist top of bag as he or she twisted top on the jar.
4. For task analysis step 3, if necessary, present *S* with a larger tie string to practice twisting. Use verbal help. If *S* does not respond correctly, demonstrate; if needed, assist *S* physically. Fade cue and reduce to normal size tie string as learning takes place.
5. For task analysis step 4, if necessary, mark on trash bag (using a piece of tape) around the circumference of the bag the point at which the bag is considered 3/4 full. This will show *S* where to begin twisting and the approximate place for the tie string to be twisted. Remove tape once learning has taken place.
6. Reinforce continuously each step as learning first takes place. Reduce to intermittent reinforcement when continuous is no longer necessary.

EMPTYING WASTEBASKET INTO TRASH CAN

Instructional Objective: Given a wastebasket filled with trash and a trash can, *S* will empty the wastebasket into the trash can, with 100% accuracy for 3 consecutive training days.

Prerequisite Skills: Palmar grasp with both hands and adequate strength to lift wastebasket.

Task Analysis:

1. *S* looks at wastebasket.
2. *S* touches the wastebasket.
3. *S* picks up wastebasket.
4. *S* moves wastebasket toward trash can.
5. *S* sets wastebasket on floor beside trash can.
6. *S* places hand on lid of trash can.

7.   *S* grasps handle of lid.
8.   *S* lifts up lid from trash can.
9.   *S* places lid down beside can.
10. *S* picks up wastebasket.
11. *S* tilts wastebasket over opening of trash can.
12. *S* turns wastebasket completely over.
13. *S* shakes wastebasket until empty.
14. *S* looks into wastebasket to make sure it is empty.
15. *S* places wastebasket down.
16. *S* picks up any trash that fell on floor.
17. *S* picks up trash can lid.
18. *S* places lid on top of trash can.
19. *S* returns wastebasket to proper place.

Teaching Suggestions: Some *Ss* may keep holding the wastebasket while taking the lid off the trash can. The task can be completed this way but tends to be clumsy and sloppy. Model the correct way to do steps 5 and 10 and direct *S* verbally.

WASHING DISHES

Instructional Objectives: Given 4 place settings, 4 cooking pans, stoppers, sinks, hot and cold water, dish rag, dish rack, and detergent, *S* will wash dishes in 30 minutes, with 100% accuracy for 3 consecutive training days.

Prerequisite Skills: Pincer and palmar grasps and mobility of both upper extremities.

Task Analysis:

1.   *S* cleans out wash and rinse sinks.
2.   *S* distinguishes between hot and cold water.
3.   *S* adjusts hot and cold water to appropriate temperature.
4.   *S* places stopper so that rinse sink begins to fill.
5.   *S* fills rinse sink half full.
6.   *S* places stopper so that wash sink begins to fill.
7.   *S* identifies and picks up detergent.
8.   *S* adds detergent to wash sink (a 1 second squeeze of bottle).
9.   *S* fills wash sink half full.
10. *S* places all dirty dishes in wash sink, except cooking pans.
11. *S* scrubs each piece thoroughly.
12. *S* rinses each piece thoroughly.
13. *S* places each piece in dish rack.
14. *S* places all cooking pans in wash sink.
15. *S* repeats steps 11–13.

16. *S* manipulates stopper so that sink drains completely and stopper collects debris.
17. *S* cleans out wash and rinse sinks.
18. *S* empties debris from stopper.

Teaching Suggestions: For task analysis step 3, color code the faucets red for hot and blue for cold. As learning takes place fade cues.

For task analysis step 9, a piece of tape can be extended around the circumference of the inside of the wash sink to show *S* the halfway point of the sink. *S* is to fill sink with water up to tape. Once the halfway point is learned, remove tape from sink.

DRYING DISHES

Instructional Objective: Given clean dishes in dish rack and clean towel, *S* will dry and put away dishes in appropriate place in 30 minutes, with 100% accuracy for 3 consecutive training days.

Prerequisite Skills: Pincer and palmar grasps and mobility of both upper extremities.

Task Analysis:
1. *S* holds unfolded towel in one hand.
2. *S* holds piece in opposite hand.
3. *S* dries entire surface of piece with towel.
4. *S* places dry piece in appropriate storage cabinet.
5. *S* repeats steps 1–4 until all pieces are dried and put away.

CLEANING A REFRIGERATOR

Instructional Objective: Given a full and dirty refrigerator, a sponge or rag, a bucket of detergent, and a wastebasket, *S* will empty and clean the refrigerator in 45 minutes, with 100% accuracy for 3 consecutive training days.

Prerequiste Skills: Palmar grasp and extension of one arm.

Task Analysis:
1. *S* adds a small amount of detergent.
2. *S* fills bucket approximately half full with warm water.
3. *S* places a wastebasket beside refrigerator.
4. *S* opens refrigerator door.
5. *S* removes all items from refrigerator and places them on a nearby surface.
6. *S* throws any spoiled food in wastebasket.
7. *S* rinses sponge in water.

8. S removes shelves one at a time.
9. S scrubs 1 shelf at a time.
10. S returns each shelf as it is washed.
11. S scrubs inside shelves of refrigerator door.
12. S removes and cleans all vegetable bins.
13. S returns vegetable bins.
14. S replaces food neatly in proper places.
15. S closes refrigerator door.
16. S rinses sponge in bucket.
17. S wipes outside of refrigerator.
18. S rinses out bucket and sponge.

SETTING A TABLE

Instructional Objective: Given a table, 4 placemats, 4 glasses, 4 plates, 4 napkins, and the proper amount of utensils for a 4-place dinner setting, S will set the table in 15 minutes, with 100% accuracy for 3 consecutive training days.

Prerequisite Skills: Pincer grasp, full extension of one arm, and fine motor control of fingers.

Task Analysis:
1. S puts 4 placemats in appropriate positions.
2. S picks up 1 plate.
3. S places plate on placemat.
4. S picks up another plate.
5. S places plate on another placemat.
6. S picks up another plate.
7. S places plate on another placemat.
8. S picks up remaining plate.
9. S places plate on remaining placemat.
10. S picks up 4 napkins.
11. S places each napkin at left side of plate.
12. S picks up four forks.
13. S places each fork on napkin.
14. S picks up 4 knives.
15. S places knives at right side of plates.
16. S picks up four spoons.
17. S places spoons next to knives (right side).
18. S picks up 1 glass.
19. S places glass at top of knife.
20. S picks up another glass.
21. S places glass at top of another knife.

22. *S* picks up another glass.
23. *S* places glass at top of another knife.
24. *S* picks up remaining glass.
25. *S* places glass at top of remaining knife.

Teaching Suggestions: The entire table setting can be visually cued. Tape colored rectangles on the table to indicate where the placemats are to be placed. Each placemat is printed with the objects to be placed. Each object and drawing are color cued. This visual cueing is gradually faded by moving from colored drawn objects to colored outlines of the objects. Visual cueing is slowly faded, one object at a time.

MAKING A BED

Instructional Objective: Given a bed, pillow, 2 sheets, pillowcase, blanket, and bedspread, and chair or table to put linens on, *S* will make the bed in 20 minutes, with 100% accuracy for 3 consecutive training days.

Prerequisite Skills: Pincer or palmar grasp and full extension of one upper extremity.

Task Analysis:

1. *S* puts linens on chair or chest near bed.
2. *S* differentiates between bottom and top sheets.
3. *S* takes bottom sheet from stack on chair.
4. *S* unfolds sheet on bed.
5. *S* grasps bottom of sheet (narrow hem) with both hands.
6. *S* pulls bottom of sheet to bottom of mattress.
7. *S* grasps top of sheet (wide hem) with both hands.
8. *S* pulls top of sheet to top of mattress.
9. *S* centers and straightens sheet.
10. *S* smoothes wrinkles in sheet.
11. *S* tucks right side of sheet under mattress.
12. *S* tucks left side of sheet under mattress.
13. *S* takes top sheet from chair.
14. *S* unfolds sheet on bed.
15. *S* grasps bottom of sheet (narrow hem) and pulls to bottom of mattress.
16. *S* grasps top of sheet (wide hem) and pulls to top of bed.
17. *S* centers, straightens, and smoothes sheet.
18. *S* takes blanket from chair.
19. *S* unfolds blanket on bed.
20. *S* grasps bottom of blanket with both hands and pulls to bottom of bed.
21. *S* grasps top of blanket and pulls to top of bed.

22. *S* centers and straightens blanket over top sheet.
23. *S* smoothes all wrinkles.
24. *S* tucks both top sheet and blanket under mattress at bottom of bed.
25. *S* folds top of sheet back to cover top of blanket.
26. *S* takes spread from chair.
27. *S* pulls bottom of spread to bottom of bed.
28. *S* centers and smoothes out spread.
29. *S* pulls top of spread to top of bed and smoothes.
30. *S* folds top of spread back about twice the width of pillow.
31. *S* takes pillow from chair.
32. *S* places pillow on bed lengthwise in front of self.
33. *S* holds one edge of open end of pillowcase in each hand.
34. *S* pulls pillow case over bottom of pillow about 4 inches.
35. *S* pulls pillow up against his or her chest, holding it with his or her chin.
36. *S* shakes pillow down halfway into pillowcase.
37. *S* shakes pillow remainder of the way into pillowcase.
38. *S* lays pillow at top of bed.
39. *S* folds spread up over pillow.
40. *S* smoothes out all wrinkles of spread, including top of pillow.

Teaching Suggestions: If *S* has difficulty centering the sheets, blanket, or spread on the bed, use two pieces of tape, one on the bed and one on the sheet, blanket, or spread. Have *S* match the pieces of tape to center the sheet, blanket, or spread. Gradually fade the tape by shortening it until *S* can center them without cues.

Use a large pillowcase while *S* is learning to put the case on the pillow so it will slide more easily. If you normally use a smaller case, fade back to this after *S* has learned to put on the larger case.

SORTING CLOTHES

Instructional Objective: Given 2 sheets, 2 towels, 2 washcloths, 2 white shirts, 2 colored shirts, 2 wash and wear dresses, 2 pairs of white socks, 2 pairs of colored socks, 2 pairs of jeans, 2 pairs of wash and wear pants, 4 pairs of underwear, and a laundry basket, *S* will sort clothes according to color and material type, with 100% accuracy for 3 consecutive training days.

Prerequisite Skills: Palmar grasp and extension of one upper extremity.

Task Analysis:

1. *S* separates linens from other clothing items.
2. *S* separates white clothes and white underwear from colored and other clothing.

3. *S* separates colored clothing and colored underwear from jeans.
4. *S* separates jeans from other 3 piles of clothes.

WASHING CLOTHES BY HAND

Instructional Objective: Given dirty clothes, liquid detergent, and sink area, *S* will wash clothes thoroughly, with 100% accuracy for 3 consecutive training days.

Prerequisite Skills: Sorting clothes and pincer or palmar grasp.

Task Analysis:

1. *S* removes objects from pockets.
2. *S* cleans out wash and rinse sinks.
3. *S* regulates water temperature — cold.
4. *S* places stopper over drain.
5. *S* puts 1½ capfuls of liquid detergent in sink.
6. *S* fills sink ¾ of the way full.
7. *S* places garments in water and lets soak.
8. *S* holds garment in both hands and rubs together gently on badly soiled areas until spots disappear.
9. *S* squeezes water out of garment.
10. *S* fills rinse sink ¾ of the way full.
11. *S* places garments in clean water.
12. *S* dips garment up and down to get suds out.
13. After dipping several times, *S* lets water drain out.
14. *S* washes out sink.
15. *S* repeats steps 10–14 once more.
16. *S* squeezes water from garments.
17. *S* places garments in basket for hanging.

Teaching Suggestions: If *S* experiences difficulty measuring 1½ capfuls of liquid detergent (step 5), draw a line around the inside of the cap at the ½ capful point. Have *S* practice pouring to that point with water. When *S* is successful 5 consecutive times, fade cue.

If *S* experiences difficulty filling the sink ¾ of the way full, place a piece of tape at that point (¾) around the circumference of the sink. Have *S* practice filling sink to that point with plain water. Fade cue as learning takes place. Use same cue for rinse sink (step 10).

If *S* experiences difficulty on step 8, getting soiled areas clean, have available exactly the same item in clean condition. Have *S* compare the two, pointing out the soiled areas. Physically aid *S* in scrubbing soiled spots if necessary. Fade all assistance and cueing as learning takes place.

If *S* experiences difficulty on steps 9 and 16, wringing clothes, provide a wet sock (small soft object) for *S* to wring. Offer physical assistance at first until *S* obtains twisting motion. Reduce assistance until no assistance is necessary. Fade all cues as learning is achieved.

WASHING CLOTHES BY MACHINE

Instructional Objective: Given a washing machine, sorted soiled clothes, detergent, measuring cup, and laundry basket, *S* will wash clothes, with 100% accuracy for 3 consecutive training days.

Prerequisite Skills: Full extension of one upper extremity, and pincer or palmar grasp.

Task Analysis:
1. *S* gets detergent from storage area.
2. *S* opens lid of washer.
3. *S* puts clothes into washer, one at a time, until the washer is half full.
4. *S* puts clothes in evenly so that machine is balanced.
5. *S* measures proper amount of detergent in cup.
6. *S* adds detergent to washer.
7. *S* turns wash cycle selector to appropriate wash cycle.
8. *S* shuts lid of washer.
9. *S* presses "Start" button.
10. *S* lifts lid when washer stops completely.
11. *S* removes clothes one at a time from washer and shakes.
12. *S* places each piece of clothing into laundry basket.
13. *S* places one hand inside washer and moves along washer drum to check for clothes stuck to side.
14. *S* removes all debris at bottom of washer drum.

Pretest:
1. Do not provide consequences or physical assistance during the pretest.
2. Place *S* in the training area with a washing machine; clothes should already be sorted before loading into machine. Clothes should be in a laundry basket in general area.
3. Say to *S*, "Get the clothes, put them in the washer, and turn it on." Do not give any further verbal cues.
4. Watch *S* to determine which steps of the program he or she completes correctly.
5. Record a plus (+) for each step *S* completes correctly. Record a minus (−) for each step *S* does incorrectly or omits.
6. *S* may be able to do some of the steps before training begins. If this occurs, *do not* eliminate these steps from the training sequence.

Teaching Procedures:
1. Say to *S*, "I will show you how to wash clothes." Explain each step as *T* models. Proceed through task analysis steps 1–9.
2. When *T* finishes modeling steps 1–9, *S* begins with step 1 with *T* guiding until *S* reaches step 9.
3. For task analysis step 3, a piece of tape can be extended around the circumference of the inside of the washer showing *S* the half-way point and how to distribute the clothes evenly around the washer.
4. For task analysis step 5, have available a ½-cup measuring cup. Instruct student to fill cup to the top. Gradually fade ½-cup measuring cup and introduce a regular cup with a red line drawn around the half-way point. Have *S* pour detergent up to line. Gradually fade cue (line).
5. For task analysis step 7, have available a clothes chart color coded, e.g., a red square next to permanent press clothes (use pictures of clothes). Match colors on chart to colors of wash settings on dial of machine. Place black strips of paper between each wash cycle. Fade cueing as learning takes place.
6. After *S* completes task analysis steps 1–9, *T* models steps 10–14, explaining steps while modeling.
7. *T* then guides *S* through steps 10–14, cueing and reminding when necessary. Fade cues and reminders as learning takes place.
8. Reinforce continuously each step as learning first takes place. Reduce to intermittent reinforcement when continuous is no longer necessary.

HANGING CLOTHES ON LINE

Instructional Objective: Given clean clothes, clothesline, and clothespins, *S* will hang clothes on line, with 100% accuracy for 3 consecutive training days.
Prerequisite Skills: Pincer and palmar grasps and full extension of both arms.
Task Analysis:
1. *S* wipes clothesline with damp cloth.
2. *S* carries clothes basket to line.
3. *S* carries clothespin basket to line.
4. *S* picks up one garment from basket.
5. *S* shakes garment to straighten it out.
6. *S* picks up clothespin in one hand while still holding garment in other hand.
7. *S* holds one end of garment adjacent to clothesline.

8. *S* attaches one end of garment to line with clothespin.
9. *S* stretches garment so that it hangs parallel to the line.
10. *S* attaches other end of garment to the line.
11. *S* repeats steps 4-10 until all garments are hung on line to dry.

Teaching Suggestions: If *S* experiences difficulty on step 6, bending over to pick clothespin from basket, attach clothespins to *S's* shirt. *S* then is able to reach clothespin without losing grasp on garment or dropping it on the ground. If *S* experiences difficulty on step 8, attaching garment to line with clothespin, have available a sponge ball for *S* to practice the squeezing motion. Once this motion is learned, provide a staple remover which requires the squeezing motion using first two fingers pressing against thumb. Next introduce the clothespin. Offer any type of assistance that is needed.

DRYING CLOTHES BY MACHINE

Instructional Objective: Given a dryer and clean, wet clothes, *S* will dry the clothes, with 100% accuracy for 3 consecutive training days.

Prerequisite Skills: Pincer or palmar grasp and extension of one upper extremity.

Task Analysis:

1. *S* opens lid of dryer.
2. *S* places clothes in dryer one at a time.
3. *S* adjusts temperature control to proper setting.
4. *S* sets timer for length of drying time.
5. *S* removes lint filter.
6. *S* checks lint filter, and cleans it if necessary.
7. *S* replaces lint filter.
8. *S* closes lid of dryer.
9. *S* depresses "Start" button.
10. When dryer stops, *S* opens lid of dryer.
11. *S* removes dry clothes one at a time.
12. *S* removes lint filter.
13. *S* cleans lint filter.
14. *S* replaces lint filter.
15. *S* closes lid of dryer.

Teaching Suggestions: For task analysis step 3, have available a clothes chart color coded exactly like the wash chart and like the color codes on the washing machine dial, e.g., a red square next to permanent press clothes (use pictures of clothes). Match colors on chart to colors of cycle settings on dial of dryer. Place black strips of paper between each cycle to indicate starting points of each drying cycle. Fade cueing as learning takes place.

FOLDING TOWELS

Instructional Objective: Given a table and 5 towels in a pile, *S* will fold the towels in 15 minutes, with 100% accuracy for 3 consecutive training days.
Prerequisite Skills: Pincer and palmar grasps and mobility of both upper extremities.
Task Analysis:

1. *S* places towel flat on table.
2. *S* smoothes wrinkles.
3. *S* picks up one hem and places it along other hem edge.
4. *S* smoothes wrinkles.
5. *S* folds towel in half.
6. *S* smoothes wrinkles.
7. *S* folds towel in half again.
8. *S* smoothes wrinkles.
9. *S* places folded towel on top of previously folded towels.

FOLDING A SHEET

Instructional Objective: Given a table and a sheet, *S* will fold a sheet in 10 minutes, with 100% accuracy for 3 consecutive training days.
Prerequisite Skills: Folding towels.
Task Analysis:

1. *S* places sheet on folding table.
2. *S* spreads sheet out on table.
3. *S* holds bottom right corner (narrow hem).
4. *S* matches bottom right corner to top right corner (wide hem).
5. *S* holds bottom left corner.
6. *S* brings bottom left corner to top left corner and matches corners.
7. *S* smoothes all wrinkles.
8. *S* holds fold (bottom) at left side.
9. *S* brings bottom of left side up to top left corner, matching corners.
10. *S* holds fold (bottom) at right side.
11. *S* brings bottom of right side up to top right corner, matching corners.
12. *S* smoothes all wrinkles.
13. *S* holds top of right side in preferred hand and bottom of right side in opposite hand.
14. *S* brings right side to left side of sheet, matching corners and edges.
15. *S* smoothes all wrinkles.
16. *S* holds folded right side of sheet with both hands.

17. *S* brings right side to left side of sheet, matching corners.
18. *S* smoothes all wrinkles.

7

FOOD SERVICE
SKILLS SUBDOMAIN

Food service and preparation is an important skill area for vocational and independent living. Recent U.S. Department of Labor surveys indicate that food service is one of the primary sources of employment for mentally retarded workers. Furthermore, these skills are critical to independent living or semi-independent living in a group home. The number of skills outlined below are only a very small proportion of those that a creative teacher could identify for instruction.

1. Opening a Can (Manual Opener)
2. Making Orange Juice from Frozen Concentrate
3. Making Instant Iced Tea
4. Making Buttered Toast
5. Making a Meat Sandwich
6. Packing a Sack Lunch
7. Turning on an Electric Stove
8. Boiling Water
9. Cooking Hot Dogs
10. Making a Hard-Boiled Egg
11. Preparing Canned Soup
12. Frying a Hamburger
13. Frying Bacon
14. Setting Oven Temperature
15. Cooking a Frozen Dinner
16. Slicing
17. Dicing
18. Busing Restaurant Table

OPENING A CAN (MANUAL OPENER)

Instructional Objective: Given an unopened can, manual can opener, and a trash receptacle, *S* will open the can within 3 minutes, with 100% accuracy for 3 consecutive training days.

Prerequisite Skill: Pincer and palmar grasps and use of both arms.

Task Analysis (right-handed; reverse hands if left-handed):

1. *S* places can on counter.
2. *S* picks up can opener by grasping top handle of opener with right hand.
3. *S* places cutting edge of opener over rim of can.
4. *S* grasps both handles of opener with left hand and squeezes together so that hole is punched in can.
5. *S* grasps turning key with right hand so that thumb is on under side of end of key closest to *S* and first two fingers are on top side of end farthest away.
6. *S* turns key away from him 180°
7. *S* repeats steps 5 and 6 until can is opened.
8. *S* drops left hand to hold only bottom handle of opener and grasps top handle with right hand.
9. *S* pulls handles apart and lifts.
10. *S* puts opener on counter.
11. *S* pushes one side of lid down.
12. *S* grasps opposite edge of lid with thumb and index finger of opposite hand.
13. *S* removes lid from can.
14. *S* moves to trash receptacle.
15. *S* lifts lid from trash receptacle.
16. *S* throws lid from can into trash receptacle.
17. *S* replaces trash receptacle top.

Teaching Suggestions: In task analysis step 3, *S* may have difficulty identifying the cutting edge of the opener. Mark the side of the edge with a small circle of colored tape. Point out the edge to *S*.

Position of hands when turning the key may also be difficult. Facilitate this learning by cutting "fingerprints" from colored tape and placing them in position on the key where fingers should go. Place *S's* fingers over the prints.

MAKING ORANGE JUICE FROM FROZEN CONCENTRATE

Instructional Objective: Given a can of frozen orange juice, spoon, water, pitcher, can opener, and a trash receptacle, *S* will make orange juice in 15 minutes, with 100% accuracy for 3 consecutive training days.

Prerequisite Skills: Opening can.
Task Analysis:
1. *S* opens can.
2. *S* holds can inverted over pitcher without spilling on counter.
3. *S* picks up spoon in preferred hand.
4. *S* inserts spoon into concentrate as needed until all concentrate is in pitcher.
5. *S* measures correct amount of water with juice can.
6. *S* adds water to pitcher.
7. *S* repeats steps 5 and 6 as necessary.
8. *S* places empty can in trash receptacle.
9. *S* picks up spoon in preferred hand.
10. *S* grasps pitcher with opposite hand.
11. *S* stirs contents of pitcher.
12. *S* continues stirring until orange juice is thoroughly mixed (no lumps).
13. *S* places spoon in sink to be washed.
14. *S* places orange juice in refrigerator.
Pretest:
1. Do not provide consequences or physical assistance during the pretest.
2. Place *S* in the training area with the necessary materials.
3. Say to *S*, "Make the orange juice." Give no further verbal clues.
4. Watch *S* to determine which steps he or she completes correctly.
5. Record a plus (+) for each step *S* completes correctly. Record a minus (–) for each step *S* does incorrectly or omits.
6. *S* may be able to do some of the steps in the program before training begins. If this occurs, *do not* eliminate these steps from the training sequence.
Teaching Procedures:
1. *T* uses black magic marker to draw a big circle around the number 3 on the juice can, indicating that 3 cans of water are to be used to make the juice.
2. *T* says, "Watch me. I will make orange juice."
3. *T* proceeds through task analysis steps 1–14, giving special attention to the number 3 on the can with the black circle drawn around it.
4. *T* uses several other orange juice cans with the number 3 circled. *T* asks *S*, "How many cans of water will you use to make this orange juice?"
5. Reinforce with praise or tangibles for correct responses.
6. Instruct *S*, "Now you make the orange juice."
7. Guide *S* through steps 1–14, giving verbal and tactile cues only as necessary.

8. Reinforce with praise or tangibles when *S* performs a new step correctly and / or when task has been learned.
9. Repeat task analysis steps 1–14, gradually fading out the circle drawn around the number 3. To do this begin with black magic marker, then use black pen, then pencil, and then gradually fade out the pencil until it no longer appears and *S* can look for the number without any cues.
10. Task is considered learned when *S* completes the task correctly for 3 consecutive days.

MAKING INSTANT ICED TEA

Instructional Objective: Given a jar of instant iced tea, glass, teaspoon, and water, *S* will be able to make a glass of instant iced tea with no errors, for 3 consecutive training days.

Prerequisite Skills: Pincer and palmar grasps.

Task Analysis:
1. *S* locates jar of instant iced tea on shelf.
2. *S* places jar on counter.
3. *S* locates 8-oz glass on shelf.
4. *S* places glass on counter.
5. *S* locates teaspoon.
6. *S* places teaspoon by glass on counter.
7. *S* twists top off instant iced tea jar.
8. *S* places top on counter.
9. *S* picks teaspoon up.
10. *S* dips teaspoon into jar.
11. *S* lifts teaspoon up.
12. *S* taps teaspoon against jar to level teaspoon.
13. *S* places tea in glass.
14. *S* places top back on jar.
15. *S* places glass under faucet.
16. *S* turns cold water on at medium force.
17. *S* fills glass until liquid is 1 inch from the top.
18. *S* turns faucet off.
19. *S* stirs liquid until all tea is dissolved.

Teaching Suggestions: If *S* experiences difficulty on task analysis step 7, twisting the top off, apply a rubber jar gripper to the lid of the jar. This will make the twisting easier for *S* if he or she does not have the strength to twist a regular top.

If *S* experiences difficulty on step 14, putting top back on jar, have available a larger jar with larger grooves to practice the skill of screwing and unscrewing the lid.

If *S* experiences difficulty on step 17, filling glass until liquid is 1 inch from the top, place a piece of tape 1 inch from the top so that *S* can more easily see the water level.

MAKING BUTTERED TOAST

Instructional Objective: Given a toaster, plate, knife, bread, and butter, *S* will toast and butter bread in 15 minutes, with 100% accuracy for 3 consecutive training days.
Prerequisite Skills: Operating a toaster and pincer or palmar grasp.
Task Analysis:

1.   *S* takes 2 slices of bread from package.
2.   *S* places bread in slots of toaster without bending or breaking.
3.   *S* adjusts toaster to desired setting.
4.   *S* pushes operating bar until it catches.
5.   *S* allows bread to toast.
6.   When toast pops up, *S* takes 1 slice out and places it on plate.
7.   *S* slices butter not more than 1/4 inch thick and spreads it on toast without tearing toast.
8.   *S* repeats step 7 until entire piece is buttered.
9.   *S* repeats steps 6–8 for other slice of toast.
10.   *S* never uses metal or other electrical conductors to get stuck toast out of toaster. (When removing stuck toast, toaster must be unplugged also.)

MAKING A MEAT SANDWICH

Instructional Objective: Given a jar of mayonnaise, 2 slices of bread, a package of meat, knife, plate, and cutting board, *S* will make a meat sandwich in 15 minutes, with 100% accuracy for 3 consecutive training days.
Prerequisite Skills: Pincer and palmar grasps.
Task Analysis:

1.   *S* washes hands.
2.   *S* places 2 slices of bread on cutting board side by side.
3.   *S* opens mayonnaise jar.
4.   *S* spreads mayonnaise on 1 slice of bread.
5.   *S* spreads mayonnaise on other slice of bread.

6. *S* replaces lid on mayonnaise jar.
7. *S* opens package of meat.
8. *S* takes 1 piece of meat out of package.
9. *S* places meat on one slice of bread.
10. *S* closes package of meat.
11. *S* places other piece of bread on top of meat.
12. *S* cuts sandwich in half.
13. *S* places sandwich on plate.

Teaching Suggestions: Task analysis step 2 can be visually cued by having outlines for bread placement drawn on the cutting board. Step 3 can be visually cued by bold arrows taped on the mayonnaise jar indicating the correct way for opening. A model sandwich can be pre-prepared and provided to further aid the student.

PACKING A SACK LUNCH

Instructional Objective: Given a paper lunch bag, 1 piece of fruit, 2 sandwiches, and a thermos, *S* will pack the lunch in the bag in 5 minutes, with 100% accuracy for 3 consecutive training days.
Prerequisite Skills: Making a meat sandwich and filling a thermos.
Task Analysis:
1. *S* looks at lunch bag.
2. *S* opens the bag.
3. *S* looks at thermos.
4. *S* puts thermos in the bag.
5. *S* looks at the sandwiches.
6. *S* puts 1 sandwich in the bag.
7. *S* puts other sandwich in the bag.
8. *S* looks at the fruit.
9. *S* puts fruit in the bag.
10. *S* folds the bag over at top down to the food for carrying.

TURNING ON AN ELECTRIC STOVE

Instructional Objective: Given an electric stove, *S* will turn on stove burner within 1 minute, with 100% accuracy for 3 consecutive training days.
Prerequisite Skills: Pincer grasp.
Task Analysis:
1. *S* stands approximately 1 foot away from stove top.
2. *S* places hand on control knob of specified burner.

3. *S* turns knob in appropriate direction to designated temperature (low, medium, high).
4. *S* leaves knob on for a few seconds.
5. *S* turns knob back to "Off" position.

BOILING WATER

Instructional Objective: Given an electric stove, medium-size saucepan, and water, *S* will boil water, with 100% accuracy for 3 consecutive training days.

Prerequisite Skills: Turning on a stove and palmar grasp.

Task Analysis:
1. *S* locates proper size pan in cabinet.
2. *S* fills pan with water, leaving water level at least 1 inch, but not more than 3 inches, below lip of pan.
3. *S* places pan on burner.
4. *S* lights appropriate burner.
5. *S* adjusts heat to high heat.
6. *S* turns pan handle so that it extends toward rear of stove top.
7. *S* observes pan entire time burner is lit to ensure safety.
8. *S* allows water to come to a full boil.
9. *S* turns burner control knob to "Off" when boiling is accomplished.

Pretest:
1. Do not provide consequences or physical assistance during the pretest.
2. Place *S* in the training area.
3. Say to *S*, "Get the pot and boil the water."
4. Watch *S* to determine which steps of the program he or she completes correctly.
5. Record a plus (+) for each step *S* completes correctly. Record a minus (−) for each step *S* does incorrectly or omits.
6. *S* may be able to do some of the steps in the program before training begins. If this occurs, *do not* eliminate these steps from the training sequence.

Teaching Procedures:
1. Say to *S*, "We are going to boil water to make coffee" (rationale: give purpose or meaning to task). Say, "Watch me."
2. Proceed with task analysis step 1, verbalizing the action.
3. Say to *S*, "You find the pot."
4. Require *S* to do step 1 with no help if possible. If necessary, give verbal help, provide demonstration, or physically assist, in that order.

5. Proceed through remaining steps in this manner until *S* can correctly do steps 1–9 unassisted.
6. Provide continuous reward.
7. In teaching task analysis step 2, provide visual cue on inside of pot to designate water level, fading gradually.
8. In teaching step 4, provide visual cues to direct which buttons control which burner.
9. In teaching step 5, provide visual cue for high heat setting by using color, picture, or number. Gradually fade.
10. *S* will probably have difficulty standing and watching water until it boils. If necessary, verbally cue.

COOKING HOT DOGS

Instructional Objective: Given 2 hot dogs, water, medium-size saucepan, and a stove, *S* will boil 2 hot dogs in 15 minutes, with 100% accuracy for 3 consecutive training days.
Prerequisite Skills: Turning on stove and boiling water.
Task Analysis:
1. *S* prepares saucepan with water to boil.
2. *S* removes package of hot dogs from the refrigerator.
3. *S* opens package of hot dogs and places 2 of them in the saucepan without tearing or disfiguring hot dogs.
4. *S* turns on burner to high heat setting.
5. *S* allows pan of water with hot dogs to come to boil.
6. *S* allows hot dogs to boil for a minimum of 3 minutes but not more than 6 minutes.
7. *S* turns burner knob to "Off" position.

MAKING A HARD-BOILED EGG

Instructional Objective: Given a kitchen timer, pot, stove, water, spoon, plate, and an egg, *S* will hard-boil an egg, with 100% accuracy for 3 consecutive training days.
Prerequisite Skills: Turning on a stove and boiling water.
Task Analysis:
1. *S* fills pot with water to appropriate level.
2. *S* gently places egg in pot of water.
3. *S* adjusts stove burner to high heat setting.
4. *S* places pot on lit burner.

5. *S* allows water to come to a boil.
6. *S* sets timer for 10 minutes.
7. When timer rings, *S* turns stove burner control to "Off."
8. *S* removes egg from water with a spoon and sets it on a plate.

PREPARING CANNED SOUP

Instructional Objective: Given a manual can opener, can of soup, water, trash receptacle, pot, bowl, spoon, and an electric stove, *S* will prepare soup in 20 minutes, with 100% accuracy for 3 consecutive training days.
Prerequisite Skills: Opening can with manual can opener and turning on a stove.
Task Analysis:
1. *S* opens can of soup with manual can opener.
2. *S* puts soup can lid in trash receptacle.
3. *S* pours syup into pot.
4. *S* turns on water.
5. *S* measures proper amount of water in can.
6. *S* turns off water.
7. *S* adds water to pot.
8. *S* throws can into trash receptacle.
9. *S* puts pot on burner.
10. *S* lights stove burner.
11. *S* adjusts burner knob to medium heat/high heat setting.
12. *S* stirs soup occasionally.
13. *S* allows soup to begin to bubble (boil).
14. *S* removes pot from burner.
15. *S* places pot on unlit burner.
16. *S* turns burner knob to "Off."
17. *S* picks up pot.
18. *S* pours soup into soup bowl.
19. *S* replaces pot on unlit burner.
Teaching Suggestions: Facilitate task analysis step 5 by using tape as cue on top of can to indicate level of water.

FRYING A HAMBURGER

Instructional Objective: Given 1 package of ground beef, salt in shaker, plate, frying pan, spatula, and 1 bun, *S* will fry a hamburger within 30 minutes, with 100% accuracy for 3 consecutive training days.

Prerequisite Skills: Turning on a stove and palmar grasp.
Task Analysis:
1.   *S* grasps one palmful of meat (@ ¹/₅ lb) in preferred hand.
2.   *S* shapes meat into round patty.
3.   *S* flattens meat patty.
4.   *S* places patty in frying pan.
5.   *S* turns burner on to medium temperature.
6.   *S* places frying pan on lit burner.
7.   *S* observes patty as it cooks.
8.   *S* allows side of patty to brown.
9.   *S* picks up spatula in preferred hand.
10.   *S* grips handle of pan with opposite hand.
11.   *S* turns patty to opposite side.
12.   *S* places spatula on counter adjacent to stove burner.
13.   *S* picks up salt shaker.
14.   *S* puts 2 to 4 shakes of salt evenly on top of patty.
15.   *S* allows this side of patty to brown.
16.   *S* repeats step 9.
17.   *S* repeats step 10.
18.   *S* picks up patty with spatula.
19.   *S* places patty on bun on plate.
20.   *S* turns off stove burner.

Teaching Suggestions: Proper holding of the pan and spatula should be given special attention to ensure safety.

FRYING BACON

Instructional Objective: Given 4 strips of bacon, frying pan, fork, and paper towels, *S* will fry bacon within 30 minutes, with 100% accuracy for 3 consecutive training days.
Prerequisite Skills: Turning on an electric stove and palmar grasp.
Task Analysis:
1.   *S* tears off 2 to 4 paper towels.
2.   *S* folds paper towels and places on counter adjacent to stove.
3.   *S* places bacon in frying pan.
4.   *S* flattens bacon out in pan so that strips are not twisted and are parallel to one another.
5.   *S* lights stove burner.
6.   *S* adjusts heat setting to medium heat.
7.   *S* places pan on lit burner.
8.   *S* observes bacon as it cooks.

9. *S* allows this side of bacon to brown.
10. *S* picks up fork in preferred hand.
11. *S* grasps handle of pan with opposite hand.
12. *S* turns strip of bacon on to opposite side.
13. *S* repeats step 12 until all 4 strips of bacon are turned.
14. *S* allows this side of bacon to brown.
15. *S* picks up strip of bacon with fork.
16. *S* places strip of bacon on towels.
17. *S* repeats steps 15 and 16 until all bacon is on towels.
18. *S* turns off stove burner.
19. *S* allows bacon grease to drain from bacon.

SETTING OVEN TEMPERATURE

Instructional Objective: Given an oven and the command "Set the oven," *S* will correctly set the oven to the designated temperature, with 100% accuracy for 3 consecutive training days.
Prerequisite Skills: Identification of numbers 200–500 at intervals of 25 (i.e., 200, 225, 250, 275...) and pincer grasp.
Task Analysis:
1. *S* looks at temperature control knob.
2. *S* reaches toward temperature control knob.
3. *S* grasps knob with fingers.
4. *S* turns knob until designated temperature matches the dot above the knob.
5. *S* removes hand from temperature control knob.
6. *S* looks at the "Off–Bake–Broil" knob.
7. *S* reaches toward "Off–Bake–Broil" knob.
8. *S* turns knob so that "Bake" matches the dot above the knob.
9. *S* removes hand from "Off–Bake–Broil" knob.
Pretest:
1. Do not provide consequences or physical assistance during the pretest.
2. Place *S* in the training area with the materials listed above.
3. Say to *S*, "Set the oven to ___°." Give no further verbal cues.
4. Watch *S* to determine which steps of the program he or she completes correctly.
5. Record a plus (+) for each step *S* completes correctly. Record a minus (–) for each step *S* does incorrectly or omits.
6. *S* may be able to do some of the steps in the program before training begins. If this occurs, *do not* eliminate these steps from the training sequence.

Teaching Procedures:

1. *T* places a piece of masking tape with a red elongated dot just above temperature control knob covering the existing dot on the stove.
2. *T* prepares a set of 3 " by 5 " cards, with numerals ranging from 200 to 500 at 25-degree intervals (i.e., 200, 225, 250, 275, . . .).
3. *T* takes one card (200) and tells *S*, "Watch me. I am going to set the oven to 200 (pointing to the card)."
4. *T* proceeds through task analysis steps 1–5, giving verbal cues as to how to adjust the temperature control knob using the elongated dot as an indicator.
5. *T* hands *S* the same card with the instructions, "Now you set the oven to this temperature."
6. *T* guides *S* through steps 1–5, giving verbal and tactile cues only as necessary.
7. Reinforce with praise or tangibles as appropriate.
8. Proceed through task analysis steps 1–5, using all 13 flash cards. When *S* can set the oven correctly in 12 out of 13 attempts proceed to next step.
9. *T* places a piece of masking tape with a red elongated dot just above the "Off–Bake–Broil" knob so that it covers the existing dot. Just above the elongated dot *T* writes with red pen the word "Bake."
10. *T* says to *S*, "Watch me. I will turn the oven on to Bake."
11. *T* proceeds through task analysis steps 6–9, emphasizing that the word "Bake" on the knob must be aligned with the word "Bake" over the dot.
12. *T* instructs *S*, "Now you turn the oven on to 'Bake.'"
13. *T* guides *S* through steps 6–9, giving verbal and tactile cues only as necessary.
14. Reinforce with praise or tangibles as appropriate.
15. Repeat task analysis steps 1–9, gradually fading out all visual cues. To do this:
    a. Make the dot over the temperature control knob smaller and smaller until it is an actual dot. Then remove masking tape completely.
    b. Repeat same fading procedure for dot over "Off–Bake–Broil" knob. Also fade the word "Bake" on the masking tape. Write it in black ink, then use pencil, making the pencil lighter and lighter. Eventually remove tape.

COOKING A FROZEN DINNER

Instructional Objective: Given an oven and a frozen dinner, *S* will correctly cook the dinner, with 100% accuracy for 3 consecutive training days.

Prerequisite Skills: Ability to set oven to designated temperature, ability to use kitchen timer, and ability to match numbers.

Task Analysis:

1. *S* looks at temperature on box of TV dinner.
2. *S* looks at temperature control knob on oven.
3. *S* reaches toward temperature control knob.
4. *S* grasps knob with fingers.
5. *S* turns knob until designated temperature matches dot above knob.
6. *S* removes hand from temperature control knob.
7. *S* looks at "Off–Bake–Broil" knob.
8. *S* reaches toward "Off–Bake–Broil" knob.
9. *S* turns knob so that "Bake" matches the dot above the knob.
10. *S* removes hand from "Off–Bake–Broil" knob.
11. *S* picks up TV dinner box.
12. *S* holds box in left hand (if *S* is right-handed).
13. *S* uses right hand to pull strip all around box.
14. *S* removes TV dinner tray from box.
15. *S* holds TV dinner in left hand and opens oven door with right hand.
16. *S* places TV dinner on rack in center of oven.
17. *S* closes oven door.
18. *S* looks on TV dinner box for minutes of baking time.
19. *S* sets kitchen timer for correct number of baking minutes.
20. When bell rings, *S* turns "Off–Bake–Broil" knob to "Off."
21. *S* opens oven door.
22. *S* picks up 2 pot holders.
23. *S* places 1 pot holder appropriately in each hand.
24. *S* removes TV dinner from oven.
25. *S* places TV dinner on top of stove (not on a burner).
26. *S* closes oven door.

Teaching Procedures:

1. Using red magic marker, *T* circles the temperature on the TV dinner box.
2. *T* places a piece of masking tape with a red elongated dot just above temperature control knob covering the existing dot on the stove.
3. *T* places a piece of masking tape with a red elongated dot just above the "Off–Bake–Broil" knob so that it covers the existing dot. Just above the elongated dot, *T* writes with red pen the word "Bake."
4. *T* says to *S*, "Watch me. I am going to set the oven to cook this TV dinner."
5. *T* proceeds through task analysis steps 1–10, giving special instructions on matching the number on the box to the correct setting on the temperature control knob. *T* also emphasizes that the TV dinner

must be baked, and that the word ''Bake'' on the ''Off–Bake–Broil'' knob must be aligned with the word ''Bake'' over the dot.

6.   *T* instructs *S*, ''Now you set the oven to cook the TV dinner.''
7.   *T* guides *S* through steps 1–10, giving verbal and tactile cues only as necessary.
8.   Reinforce with praise or tangibles as appropriate.
9.   When *S* can set the oven to the correct temperature without assistance for 3 consecutive days, proceed to next step.
10. *T* says to *S*, ''Watch me. I will put the TV dinner in the oven.''
11. *T* proceeds through task analysis steps 11–17, giving appropriate verbal instructions as necessary.
12. *T* instructs *S*, ''You put the dinner in the oven.''
13. *T* guides *S* through steps 11–17, giving verbal and tactile cues only as necessary.
14. Reinforce with tangibles or praise as appropriate.
15. *T* circles baking time on TV dinner box with blue magic marker.
16. *T* says, ''Watch me. I will cook this dinner for the correct number of minutes.''
17. *T* proceeds through task analysis steps 18–26, giving appropriate verbal instructions as necessary.
18. *T* instructs *S*, ''Now you cook this TV dinner.''
19. *T* guides *S* through steps 18–26, giving appropriate verbal instructions as necessary.
20. Repeat task analysis steps 1–26, gradually fading out all visual cues. To do this:
     a.   Make the circles on the box (around the temperature and the minutes) lighter and lighter. Fade the circle from the magic marker to pen, then to pencil. Gradually fade out completely.
     b.   Fade the elongated dot and the word ''Bake'' over the ''Off–Bake–Broil'' knob. To do this, fade the word from the red magic marker to red pencil. Then remove the masking tape completely.

SLICING

Instructional Objective: Given a cutting board, knife, and a vegetable, *S* will slice the vegetable with no errors, with 100% accuracy for 3 consecutive training days.
Prerequisite Skills: Palmar grasp and full use of one arm.
Task Analysis:
1.   *S* looks at vegetable.
2.   *S* reaches toward vegetable with left hand (if *S* is right-handed).

3. *S* picks up vegetable with left hand.
4. *S* places vegetable on cutting board.
5. While holding vegetable with left hand, *S* looks at knife.
6. *S* reaches toward knife with right hand.
7. *S* picks up knife with right hand.
8. While holding vegetable with left hand, *S* uses knife to slice the vegetable approximately 1/4 inch from right end.
9. *S* repeats step 8 until all of vegetable has been sliced.
10. *S* places knife to the side.

DICING

Instructional Objective: Given a cutting board, knife, bowl, and a vegetable, *S* will correctly dice the vegetable and scrape the diced pieces into a bowl, with 100% accuracy for 3 consecutive training days.
Prerequisite Skills: Palmar grasp and full use of one arm.
Task Analysis:
1. *S* looks at vegetable.
2. *S* reaches toward vegetable with left hand (if *S* is right-handed).
3. *S* picks up vegetable with left hand.
4. *S* places vegetable on cutting board.
5. While holding vegetable with left hand, *S* looks at knife.
6. *S* reaches toward knife with right hand.
7. *S* picks up knife with right hand.
8. While holding vegetable with left hand, *S* uses knife to slice the vegetable approximately 1/4 inch from right end.
9. *S* repeats step 8 until all of vegetable has been sliced.
10. *S* places knife to the side.
11. *S* moves all sliced pieces of the vegetable to the side or off the cutting board.
12. *S* picks up 1 slice of the vegetable.
13. *S* places slice on the cutting board.
14. *S* holds vegetable slice with left hand.
15. *S* picks up knife with right hand.
16. While holding vegetable with left hand, *S* uses knife to slice the vegetable approximately 1/4 inch from right end.
17. *S* repeats step 16 until all of vegetable slice has been sliced.
18. *S* turns cutting board 90 degrees.
19. *S* repeats steps 16 and 17 until all of vegetable has been sliced in the other direction.
20. *S* uses knife to scrape diced pieces into bowl.
21. *S* repeats steps 12–20 until all slices have been diced.

Teaching Suggestions: For task analysis steps 12–19, use a toothpick and red food coloring, dip the toothpick in the coloring, and draw lines at ¼-inch intervals on a vegetable slice. Then, using a toothpick and green food coloring, dip toothpick in the coloring and draw lines at ¼-inch intervals perpendicular to the red lines already drawn. Proceed through steps 12–19, giving *S* special instructions to slice on the red lines first, turn the cutting board, and then slice on the green lines.

BUSING RESTAURANT TABLE

Instructional Objective: Given 4 plates, 4 glasses, 4 settings of silverware, 4 napkins, 1 ashtray, several pieces of change (tip), 1 table, 2 bench seats, plate tray, and cleaning rag, *S* will bus the table in 1 minute, with 90% accuracy for 3 consecutive training days.

Prerequisite Skills: Pincer and palmar grasps.

Task Analysis:

1. *S* approaches table with tray and cleaning rag.
2. *S* places tray on bench adjacent to table.
3. *S* places rag on table.
4. *S* stacks up plates.
5. *S* picks up plates.
6. *S* places plates in tray.
7. *S* picks up 2 glasses.
8. *S* places 2 glasses in tray.
9. *S* repeats steps 7 and 8.
10. *S* gathers up silverware in both hands quickly.
11. *S* places silverware in tray.
12. *S* gathers up napkins in both hands quickly.
13. *S* places napkins in tray.
14. *S* picks up ashtray in preferred hand.
15. *S* empties ashtray in tray.
16. *S* picks up cleaning rag in opposite hand.
17. *S* wipes out ashtray.
18. *S* places ashtray on back edge of table.
19. *S* places cleaning rag on table.
20. *S* scoops up change at edge of table using both hands.
21. *S* places change in ashtray.
22. *S* picks up cleaning rag in preferred hand.
23. *S* wipes off table top thoroughly with cleaning rag.
24. *S* visually checks bench seats.

25.   *S* wipes off bench seats as necessary.
26.   *S* places cleaning rag in tray.
27.   *S* picks up tray.
28.   *S* takes tray to dishwashing area.

8

HOME INDUSTRY SKILLS SUBDOMAIN

Home industry skills represent another cluster of vocational behaviors in which the handicapped student should receive instruction. These skills include basic tool use and identification; for example, competency in use of a hammer, screwdriver, wrench, and saw will allow for the construction of different materials and objects. In addition to enabling employment in jobs like farmer's helper, or carpenter's helper, these skills will also facilitate independent living. The skills provided in this subdomain emphasize proficiency in the use of basic tools. They include:

1. Sorting Nails (or Bolts)
2. Bolting Wood Together
3. Gluing Mitered Corners Together
4. Hammering Two Boards Together
5. Removing a Nail
6. Putting Screws in a Board
7. Unscrewing Screws
8. Using a Wrench to Tighten a Nut and Bolt
9. Sawing a Board
10. Sanding a Board
11. Staining a Board
12. Painting a Board
13. Stripping Paint from a Board

SORTING NAILS (OR BOLTS)

Instructional Objective: Given a cup of 20 nails, in sizes 1, 2, 3, and 4 inches, and 4 boxes, *S* will sort the nails by size into the 4 boxes, with 100% accuracy for 3 consecutive training days.

Prerequisite Skills: Pincer grasp and potential for visual and/or tactile discrimination.

Task Analysis:

1.   S pours nails out onto surface and spreads apart.
2.   S picks out a nail.
3.   S places nail in nondominant hand.
4.   S looks carefully at remaining nails and chooses another that appears to be the same length.
5.   S places second nail in nondominant hand beside first for comparison.
6.   S leaves nail in hand if identical in length; replaces in pile if different.
7.   S repeats steps 4–6 until all nails of one size are together in hand (even if S must try every nail in pile).
8.   S places nails in hand in box 1.
9.   S repeats steps 2–7 for second size of nails.
10.   S repeats steps 2–7 for third size of nails.
11.   S collects remaining nails on surface, compares for common size, and places in fourth box.

Teaching Procedures:

1.   For a pretask familiarization, have S separate into 4 boxes like objects (of 4 different types) mixed together (e.g., have mixed together 4 washers, 4 screws, 4 nails, and 4 bolts).
2.   Next, have S sort materials that are different in two ways (e.g., give S strips of construction paper — 4 green, 4 yellow, 4 red, and 4 blue — but have them vary in length from one color to the next). Have S notice and say aloud the two ways that they differ from each other.
3.   Then have S sort paper strips all of the same color but of four varying lengths. Have S isolate those alike and place in one box before going on to next size.
4.   Have S practice feeling and aligning head to head nails of different lengths and naming the longer one.

BOLTING WOOD TOGETHER

Instructional Objective: Given 2 pieces of wood and a nut and bolt, S will bolt the 2 pieces of wood together in 10 minutes, with 100% accuracy for 3 consecutive training days.

Prerequisite Skills: Pincer grasp and eye-hand coordination to align holes and nut to bolt.

Task Analysis:
1. *S* places wood pieces and bolt and nut on top of work station.
2. *S* picks up 1 piece of wood with left hand.
3. *S* picks up other piece of wood with right hand.
4. *S* places 2 wood pieces together.
5. *S* aligns drilled bolt holes on top of one another.
6. *S* grasps both aligned pieces of wood in one hand.
7. *S* picks up bolt with other hand.
8. *S* aligns bolt with hole.
9. *S* inserts bolt through hole.
10. *S* holds bolt in hole with one finger and picks up nut with other hand.
11. *S* aligns nut with bolt.
12. *S* turns nut on bolt until finger tight.
13. *S* places assembled wood on table.

Pretest:
1. Do not provide consequences or physical assistance during the pretest.
2. Place *S* in the training area with the appropriate materials on a flat surface.
3. Tell *S*, "Bolt together these two pieces of wood."
4. Watch *S* to determine which steps he or she completes correctly.
5. Record a plus (+) for each step *S* completes correctly. Record a minus (−) for each step *S* does incorrectly or omits.
6. *S* may be able to do some of the steps of the program before training begins. If this occurs, *do not* eliminate these steps from the training sequence.

Teaching Procedures:
1. *T* will model skill, giving verbal explanation of each task analysis step (1–13).
2. *T* will give *S* materials and command, "Bolt together these two pieces of wood." *T* will give physical assistance and verbal cues throughout the completion of the task when *T* notes omissions, hesitations, or uncertain moves.
3. *T* will have *S* repeat task, gradually decreasing frequency of physical, then verbal, cues.
4. *T* will give command, and *S* will complete task without any physical or verbal cues on 5 out of 5 trials.
5. *T* will acknowledge correct moves and give praise for appropriate behaviors throughout completion of task on all levels.

6. To assist in showing how to align holes and hold in place, *T* can give *S* 2 pieces of paper with pre-punched holes and have *S* place brads through each of the sets of holes and fasten; or *S* can be given 2 pieces of cardboard with pre-punched holes and can place pegs or pencils through each set of holes.

7. To practice eye-hand coordination required to place the nut onto the bolt, have *S* place a handful of washers, one by one, onto a stationary stick, nail, pencil, etc., held tightly in wood.

8. To practice skills used in aligning nut onto bolt and turning, give *S* small jars and jar lids and have *S* place and tighten lid on jar. For this skill, have *S* simply practice screwing and unscrewing nut onto bolt in isolation.

9. To practice thumb and first finger movement used in screwing the nut, have *S* turn knob on bottom or back of a wind-up clock that sets the hands or is the winding mechanism, or have *S* twist dial on a combination lock.

GLUING MITERED CORNERS TOGETHER

Instructional Objective: Given 2 boards with mitered edges and a bottle of contact cement with a brush inside, *S* will glue the two edges together in 30 minutes, with 100% accuracy for 3 consecutive training days.

Prerequisite Skills: Pincer grasp, minimal arm strength to hold boards together, and ability to tell time to the minute.

Task Analysis:

1. *S* places several sheets of paper on work surface.
2. *S* places boards and gluing materials on work surface.
3. *S* places can of contact cement and screwdriver in front of self on work surface.
4. *S* grasps can of contact cement with one hand.
5. *S* places can of contact cement by left corner of newspaper.
6. *S* places mitered boards in front of self.
7. *S* grasps one mitered board.
8. *S* picks up brush.
9. *S* dips tip of brush in contact cement.
10. *S* strokes small amount of contact cement on one end of both mitered boards.
11. *S* sets aside boards on newspaper for 15 minutes.
12. *S* replaces cap on bottle of contact cement.
13. *S* picks up both mitered boards.
14. *S* lines up bottom edges of mitered boards.

15. *S* presses together mitered edges while keeping them correctly positioned.
16. *S* presses pieces of wood together for 1 minute.
17. *S* places glued pieces on small piece of newspaper.
18. *S* throws away rest of newspaper.

Teaching Procedures:
1. To illustrate to *S* the need to place substance on both surfaces and the need for a waiting period, give *S* two pieces of paper and bottle of rubber cement. Have *S* rub rubber cement on both pieces of paper. Let dry; then press together. Have *S* do the same task two more times, once when cement is applied to only one surface, and once when they are placed together while still wet. Have *S* state aloud problems with the two latter methods as opposed to first.
2. Have *S* study the formation of picture frames at the corners before performing activity.
3. Have *S* glue together with white glue two pieces of paper to practice alignment and pressing the two together.

HAMMERING TWO BOARDS TOGETHER

Instructional Objective: Given a hammer, two 3-foot long 2″ by 4″ boards, and a box of assorted nails, *S* will nail the boards together at the middle and at each end in 15 minutes, with 100% accuracy, for 3 consecutive training days.

Prerequisite Skills: Palmar grasp, extension of one arm, and eye-hand coordination.

Task Analysis:
1. *S* places 1 board in front of self.
2. *S* places second board on top of first board.
3. *S* aligns the 2 boards so that all edges match.
4. *S* picks up nail.
5. *S* positions nail at one end of board with sharp end down.
6. *S* picks up hammer while still holding nail in position.
7. *S* grasps shaft of hammer with fist.
8. *S* positions blunt end of hammer on head of nail.
9. *S* raises hammer.
10. *S* brings hammer down on nail head with a striking force.
11. *S* continues to hold boards aligned correctly with free hand.
12. *S* repeats step 10, holding nail upright until head of nail is even with board surface.

13.   *S* repeats steps 4–12 at middle position on boards.
14.   *S* repeats steps 4–12 at end position on boards.

Teaching Suggestions: Have *S* practice hammering nails into single boards to develop the necessary strength and the eye-hand coordination required to meet hammerhead to nail head (begin with large nails with large heads and decrease size gradually), to achieve goal of driving nail into board so that nail head is flush with wood surface.

REMOVING A NAIL

Instructional Objective: Given a board with protruding nail, *S* will remove the nail during a 5-minute work period, with 100% accuracy for 3 consecutive training days.

Prerequisite Skills: Palmar grasp, total arm movement, eye-hand coordination.

Task Analysis:
1.   *S* places board with nail in front of self on work surface.
2.   *S* picks up hammer.
3.   *S* holds hammer so that hammerhand is pointing down toward nail.
4.   *S* twists hammerhead so that prong side faces nail.
5.   *S* aligns middle of prongs with nail.
6.   *S* slips prongs around nail as far as possible.
7.   *S* holds board steady with other hand.
8.   *S* pulls handle in opposite direction of nail.
9.   *S* uses sufficient force to remove nail.
10.   *S* removes nail from prongs of hammer.

Teaching Suggestions: To illustrate the leverage principle involved in placing hammerhead on board and exerting pressure upward from board, show *S* analogous situations; i.e., demonstrate and have *S* do the following: remove the top from an empty paint can with a screw driver, remove a hub cap with a tire iron, or remove a bottle cap with a bottle opener. Show *S* how the tool must always touch the surface and pressure must be exerted away from that surface.

PUTTING SCREWS IN A BOARD

Instructional Objective: Given a 2 ′ by 4 ′ board, screws, screwdriver, hammer, and a nail, *S* will screw the screw completely into the board within 5 minutes, with 100% accuracy for 3 consecutive training days.

Prerequisite Skills: Pincer and palmar grasps and wrist rotation.

Task Analysis:
1. *S* looks at board.
2. *S* places board in front of self.
3. *S* looks at nail.
4. *S* picks up nail.
5. *S* turns nail so that pointed end faces downward.
6. *S* touches pointed end of nail to board.
7. *S* looks at hammer.
8. *S* picks up hammer.
9. *S* turns hammer so that metal head is facing upward.
10. *S* turns hammer so that flattened end of the head faces head of nail.
11. *S* aims hammer toward head of the nail.
12. *S* strikes head of nail with hammer so as to force nail straight into board only a short distance.
13. *S* puts hammer down.
14. *S* takes nail out of board.
15. *S* puts nail down.
16. *S* looks at screw.
17. *S* picks up screw.
18. *S* turns screw so that pointed end is pointing downward.
19. *S* places pointed end of screw into hole made with nail.
20. *S* looks at screwdriver.
21. *S* picks up screwdriver.
22. *S* turns screwdriver so that flat, pointed end points downward.
23. *S* places flat, pointed end of screwdriver into slot on head of screw.
24. *S* turns screw in clockwise manner with screwdriver.
25. *S* continues this motion until screw is completely into board.

UNSCREWING SCREWS

Instructional Objective: Given 2 boards screwed together and a screwdriver, *S* will unscrew the boards by completely removing the screw during a 10-minute work period, with 100% accuracy for 3 consecutive days.
Prerequisite Skills: Palmar grasp, eye-hand coordination, and wrist rotation.
Task Analysis:
1. *S* places board in front of self with heads of screws facing up.
2. *S* grasps handle of screwdriver.
3. *S* picks up screwdriver.
4. *S* positions flat, pointed end of screwdriver in groove of screw.

5. *S* holds board with other hand to steady.
6. *S* turns screw clockwise to loosen.
7. *S* repeats step 6 until screw is free.
8. *S* unscrews screw by hand when loose enough to do so.
9. *S* picks up screw and sets aside on work surface.
10. *S* repeats steps 4–9 for other two screws.

Teaching Procedures:
1. Have *S* practice screwing and unscrewing jar lids to imprint results of clockwise and counterclockwise motion in mind.
2. Have *S* hold nut in nondominant hand and a bolt in dominant hand. Holding nut stationary, have *S* use dominant hand to screw and unscrew bolt, noticing clockwise and counterclockwise movements and associating direction with moving in and out of bolt. Associate this movement with movement of a screw.
3. To gain skill in wrist and hand movements associated with a screwdriver, have *S* practice repeatedly twisting either a door knob, while grasping tightly, or a dowel placed into a tight fitting hole drilled into a plank.

USING A WRENCH TO TIGHTEN A NUT AND BOLT

Instructional Objective: Given the command "Tighten the nut," *S* will use a wrench to tighten the nut during a 5-minute work period, with 100% accuracy for 3 consecutive training days.

Prerequisite Skills: Palmar grasp and 5-finger manipulative skills.

Task Analysis:
1. *S* looks at the materials.
2. *S* places board in front of self on work surface.
3. *S* places board with nut side facing up.
4. *S* screws down nut with fingers as far as it will go easily.
5. *S* looks at wrench.
6. *S* picks up wrench.
7. *S* moves wrench to nut.
8. *S* aligns head of wrench with nut.
9. *S* uses thumb and forefinger to adjust width of wrench.
10. *S* adjusts wrench so that it fits nut.
11. *S* slides wrench around nut.
12. *S* grasps handle of wrench.
13. *S* turns handle in a clockwise direction.
14. *S* holds bottom side of bolt with hand, screwdriver, pliers, or another wrench to keep nut and bolt from turning as one unit.

15. *S* continues to exert pressure until nut is tight.
16. *S* removes wrench from nut.

Teaching Procedures:
1. To develop skill of placing wrench onto nut, have *S* practice grasping and lifting cups with kitchen tongs. (Mark spots on the cup to be picked up to encourage precision.)
2. To develop 5-finger movement required to adjust wrench, have *S* practice moving hands and fingers on knobs on a wind-up clock.

SAWING A BOARD

Instructional Objective: Given a saw, ruler, and a board, *S* will saw a 1-foot long piece off the board in 20 minutes, with 100% accuracy for 3 consecutive work days.

Prerequisite Skills: Pincer and palmar grasps and extension of one arm.

Task Analysis:
1. *S* places board and ruler in front of self.
2. *S* places ruler on top of board.
3. *S* lines up edge of ruler with edge of board at one end.
4. *S* picks up pencil.
5. *S* makes mark at end of ruler on board.
6. *S* marks at another point on other edge.
7. *S* aligns marks and draws a solid line.
8. *S* sets ruler aside.
9. *S* places board on work surface with marked end extending over edge of worktable.
10. *S* picks up saw.
11. *S* grasps saw in fist of preferred hand.
12. *S* holds board down with other hand.
13. *S* aligns teeth of saw with marks on board.
14. *S* pulls saw backward.
15. *S* pushes saw forward.
16. *S* repeats steps 14 and 15 in same position until board is sawed through.
17. *S* picks up sawed off piece and places at work station.

Teaching Procedures:
1. Supply *S* with instruction on measurement — worksheets on use of ruler, measurement equivalents, difference in use of ruler, yardstick, and tape measure, and so on.
2. Have *S* cut 1 foot off 3-foot piece of paper. Show how to align ruler with end of paper; make a few small marks in various places, align small marks with ruler, and draw solid line.

3.   Have S cut with scissors along predrawn lines to practice eye-hand co-ordination skills.
4.   Draw lines on piece of Styrofoam and have S "saw" through with a knife.

SANDING A BOARD

Instructional Objective: Given sandpaper and a piece of wood needing sanding, S will sand all surfaces of wood until smooth during a 15-minute work period, with 100% accuracy for 3 consecutive training days.
Prerequisite Skills: Pincer grasp and use of one arm.
Task Analysis:
1.   S looks at piece of wood.
2.   S touches piece of wood.
3.   S places piece of wood in front of self.
4.   S looks at sandpaper.
5.   S touches sandpaper.
6.   S picks up sandpaper.
7.   S folds sandpaper to hand size (folds into fourths).
8.   S grasps wood with other hand.
9.   S places sandpaper on top of wood.
10.   S rubs sandpaper forward across surface of wood.
11.   S rubs sandpaper back across surface of wood.
12.   S repeats steps 10 and 11 until smooth.
13.   S turns piece of wood so that another area to be sanded faces up.
14.   S repeats steps 10–13 until all sides are smooth (uses different fourth of sandpaper for different sides).

STAINING A BOARD

Instructional Objectives: Given a board, staining materials, and news-paper, S will stain 4 sides of a board during a 40-minute work period, with 100% accuracy for 3 consecutive training days.
Prerequisite Skills: Palmar grasp and use of one arm.
Task Analysis:
1.   S places several sheets of paper on work surface.
2.   S places board and staining materials on newspaper.
3.   S places can of stain and screwdriver in front of self on work surface.
4.   S grasps stain can with hand.
5.   S picks up screwdriver with other hand.
6.   S inserts flat, pointed end of screwdriver under edge of lid of stain can.

7.   *S* twists screwdriver under edge of lid of stain can.
8.   *S* repeats steps 6 and 7 around can until lid is free.
9.   *S* lays down screwdriver.
10.   *S* removes lid from can of stain.
11.   *S* stirs stain until all residue is mixed.
12.   *S* places can of stain on corner of newspaper.
13.   *S* places board in front of self on work surface.
14.   *S* picks up paintbrush.
15.   *S* dips tip of brush in stain.
16.   *S* scrapes excess stain from brush on side of can.
17.   *S* moves tip of brush to left of board.
18.   *S* places brush tip flat on top edge of board.
19.   *S* slowly spreads stain along surface using short strokes.
20.   *S* completely covers top surface of the board.
21.   *S* lays brush on newspaper.
22.   *S* waits 5 minutes.
23.   *S* picks up rag.
24.   *S* folds rag to hand size.
25.   *S* places cloth (while held in hand) on top of board.
26.   *S* wipes excess stain off board.
27.   *S* repeats steps 14–26 until all sides of board are stained.
28.   *S* picks up lid of stain can.
29.   *S* places lid on stain can.
30.   *S* presses lid tightly on can.
31.   *S* picks up rag.
32.   *S* wipes stain from outside of can.
33.   *S* removes cap from turpentine.
34.   *S* pours turpentine into a can until ⅓ full.
35.   *S* places brush in can and swishes around.
36.   *S* wipes brush on side of can.
37.   *S* wipes brush on rag.
38.   *S* repeats steps 35–37 two more times.
39.   *S* lays brush out on piece of newspaper to dry.
40.   *S* replaces cap on turpentine.
41.   *S* empties contents of can outside on ground.
42.   *S* throws rag and newspaper in trash.

Teaching Procedures:
1.   *S* can practice many skills by first using water in a can and "painting" on cardboard. Practice in this way especially to emphasize wiping brush on edge of can, dipping brush into liquid only halfway up bristles, and clean-up procedures.

2. To help illustrate technique of wiping off stain, refer to task analysis steps for "Sanding a Board."
3. To practice full or total arm movement, have S rake leaves with a rake from one small area. To practice arm movement and demonstrate application then removal of a substance, have S clean a large window with a squeegee (apply soap on complete surface with one side of tool; then remove from surface with other side).

PAINTING A BOARD

Instructional Objective: Given a board, paint, paintbrush, rags, newspaper, screwdriver, and paint shirt, S will paint four sides of a board during a 60-minute work period, with 100% accuracy for 3 consecutive training days.
Prerequisite Skills: Palmar grasp and use of one arm.
Task Analysis:

1. S puts on paint shirt to protect clothes.
2. S places several pieces of newspaper on work surface.
3. S places a board and painting materials on the newspaper.
4. S places a can of paint and a screwdriver in front of self on work surface.
5. S grasps paint can with left hand (if right-handed).
6. S picks up screwdriver with right hand.
7. S inserts flat, pointed end of screwdriver under edge of lid of paint can.
8. S twists screwdriver to pry up lid of paint can.
9. S repeats steps 7 and 8 around can until lid is free.
10. S lays down screwdriver.
11. S stirs paint with paint stirrer until color and texture are uniform.
12. S places can of paint on left corner of newspaper.
13. S places a board in front of self on work surface.
14. S picks up paintbrush.
15. S dips tip of brush in paint.
16. S scrapes excess paint from brush on side of can.
17. S moves tip of brush to left of board.
18. S places brush tip flat on top edge of board.
19. S slowly spreads paint along surface using short strokes.
20. S completely covers top surface of the board.
21. S lays brush on newspaper.
22. S turns board on one side.
23. S picks up brush.
24. S dips tip of brush in paint.
25. S scrapes excess paint from brush on edge of can.

26. *S* places tip of brush flat on left side of board.
27. *S* slowly spreads paint along surface using short strokes.
28. *S* completely covers top surface of board.
29. *S* dips brush in paint.
30. *S* removes excess paint using lip of can.
31. *S* moves edge of brush to left of unpainted side of board.
32. *S* places brush flat on surface of unpainted side.
33. *S* slowly spreads paint along surface using short strokes.
34. *S* completely covers side of board.
35. *S* lays brush down on newspaper.
36. *S* places fingers on each end of board.
37. *S* turns board up on edge.
38. *S* turns board so that unpainted side is toward front of work surface.
39. *S* picks up paintbrush.
40. *S* dips brush in paint.
41. *S* removes excess paint from brush using edge of can.
42. *S* moves brush to top of unpainted surface.
43. *S* places edge of brush flat on surface.
44. *S* slowly spreads paint along surface using short strokes.
45. *S* completely covers surface.
46. *S* lays paintbrush down.
47. *S* leaves board on end to dry.
48. *S* picks up lid of paint can.
49. *S* places lid on top of can.
50. *S* presses lid tightly onto can.
51. *S* picks up rag.
52. *S* wipes paint from outside of paint can.
53. *S* fills another can ⅓ full with water or turpentine (depending on whether paint is a latex or oil-based paint).
54. *S* places brush in can and swishes around.
55. *S* wipes brush on side of can.
56. *S* wipes brush on rag.
57. *S* repeats steps 53–56 two more times.
58. *S* lays brush out on piece of newspaper to dry.
59. *S* empties contents of can outside.
60. *S* throws away rags and newspaper.
61. *S* replaces cap on turpentine.

Depending on the age and entry level of *S*, some prerequisite skills for doing the task might include a good pencil grasp and visual discrimination.

Pretest:

1. Do not provide consequences or physical assistance during the pretest.

2. Place *S* in the training area with the appropriate materials on a flat surface.
3. Tell *S*, "Paint this board on the four long sides."
4. Watch *S* to determine which steps he or she completes correctly.
5. Record a plus (+) for each step *S* completes correctly. Record a minus (−) for each step *S* does incorrectly or omits.
6. *S* may be able to do some of the steps of the program before training begins. If this occurs, *do not* eliminate these steps from the training sequence.

Teaching Procedures:

1. *T* will model skill, giving verbal explanation of each step (steps 1–61).
2. *T* will give *S* materials and command, "Paint this board on the four long sides." *T* will give physical assistance and verbal cues throughout the completion of the task when he or she notes omissions, hesitations, or uncertain moves.
3. *T* will have *S* repeat task, gradually decreasing frequency of physical, then verbal, cues.
4. *T* will give command, and *S* will complete task without any physical or verbal cues with 100% accuracy.
5. *T* will acknowledge correct moves and give praise for appropriate behavior throughout completion of task on all levels.
6. To practice total arm movement and to illustrate importance of covering entire surface, have *S* wash a blackboard with a sponge, emphasizing a consistent pattern in straight lines, complete coverage, frequent re-dipping, and proper squeezing.
7. Practice in isolation with water in a can and "paint" on cardboard. This way *T* can emphasize wiping of brush on edge of can, dipping brush into liquid only halfway up bristles, and clean-up procedures.
8. In advance of teaching this activity, illustrate turning of board to prevent wet side from touching paper by using a child's rectangular building block. In an activity with *S*, hand *S* the block and say, "Never let the side with a red X touch the table, but you must change its position each time I mark it." Have a red magic marker and proceed to mark four sides of the block, one at a time, having *S* deal with turning the block after each mark. Perform this activity until he or she learns to turn block on its end.

STRIPPING PAINT FROM A BOARD

Instructional Objective: Given a painted board, paint remover, scraper, rags, paintbrush, newspapers, 2 cans, cleaning solution, and a workshirt, *S* will remove all the paint from the board, with 100% accuracy for 3 consecutive training days.

Prerequisite Skills: Palmar grasp, movement of one arm, and fine finger movement.

Task Analysis:

1. *S* puts on workshirt to protect clothes.
2. *S* places several sheets of newspaper on work surface.
3. *S* places a board and stripping materials on newspaper.
4. *S* places a can of stripper in front of self on work surface.
5. *S* opens the can of stripper.
6. *S* pours a small amount of stripper into a can.
7. *S* puts cap back on can.
8. *S* picks up brush with hand.
9. *S* touches tip of brush in stripper.
10. *S* places wide surface of brush on one end of top of board.
11. *S* slowly spreads stripper along surface using short strokes.
12. *S* completely covers top surface of the board.
13. *S* places brush on newspaper.
14. *S* waits until paint "bubbles" up.
15. *S* picks up scraper.
16. *S* moves scraper to one side of board.
17. *S* places scraper flat side down on board.
18. *S* scrapes softened paint with short strokes.
19. *S* uses a rag to wipe removed varnish off scraper.
20. *S* repeats steps 16–18 until top surface is clean.

Harrison

9

HORTICULTURE
SKILLS SUBDOMAIN

In a predominantly rural area, landscaping and horticulture skills are important vocational behaviors for students to learn. Working in a greenhouse, a florist's shop, or a landscaping company are various placements for which handicapped students may be prepared. Ideally, horticulture skills can be taught to the young child, with increasingly complex skills presented as the student becomes older and more proficient. The development of horticulture skills is also excellent for helping the retarded student acquire appropriate leisure skills, e.g., working with plants. The following skills have been analyzed:

1. Raking Leaves
2. Weeding
3. Trimming Grass Around Tree
4. Filling Lawn Mower Gas Tank
5. Mowing Lawn
6. Washing Flower Pots
7. Filling Flower Pots with Soil
8. Sifting Soil
9. Putting Hangers on Hanging Baskets
10. Potting Cuttings in Pots Already Filled with Soil
11. Potting a Rooted Geranium Cutting
12. Repotting Plant from 3″ to 5″ Clay Pot
13. Planting a Vegetable Plant
14. Stem Cuttings
15. Leaf Cuttings
16. Disbudding

RAKING LEAVES

Instructional Objective: Given a rake, leaves, and a designated area, *S* will rake all of the leaves into a single pile, with 100% accuracy for 3 consecutive training days.

Prerequisite Skills: Palmar grasp and extension of both arms.

Task Analysis:

1. *S* holds rake with flat surface parallel to ground.
2. *S* rakes leaves toward designated area from left side of area to be raked.
3. *S* takes 1 step to his or her right.
4. *S* repeats steps 2 and 3 until he or she reaches right boundary of area.
5. *S* rakes leaves toward designated area from right side.
6. *S* takes 1 step to his or her left.
7. *S* repeats steps 5 and 6 until he or she reaches left boundary of area.
8. *S* repeats steps 2–7 until area is raked.
9. *S* rakes leaves into a single pile.
10. *S* removes leaves from rake with hand as necessary.

Teaching Suggestions: Start with a small designated area about 6′ by 6′. Mark off the area with tape or string to correspond to the steps in the task analysis. Place a plastic bag or bushel basket in the right corner of the area to show *S* his or her goal.

WEEDING

Instructional Objective: Given a flower bed with flowers and weeds and a trash bag, *S* will weed the bed thoroughly and place the weeds in the trash bag, with 100% accuracy for 3 consecutive training days.

Prerequisite Skills: Palmar and pincer grasps and extension of one arm.

Task Analysis:

1. *S* differentiates between flowers and weeds.
2. *S* places fingers at base of weed.
3. *S* pulls weed from bed.
4. *S* shakes dirt from root of weed.
5. *S* places weed in trash bag.
6. *S* repeats steps 2–5 until flower bed is thoroughly weeded.

TRIMMING GRASS AROUND TREE

Instructional Objective: Given a tree, grass, and clippers, *S* will trim grass around tree, with 100% accuracy for 3 consecutive training days.

Prerequisite Skills: Extension of one arm and adequate hand strength to squeeze clippers.

Task Analysis:

1.   S picks up clippers.
2.   S holds clippers so that he or she can operate cutting edges by squeezing handles.
3.   S identifies area to be trimmed.
4.   S places blades in area to be trimmed parallel to ground and at the proper height.
5.   S squeezes handle, trimming grass.
6.   S repeats steps 4–5 until grass is trimmed to proper height on all sides of tree.

Teaching Suggestions: Proper hand placement may be visually cued by marking the thumb area with tape.

Step 4 can be physically cued by the use of a cardboard strip about 1 ½ inches in height. This strip can be placed in the grass so that the clippers can be moved along the top edge.

FILLING LAWN MOWER GAS TANK

Instructional Objective: Given a standard gasoline lawn mower, gas, gas can, and funnel, S will fill the mower tank, with 100% accuracy for 3 consecutive training days.

Prerequisite Skills: Pincer and palmar grasps and extension of both arms.

Task Analysis:

1.   S disconnects spark plug wire from spark plug.
2.   S removes gas tank cap with preferred hand.
3.   S places tank cap on mower blade housing
4.   S removes gas can cap with preferred hand.
5.   S places can cap on ground adjacent to gas can.
6.   S picks up funnel in preferred hand.
7.   S places funnel in gas tank.
8.   S picks up gas can with both hands.
9.   S holds can so that one hand depresses vacuum release button.
10.   S slowly pours gasoline into tank.
11.   S continues until tank is full but not overflowing.
12.   S sets gas can on ground adjacent to mower.
13.   S removes funnel.
14.   S picks up tank cap.
15.   S replaces tank cap tightly.

16. *S* picks up can cap.
17. *S* replaces can cap tightly.
18. *S* connects spark plug wire to spark plug.

MOWING LAWN

Instructional Objective: Given a lawn mower and a lawn, *S* will mow the lawn, with 100% accuracy for 3 consecutive training days.
Prerequisite Skills: Filling lawn mower gas tank, starting lawn mower, strength to push mower.
Task Analysis:
1. *S* pushes mower to flat area of lawn.
2. *S* starts mower.
3. *S* adjusts controls to appropriate speed to suit conditions (higher or thicker grass — higher speed, etc.).
4. *S* grasps mower handle with both hands.
5. *S* grasps handle with palms down.
6. *S,* starting at one boundary, pushes mower along the boundary to end of area to be mowed.
7. *S* stops at end of area to be mowed.
8. *S* lightly pushes down on handle, taking weight off front wheels.
9. *S* walks handle of mower around, rotating mower 180 degrees.
10. *S* releases pressure on handle.
11. *S* places mower so that cutting area overlaps previously mowed area by 1 to 4 inches.
12. *S* pushes mower along cut area to edge of area to be mowed, maintaining overlap so that no spots are left unmowed.
13. *S* repeats steps 7–12 until entire area has been mowed.
14. *S* turns mower off.
Teaching Suggestions: The overlap required in step 11 can be cued by marking the front of the mower with tape. *S* should line up the mark with the previously cut line.

WASHING FLOWER POTS

Instructional Objective: Given a sink, water, worktable, dirty pots, and a brush, *S* will wash flower pots thoroughly, with 100% accuracy for 3 consecutive training days.
Prerequisite Skills: Discrimination between hot and cold water, and pincer and palmar grasps.

Task Analysis:
1. *S* empties any loose dirt from pot into trash can.
2. *S* places pot on counter beside sink.
3. *S* removes objects from sink.
4. *S* places stopper in sink.
5. *S* fills sink with water to proper level.
6. *S* places dirty pot in water.
7. *S* picks up brush in preferred hand.
8. *S* picks up pot in opposite hand.
9. *S* scrubs inside of pot thoroughly.
10. *S* scrubs outside of pot thoroughly.
11. *S* places pot upside down on worktable.
12. *S* repeats steps 6–11 until all pots are clean.
13. *S* pulls stopper from sink.
14. *S* thoroughly rinses debris from sink.

Pretest:
1. Do not provide consequences or physical assistance during the pretest.
2. Place *S* in the training area at sink; pots should be stacked on counter and brush should be in cabinet under sink.
3. Say to *S*, "Get the brush and wash the flower pots."
4. Watch *S* to determine which steps of the program he or she completes correctly.
5. Record a plus (+) for each step *S* completes correctly. Record a minus (–) for each step *S* does incorrectly or omits.
6. *S* may be able to do some of the steps in the program before training begins. If this occurs, *do not* eliminate these steps from the training sequence.

Teaching Procedures:
1. Say to *S*, "Watch me wash the flower pots." Proceed through steps 1–14.
2. Say to *S*, "Wash the flower pots." Require *S* to do step 1 and guide *S* through steps 2–14. Gradually fade all physical and verbal cueing. When *S* can do step 1 correctly unassisted for 2 consecutive days, proceed to step 2.
3. Say to *S*, "Wash the flower pots." Require *S* to do step 1, model step 2, require *S* to do step 2, and guide through steps 3–14. Gradually fade all physical and verbal cueing. When *S* can do steps 1 and 2 correctly unassisted for 2 consecutive days, proceed to step 3.

4. Proceed through the remaining steps in this manner until *S* can correctly do steps 1–14 unassisted. Provide praise and consumable consequences for the desired behavior. Record a plus (+) when *S* completes a step correctly without assistance; record a minus (−) for steps not completed correctly unassisted.

5. The behavior in step 5 may be facilitated by affixing colored tape to the sink to show proper water level. Show *S* that this is the level to which the water should come.

6. *S* may have difficulty distinguishing between a *thoroughly* clean pot and one that is not thoroughly clean. Show *S* a pot that is clean and one that is dirty. Point out the dirty spots in the one as opposed to the other. Have *S* find the dirty spots. Have *S* feel the dirty pot as opposed to the clean one.

7. To aid in teaching step 14 it may be necessary to continually point out debris left in sink until *S* can identify unassisted.

FILLING FLOWER POTS WITH SOIL

Instructional Objective: Given flower pots, worktable, hand shovel, and soil, *S* will fill pots with soil, with 100% accuracy for 3 consecutive training days.

Prerequisite Skills: Palmar grasp and sufficient arm and hand strength to hand shovel soil.

Task Analysis:

1. *S* places pot on worktable.
2. *S* picks up shovel in preferred hand.
3. *S* puts shovel in soil.
4. *S* brings shovel with soil to pot.
5. *S* puts soil into pot with shovel.
6. *S* repeats step 5 until soil in pot reaches proper level.
7. *S* repeats steps 3–6 until all pots are filled.

SIFTING SOIL

Instructional Objective: Given a shovel, trash receptacle, soil, bucket, piece of screening to go over top of bucket, and a large spoon, *S* will sift debris from soil, with 100% accuracy for 3 consecutive training days.

Prerequisite Skills: Palmar grasp.

Task Analysis:

1. *S* places screen on top of bucket.
2. *S* picks up shovel.

3. *S* puts shovel into soil and fills with dirt.
4. *S* empties soil from shovel onto screen.
5. *S* repeats steps 3 and 4 until screen contains proper amount of soil.
6. *S* places shovel aside.
7. *S* picks up spoon in preferred hand.
8. *S* holds screen in place with opposite hand.
9. *S* moves spoon back and forth over soil until all soil has been sifted into bucket.
10. *S* picks up screen and dumps debris into trash receptacle.
11. *S* replaces screen on top of bucket.
12. *S* repeats steps 2–10 until all soil has been sifted.

Teaching Suggestions: Draw a small circle in the center of the screen. Have *S* place the soil on the circle. As *S* begins to do steps 1–12 with minimal cueing, begin making the circle on the screen bigger until it is almost the same size as the bucket.

PUTTING HANGERS ON HANGING BASKETS

Instructional Objective: Given hanging pots, worktable, and wire hangers, *S* will put hangers on hanging baskets, with 100% accuracy for 3 consecutive training days.

Prerequisite Skills: Pincer grasp, one-hand coordination sufficient for threading hanger through basket hole, and fine motor coordination for twisting hanger hook.

Task Analysis:
1. *S* picks up hanger in preferred hand.
2. *S* grasps pot in opposite hand.
3. *S* places on hanger hook through a hole on the rim of the pot.
4. *S* releases hanger.
5. *S* twists hook with preferred hand so it will not slip through hole in rim of pot.
6. *S* repeats steps 3–5 until hanger is completely attached to pot.
7. *S* places hanging pot on worktable.
8. *S* repeats steps 1–7 until all hangers are on hanging pots.

POTTING CUTTINGS IN POTS ALREADY FILLED WITH SOIL

Instructional Objective: Given soil in pots and cuttings, *S* will pot cuttings in pots already filled with soil, with 100% accuracy for 3 consecutive training days.

Prerequisite Skills: Hand mobility.

Task Analysis:
1. *S* picks up leaf cutting.
2. *S* places leaf cutting on top of soil.
3. *S* places tip of index finger of preferred hand on end of cutting.
4. *S* presses tip of cutting into soil.
5. *S* repeats steps 1–4 until specified number of cuttings are in pot.
6. *S* puts proper amount of soil around cuttings.
7. *S* pats soil around cuttings so that cuttings stand firmly in pot.
8. *S* repeats steps 1–7 until all pots are full of cuttings.

Teaching Suggestions: Visual cueing to indicate the tip of the leaf cutting that is to be covered by soil can be provided by coloring the leaf tip with a nontoxic water-base color. The index finger used in step 3 may also be visually cued in the same manner by coloring the tip of the finger with the dye.

POTTING A ROOTED GERANIUM CUTTING

Instructional Objective: Given a rooted geranium cutting, appropriate size pot, and soil, *S* will pot a rooted geranium cutting in 10 minutes, with 100% accuracy for 3 consecutive training days.

Prerequisite Skills: Pincer and palmar grasps.

Task Analysis:
1. *S* holds cutting in preferred hand.
2. *S* positions cutting at correct position in pot.
3. *S* picks up handful of potting soil in opposite hand.
4. *S* places soil in pot around rooted cutting.
5. *S* repeats steps 3 and 4 until soil reaches appropriate level.
6. *S* places hands on rim of pot with thumbs inside rim of pot.
7. *S* firms the soil around entire plant with thumbs.

REPOTTING PLANT FROM 3″ TO 5″ CLAY POT

Instructional Objective: Given a plant in a 3″ pot, a 5″ pot, potting soil, and pot shards or pebbles, *S* will repot the plant in the 5″ pot in 10 minutes, with 100% accuracy for 3 consecutive training days.

Prerequisite Skills: Pincer and palmar grasps.

Task Analysis:
1. *S* covers drain holes in 5″ pot with pot shards or pebbles.
2. *S* turns plant in 3″ pot upside down holding hand so that plant stem protrudes between middle fingers.
3. *S* gently taps rim of 3″ pot against a solid object until plant is loose in pot.
4. *S* takes plant out of 3″ pot.

5. *S* places plant in position in 5" pot.
6. *S* holds plant upright in pot with preferred hand.
7. *S* picks up handful of potting soil with opposite hand.
8. *S* places soil around plant in pot.
9. *S* repeats steps 7 and 8 until soil reaches appropriate level.
10. *S* places hands on rim of pot with thumbs inside rim.
11. *S* firms the soil around entire plant with thumbs.

PLANTING A VEGETABLE PLANT

Instructional Objective: Given a vegetable plant, shovel, and garden spot, *S* will plant the plant, with 100% accuracy for 3 consecutive training days.
Prerequisite Skills: Palmar grasp.
Task Analysis:
1. *S* picks up shovel.
2. *S* puts shovel into soil.
3. *S* scoops up shovelful of soil.
4. *S* puts shovelful of soil adjacent to hole.
5. *S* lays shovel aside.
6. *S* holds plant in proper position in hole with preferred hand.
8. *S* puts dirt in hole around roots of plant with opposite hand.
9. When hole is full, *S* taps down (firms) soil with hands.

STEM CUTTINGS

Instructional Objective: Given plants, worktable, and flats filled with soil, *S* will take stem cuttings, with 100% accuracy for 3 consecutive training days.
Prerequisite Skills: Pincer grasp.
1. *S* places thumb and index finger of preferred hand on stem about 3 inches down the stem.
2. *S* breaks cuttings off with fingers.
3. *S* places cuttings in flat.
4. *S* repeats steps 1–3 until flats are full.
Pretest:
1. Do not provide consequences or physical assistance during the pretest.
2. Place *S* in the training area with the materials listed above.
3. Say to *S*, "Take stem cuttings from this plant."
4. Watch *S* to determine which steps of the program he or she completes correctly.
5. Record a plus (+) for each step *S* completes correctly. Record a minus (–) for each step *S* omits or performs incorrectly.

6. S may be able to do some of the steps in the program before training begins. If this occurs, *do not* eliminate these steps from the training procedure.

Teaching Procedures:

1. Using a flat filled with soil, T uses bright-colored yarn to mark off 1-inch squares (stretch pieces of yarn vertically and horizontally across top of flat). The yarn is fastened to the flat edges of flat with masking tape to ensure easy removal.
2. About 3 inches down on selected stems, T places a piece of masking tape around the stem.
3. T instructs S, "Watch me. I will break off this cutting so that it is about 3 inches long." (Teacher breaks it just above the masking tape.)
4. Instruct S, "Now you break off a cutting."
5. Guide S through task analysis steps 1 and 2, giving verbal and tactile cues only as needed. Reinforce as necessary.
6. When S can break off a cutting successfully for 3 consecutive attempts with no cueing or assistance, proceed to next step.
7. Instruct S, "Watch me. I will place these cuttings in a flat."
8. Proceeding from the top left corner, T places cuttings in each 1-inch space in the flat.
9. Instruct S, "Now you place these cuttings in the flat."
10. Guide S through step 3, giving verbal and tactile cues only as needed. Reinforce with tangibles or praise as needed.
11. As S begins to do steps 1–3 with minimal cueing, begin to fade the visual cues. To do this, make the masking tape on the plant stems thinner and thinner until it disappears. On the flats, replace the bright-colored yarn with thread of the same color. Then replace the bright-colored thread with brown thread. Then remove completely so that S is placing the cuttings approximately 1 inch apart.

LEAF CUTTINGS

Instructional Objective: Given plants, worktable, knife, and flats filled with soil, S will take leaf cuttings, with 100% accuracy for 3 consecutive training days.

Prerequisite Skills: Stem cuttings.

Task Analysis:

1. S locates leaf node on leaf cutting.
2. S places fingers below node on tip with new growth.

3. *S* break off (or cuts with knife) the tip cutting.
4. *S* places tip cutting in flat.
5. *S* repeats steps 1–4 until flats are full.

DISBUDDING

Instructional Objective: Given a small, budding chrysanthemum plant, *S* will disbud the plant, with 100% accuracy for 3 consecutive training days.
Prerequisite Skills: Pincer grasp.
Task Analysis:
   1. *S* identifies central flower bud on stem.
   2. *S* carefully removes all other buds around and adjacent to the terminal bud on this stem with thumb and index finger.
   3. *S* repeats steps 1 and 2 until all stems have been disbudded.

Teaching Suggestions: Using pegboard and small plastic pegs, instruct *S* to fill pegboard and then remove pegs from board and place in box. (The finger grasp used in this activity is similar to that used in disbudding.)

10

JANITORIAL
SKILLS SUBDOMAIN

The janitorial skills subdomain consists of heavy cleaning work and usually involves physical or gross motor involvement. Mopping and buffing floors are examples of activities in this subdomain. The skills portrayed in janitorial and domestic skills subdomains are closely related and provide an excellent source of employment for many retarded individuals. There is a perpetual turnover of employees in these jobs. Below are listed a representative sample of skills in the janitorial skills area.

1. Cleaning Toilet
2. Putting Toilet Paper on a Wall-Mounted Roll
3. Refilling Paper Towel Dispenser
4. Cleaning Sink
5. Cleaning Mirror
6. Sweeping Floor
7. Vacuuming
8. Damp Mopping Floor
9. String Mopping Floor
10. Waxing Floor
11. Cleaning an Ashtray
12. Cleaning a Window
13. Waxing and Polishing a Table

CLEANING TOILET

Instructional Objective: Given a dirty toilet, scouring brush, sponge, scouring powder, disinfectant, water, and a small bucket, S will completely clean the toilet in 35 minutes, with 100% accuracy for 3 consecutive training days.

Prerequisite Skills: Palmar grasp, mobility for stooping, full extension of one upper extremity, and ability to mix disinfectant (or availability of mix).
Task Analysis:
1.   *S* removes all articles from surface of toilet.
2.   *S* picks up a sponge.
3.   *S* wets sponge in disinfectant.
4.   *S* wipes top of tank at rear of toilet with sponge.
5.   *S* wipes sides and front of toilet tank.
6.   *S* wipes handle of toilet.
7.   *S* rinses sponge in disinfectant.
8.   *S* wipes outside seat of toilet.
9.   *S* wipes areas between toilet seat and back tank.
10.   *S* rinses sponge in disinfectant mixture.
11.   *S* lifts top of toilet seat.
12.   *S* wipes under lid of toilet seat.
13.   *S* wipes toilet seat itself.
14.   *S* lifts toilet seat.
15.   *S* wipes underneath toilet seat.
16.   *S* rinses sponge in disinfectant mixture.
17.   *S* wipes rim of bowl.
18.   *S* picks up scouring powder.
19.   *S* picks up scouring brush.
20.   *S* sprinkles powder on brush over toilet.
21.   *S* wipes brush around inside of toilet bowl.
22.   *S* flushes toilet.
23.   *S* replaces brush in proper location.
24.   *S* rinses sponge.
25.   *S* wipes outside of toilet bowl.
26.   *S* rinses sponge.

PUTTING TOILET PAPER ON A WALL-MOUNTED ROLL

Instructional Objective: Given a roll of toilet paper, *S* will put the new roll on the empty spool during a 5-minute work period, with 100% accuracy for 3 consecutive training days.
Prerequisite Skills: Pincer and palmar grasps.
Task Analysis:
1.   *S* looks at roll of toilet paper.
2.   *S* picks up roll of toilet paper.
3.   *S* touches wrapper.
4.   *S* removes wrapping.

5. *S* looks at empty spool.
6. *S* holds paper in one hand.
7. *S* touches empty spool.
8. *S* pulls roll so that side bar releases spool.
9. *S* removes empty spool.
10. *S* aligns spool with hole in center of paper.
11. *S* inserts spool through roll of paper.
12. *S* spreads apart sides of wall mount to separate.
13. *S* aligns spool with roll of paper with one side of wall mount.
14. *S* aligns spool with other side of wall mount.
15. *S* locks spool in place.

REFILLING PAPER TOWEL DISPENSER

Instructional Objective: Given a wall-mounted paper towel dispenser, paper towels, and a key to the dispenser, *S* will completely refill the dispenser with towels in 10 minutes, with 100% accuracy for 3 consecutive training days.

Prerequisite Skills: Pincer and palmar grasps.

Task Analysis:
1. *S* looks at dispenser.
2. *S* picks up key to dispenser box.
3. *S* aligns key with keyhole.
4. *S* inserts key in lock.
5. *S* unlocks lock.
6. *S* lifts lid of dispenser.
7. *S* looks at package of paper towels.
8. *S* picks up package.
9. *S* removes wrapper from package.
10. *S* turns towels so that smooth side of towels faces up.
11. *S* inserts towels smooth side up in dispenser.
12. *S* completely fills dispenser.
13. *S* closes dispenser lid.
14. *S* locks dispenser.
15. *S* removes key.
16. *S* inserts finger into bottom slot of dispenser to free flap of towel.

Pretest:
1. Do not provide consequences or physical assistance during the pretest.
2. Place *S* in the training area with an empty paper towel dispenser, paper towels, and a key to the dispenser.

3. Say to S, "Refill the paper towel dispenser." Give no further verbal cues.
4. Watch S to determine which steps of the program he or she completes correctly.
5. Record a plus (+) for each step S completes correctly. Record a minus (−) for each step S does incorrectly or omits.
6. S may be able to do some of the steps in the program before training begins. If this occurs, *do not* eliminate these steps from the training sequence.

Teaching Procedures:
1. Take S to work area and say, "Watch me, I am going to show you how to refill a paper towel dispenser." Then demonstrate task analysis steps 1–16, verbalizing all actions. Require S to proceed through steps 1–16.
2. Step 3 can be visually cued by taping three or four arrows on the dispenser pointing to the keyhole.
3. In step 5, a different arrow can direct the correct turn for the key to unlock the lock.
4. In step 9, opening the paper towels, initially the towels can be almost all the way open. Then gradually less of the package should be pre-opened so that finally S is opening the package independently.
5. In step 10, the smooth side of the towels can be colored to aid S in putting the proper side up in the dispenser.
6. A "full" mark in the dispenser can be provided for step 12.
7. Assistance is given to S with verbal assistance, demonstration, and, finally, physical aid, as needed.
8. Reinforcement is given for each correct response on a continuous schedule initially and then gradually shifted to an intermittent schedule.

CLEANING SINK

Instructional Objective: Given a dirty sink, scouring powder, a sponge, and water, S will clean the sink, with 100% accuracy for 3 consecutive training days.
Prerequisite Skills: Palmar grasp and extension of one arm.
Task Analysis:
1. S removes all objects (soap, cups, etc.) from sink.
2. S turns on water.
3. S adjusts water to comfortable temperature and steady flow.
4. S places fingers under stream of water.

5. *S* gently splashes water to wet sink.
6. *S* turns off water.
7. *S* picks up can of scouring powder.
8. *S* moves can of powder to sink.
9. *S* turns scouring powder can upside down over sink.
10. *S* gently shakes can to sprinkle scouring powder in sink.
11. *S* sprinkles powder until it lightly covers sink.
12. *S* puts can of powder down.
13. *S* picks up sponge.
14. *S* moves sponge back and forth over sink.
15. *S* continues back and forth motion until entire sink is scrubbed.
16. *S* puts down sponge.
17. *S* turns on water.
18. *S* adjusts water temperature and force.
19. *S* uses hand to splash water around sink.
20. *S* continues splashing until sink is rinsed.
21. *S* picks up sponge.
22. *S* rinses out sponge.
23. *S* puts down sponge.
24. *S* turns off water.

Teaching Suggestions: Steps 10 and 11 may need much physical assistance and constant demonstration. *S* should receive immediate reinforcement when he or she has correctly sprinkled the scouring powder.

Step 15 may require *T* to point out to *S* spots in the sink not properly scrubbed. If *S* experiences difficulty in cleaning stains, add food particles so that *S* see he or she is actually cleaning the sink.

In step 20, *T* should reinforce *S* for rinsing the sink only after all traces of scouring powder and grime are gone from the sink.

CLEANING MIRROR

Instructional Objective: Given a dirty mirror, paper towels, and spray bottle of glass cleaner, *S* will completely clean the mirror in 5 minutes, with 100% accuracy for 3 consecutive training days.

Prerequisite Skills: Pincer and palmar grasps and full extension of one upper extremity.

Task Analysis:
1. *S* moves in front of mirror.
2. *S* picks up spray bottle of glass cleaner.
3. *S* points nozzle of glass cleaner toward mirror.
4. *S* places a finger on top of spray button.

5. *S* presses button for several seconds toward mirror.
6. *S* sets spray bottle down.
7. *S* picks up roll of paper towels.
8. *S* tears off several towels.
9. *S* puts down roll of towels.
10. *S* places towels on mirror.
11. *S* slowly spreads glass cleaner over surface of mirror.
12. *S* turns paper towels to a dry side.
13. *S* continues wiping surface of mirror until streaks are gone.
14. *S* replaces wet paper towels with dry ones as necessary, repeating steps 7–9 above.
15. *S* places used paper towels in trash can.

SWEEPING FLOOR

Instructional Objective: Given a broom, dustpan, and trash receptacle, *S* will sweep floor thoroughly in 30 minutes, with 100% accuracy for 3 consecutive training days.
Prerequisite Skills: Palmar grasp and use of both arms.
Task Analysis:
1. *S* moves obstacles out of way of area to be swept.
2. *S* brings broom and dustpan to area.
3. *S* places dustpan aside.
4. *S* holds broom with both hands.
5. *S* stands at a corner of area with left side of body facing in toward center of area.
6. *S* brings broom to right, or back, toward boundary line.
7. *S* follows through by bringing broom forward, as broom touches and sweeps floor.
8. *S* steps backward or forward, as appropriate, along boundary line.
9. *S* brings broom back.
10. *S* swings broom forward.
11. *S* steps in appropriate direction again, moving along boundary line.
12. *S* brings broom back.
13. *S* swings broom forward.
14. *S* repeats steps 11–13 until *S* moves around perimeter of boundary.
15. *S* steps in toward center, about 1¼ feet.
16. *S* brings broom back.
17. *S* swings broom forward.
18. *S* steps in appropriate direction along newly established perimeter.
19. *S* brings broom back.

20. *S* swings broom forward.
21. *S* steps in appropriate direction along new perimeter.
22. *S* repeats steps 19–20 until *S* moves around perimeter.
23. *S* steps toward center.
24. *S* moves around area again, sweeping (steps 19–21) until dust/dirt is at center of area.
25. *S* picks up dustpan without disturbing pile of dust/dirt.
26. *S* brings dustpan and broom to pile.
27. *S* bends down, holding bottom of dustpan to floor.
28. *S* holds broom with hand close to brushes.
29. *S* pushes pile of dust/dirt into dustpan with broom.
30. *S* repeats step 29 until all dust/dirt is in pan.
31. *S* picks up pan.
32. *S* empties contents of pan into waste container without spilling any dust/dirt.
33. *S* replaces broom and pan in proper place.

Teaching Suggestions: If *S* experiences difficulty sweeping dirt, put some visible dirt, e.g., dirt from flower pot, in a small area (6 " by 6 "). Instruct *S* to sweep dirt in a pile.

If *S* has trouble with regular size dust pan, provide a larger one at first. Eventually fade this out and have *S* use regular size.

Facilitate steps 27–29 by taping hand positions on dust pan and lower portion of broom with colored tape.

VACUUMING

Instructional Objective: Given a vacuum and a specified section of rug not larger than 10 ' by 10 ', *S* will vacuum the rug in 20 minutes, with 100% accuracy for 3 consecutive training days.

Prerequisite Skills: Recognition of dirt and extended arm movement.

Task Analysis:
1. *S* puts movable objects out of the way of area to be vacuumed.
2. *S* brings vacuum to rug.
3. *S* unwinds electric cord.
4. *S* puts electric plug of vacuum in nearest electric outlet.
5. *S* turns switch to "On."
6. *S* holds metal tube of vacuum so that cleaning attachment is flat on rug.
7. *S* stands 1 foot away from edge of area to be cleaned, at left side of area.
8. *S*, beginning at outer edge of area, pushes attachment across area.

9. *S* pulls attachment back to original position.
10. *S* steps one-half step to right.
11. *S* repeats steps 8–10 until area has been covered.
12. *S* turns switch to "Off."
13. *S* takes electric plug out of electric outlet.
14. *S* winds electric cord around vacuum.
15. *S* takes vacuum and attachments and puts them in proper place.
16. *S* puts movable obstacles back in proper place.

Teaching Suggestions: Before teaching procedure begins, tape off a section of rug for *S* to vacuum. Enlarge the area as *S* becomes more competent at the task. Also, when *S* is first learning the task, *T* may want to put pieces of paper or some type of debris on the rug so that *S* can easily see what he or she is vacuuming.

DAMP MOPPING FLOOR

Instructional Objective: Given a mop, bucket, ¼ cup of cleaning liquid, hot water, and a dirty floor, *S* will mop the floor in 30 minutes, with 100% accuracy for 3 consecutive training days.

Prerequisite Skills: Full extension of upper extremities and palmar grasp.

Task Analysis:
1. *S* picks up mop and bucket from storage area.
2. *S* identifies correct cleaning liquid.
3. *S* puts ¼ cup of cleaning liquid into bucket.
4. *S* fills bucket ½ full with hot water.
5. *S* soaks mop in cleaning solution in bucket until mop head is completely soaked.
6. *S* squeezes mop head until excess water is squeezed out.
7. *S* mops section (5 ' by 5 ') of floor.
8. *S* rings and squeezes mop head.
9. *S* repeats steps 7 and 8 until entire floor is mopped.
10. *S* allows floor to dry before walking on it.

STRING MOPPING FLOOR

Instructional Objective: Given a string mop, wringer bucket, broom, dustpan, detergent, water, and a dirty floor, *S* will mop the floor in 30 minutes, with 100% accuracy for 3 consecutive training days.

Prerequisite Skills: Sweeping floor skill and adequate strength for wringing and mopping.

Task Analysis:
1. *S* removes all items of furniture from floor area to be mopped.
2. *S* sweeps floor and empties dustpan.
3. *S* gets mop, mop pail with wringer, and detergent from storage area.
4. *S* brings items to area to be mopped.
5. *S* fills pail ½ full with warm water.
6. *S* adds detergent to water.
7. *S* grasps mop handle with both hands.
8. *S* puts mop into pail until it is covered with water.
9. *S* pulls mop up to wringer.
10. *S* threads wet mop between wringer rollers or places mop in metal cup wringer.
11. *S* steps on level to close wringer and pulls mop through or presses down on mop until excess water is squeezed out.
12. *S* mops area (5′ by 5′) of floor.
13. *S* places mop back into pail.
14. *S* threads wet mop between wringer rollers or places mop in metal cup wringer.
15. *S* steps on level to close wringer and pulls mop through or presses down on mop until excess water is squeezed out.
16. *S* mops remaining area.
17. *S* picks up mop pail and mop.
18. *S* carries mop pail and mop to sink.
19. *S* empties mop pail of all water.
20. *S* rinses mop pail with cold water.
21. *S* rinses mop.
22. *S* wrings mop dry.
23. *S* puts mop, mop pail, and detergent away.

Teaching Suggestions: In task analysis step 5, *T* may mark the inside of the bucket at the ½ full level and say to *S*, "Fill the bucket to the line." The detergent measurement can be visually cued by marking the cup with tape (step 6). The instruction of step 12 can be aided by marking the area to be mopped into smaller square sections with masking tape.

WAXING FLOOR

Instructional Objective: Given a sponge mop, a can of liquid wax, and a clean floor, *S* will wax the floor in 30 minutes, with 100% accuracy for 3 consecutive training days.

Prerequisite Skills: Palmar grasp and use of upper extremities.

Task Analysis:
1. *S* looks at area to be waxed.
2. *S* picks up can of wax.
3. *S* opens can of wax.
4. *S* moves to a corner section of the area to be waxed.
5. *S* poors small amount of wax on floor.
6. *S* grasps sponge mop with both hands.
7. *S* places sponge on top of wax on floor.
8. *S* moves sponge mop in a back and forth motion.
9. *S* spreads wax evenly on floor section.
10. *S* moves over several steps to a new section.
11. *S* pours small amount of wax on floor.
12. *S* spreads wax evenly.
13. *S* continues movements until entire floor is covered.
14. *S* closes can of wax.
15. *S* rinses out sponge.

Pretest:
1. Do not provide consequences or physical assistance during the pretest.
2. Take *S* to the training area with the materials prearranged.
3. Say to *S*, "Wax the floor." Give no further verbal cues.
4. Watch *S* to determine which steps of the program he or she completes correctly.
5. Record a plus (+) for each step *S* completes correctly. Record a minus (−) for each step *S* does incorrectly or omits.
6. *S* may be able to do some of the steps in the program before training begins. If this occurs, *do not* eliminate these steps from the training sequence.

Teaching Suggestions: Model the entire procedure for *S*, providing a detailed verbal explanation of the subject. Using physical and verbal cues, direct *S* through steps 1–4.

For steps 5 and 11, *S* may need an example to compare with the amount of wax to be poured on the floor. A construction paper "blob" (about 3 inches in diameter) could be used for comparison. Practice could be given by allowing *S* to pour water out of a bottle and compare it to the blob.

In step 6 *T* may wish to mark the mop handle with colored tape for hand position (red for left, blue for right).

Physical and verbal cueing can be used for steps 7–9.

T should instruct *S* to orally count these steps over for step 10.

Use physical and verbal cues for steps 12–15. Gradually fade all physical and then verbal cues. Praise appropriate responses.

CLEANING AN ASHTRAY

Instructional Objective: Given a dirty ashtray, a cloth, and a trash can, *S* will clean the ashtray in 2 minutes, with 100% accuracy for 3 consecutive training days.

Prerequisite Skills: Palmar grasp.

Task Analysis:

1. *S* looks at ashtray.
2. *S* moves in front of ashtray.
3. *S* picks up ashtray with preferred hand.
4. *S* carries ashtray to trash can.
5. *S* places ashtray over trash can.
6. *S* empties ashtray into trash can.
7. *S* picks up cloth.
8. *S* wipes ashtray with cloth.
9. *S* continues wiping until ashtray is clean.
10. *S* puts cloth down.
11. *S* replaces ashtray on table.

Teaching Suggestions: In teaching step 9 it may be difficult for *S* to identify what is clean. It may be helpful to provide a model of a clean ashtray for *S* to use for comparison, with *T* pointing out differences. Also, have *S* feel the clean ashtray as opposed to the unclean one.

CLEANING A WINDOW

Instructional Objective: Given a dirty window, glass cleaner, and paper towels, *S* will clean both sides of the window, with 100% accuracy for 3 consecutive training days.

Prerequisite Skills: Pincer and palmar grasps and full extension of one upper extremity.

Task Analysis:

1. *S* looks at window.
2. *S* looks at paper towels.
3. *S* picks up roll of towels.
4. *S* tears off several towels.
5. *S* looks at spray window cleaner.
6. *S* picks up can of cleaner.
7. *S* points spray nozzle hole toward window.
8. *S* places one finger on top of button.
9. *S* presses button, releasing window cleaner.
10. *S* completely covers window pane.

11.   S puts down can of cleaner.
12.   S places handful of paper towels on the window pane.
13.   S slowly wipes window until entire side of pane is clean.
14.   S turns paper towels to dry side as needed.
15.   S replaces wet paper towels with dry ones as necessary, repeating steps 2–4.
16.   S walks around to other side of the window.
17.   S repeats steps 5–15 so that entire window is cleaned.

Teaching Suggestions: Steps 14 and 15 may be troublesome for S. T should prompt S when it is time to turn or replace the wet towels.

WAXING AND POLISHING A TABLE

Instructional Objective: Given a self-polishing wax, a soft cloth, and a wooden table, S will wax and polish the table, with 100% accuracy for 3 consecutive training days.

Prerequisite Skills: Pincer and palmar grasps, mobility of arms, and use of index finger.

Task Analysis:
1.   S gets cloth and polish from closet and sets aside.
2.   S clears objects off table to be waxed.
3.   S sets container of wax down on table.
4.   S brings cloth to table to be waxed.
5.   S folds cloth to hand size and holds in one hand.
6.   S picks up polish in other hand.
7.   S pushes button, spraying polish on table.
8.   S puts hand with cloth side down on front edge of table.
9.   S, keeping cloth in contact with surface, moves cloth in circular motion to back edge of table.
10.   S moves hand with cloth over one hand width on table.
11.   S moves hand in circular motion from back edge to front of table.
12.   S applies more polish to table as needed.
13.   S repeats steps 9–12 until surface has been polished.
14.   S puts objects back on table.
15.   S puts cloth and polish back in closet.

11

OFFICE/CLERICAL SKILLS SUBDOMAIN

This subdomain provides a representative array of office and clerical skills. These include folding, stapling, packaging, and filing. Clerical skills are required in most businesses and government organizations and involve varying degrees of complexity. Clerical skills can be important vocational behaviors for students to acquire because of the availability of these jobs in many settings. Furthermore, many clerical jobs are not difficult and entirely within the learning capacity of severely handicapped students.

These skills are only a small fraction of the many office and clerical jobs that are available. They have been sequenced in a logical order and include:

1. Using a Letter Opener
2. Collating Paper
3. Stuffing Envelopes
4. Sealing Envelopes
5. Applying Pressure-Sensitive Labels
6. Punching Holes
7. Removing Staples
8. Loading a Stapler
9. Sharpening a Pencil
10. Emptying a Pencil Sharpener
11. Alphabetizing by Initial Letter
12. Filing Records by Name

USING A LETTER OPENER

Instructional Objective: Given the command "Open the mail," S will use a letter opener to open and remove the mail during a 2-minute work period, without damaging any of the mail, for 3 consecutive training days.

Prerequisite Skills: Palmar and pincer grasps.
Task Analysis:
1.   *S* picks up sealed envelope.
2.   *S* picks up letter opener.
3.   *S* turns envelope so that sealed flap is pointing upward.
4.   *S* locates top corner of envelope.
5.   *S* aligns pointed end of opener with small opening in corner of envelope.
6.   *S* inserts opener approximately 1 inch inside envelope.
7.   *S* pulls opener along edge of envelope.
8.   *S* continues pulling until entire seam is open.
9.   *S* lays down letter opener.
10.   *S* removes contents of envelope.
11.   *S* places contents on top of envelope and places to one side.

COLLATING PAPER

Instructional Objective: Given 2 stacks of paper, a stapler placed in front of *S*, and the command "Collate these papers," *S* will correctly take 1 sheet from each pile, combine the 2 sheets, staple them together, and place them in a box, 10 out of 10 times, for 3 consecutive training days.
Prerequisite Skills: Pincer grasp, left to right progression, use of stapler, and full use of both arms.
Task Analysis:
1.   *S* looks at stacks of paper.
2.   *S* reaches toward first stack of paper.
3.   *S* touches stack of paper.
4.   *S* grasps 1 sheet of paper in first stack.
5.   *S* picks up one sheet.
6.   *S* places paper in other hand.
7.   *S* looks at second stack of paper.
8.   *S* reaches toward second stack.
9.   *S* touches second stack.
10.   *S* grasps 1 sheet from second stack.
11.   *S* picks up 1 sheet from second stack.
12.   *S* puts second sheet under first sheet.
13.   *S* puts second sheet under first sheet so that left corners match.
14.   *S* looks at stapler.
15.   *S* brings papers toward stapler.
16.   *S* places left-hand corners of 2 papers (still one on top of the other) under stapler.

17. S reaches other hand toward stapler.
18. S touches stapler.
19. S pushes down on stapler so that it staples papers together.
20. S lifts up hand from stapler.
21. S removes sheets from under stapler.
22. S puts stapled papers in box.

Pretest:

1. Do not provide consequences or physical assistance during the pretest.
2. Place S in the training area with the materials listed above.
3. Say to S, "Collate these papers." Give no further verbal cues.
4. Watch S to determine which steps of the program he or she completes correctly.
5. Record a plus (+) for each step S completes correctly. Record a minus (–) for each step S does incorrectly or omits.
6. S may be able to do some of the steps in the program before training begins. If this occurs, *do not* eliminate these steps from the training sequence.

Teaching Procedures:

1. Using pencil, T prints a large "1" in the upper right-hand corner of each page in the first stack of paper. T places a large "2" in the upper right-hand corner of each page in the second stack.
2. Using pencil T makes a small rectangle ☐ in the upper left-hand corner of each page in the first stack.
3. T says to S, "I will show you how to collate papers."
4. T proceeds through task analysis steps 1–22, giving special instructions to have the papers numbered sequentially (1–2). T staples the papers together, making sure the staple is within the rectangle in the upper left-hand corner of the page.
5. T instructs S, "Now you collate these papers."
6. T guides S through steps 1–22, giving verbal and tactile cues only as necessary.
7. Reinforce as appropriate with praise or tangibles.
8. When S can do steps 1–22 correctly with no assistance other than the visual cues, proceed as described below.
9. Repeat steps 1–22 while gradually fading out all visual cues. To do this make the numbers gradually smaller and lighter until they are no longer needed. Also make the rectangle lighter and lighter until it is no longer visible.
10. This skill is considered learned when S can correctly complete all steps of the task without assistance for 3 consecutive training days.

STUFFING ENVELOPES

Instructional Objective: Given envelopes and folded pieces of paper, *S* will be able to stuff the envelopes correctly, 10 out of 10 times, for 3 consecutive training days.
Prerequisite Skills: Palmar grasp with both hands.
Task Analysis:
1.   *S* looks at envelope.
2.   *S* reaches toward envelope.
3.   *S* touches envelope.
4.   *S* grasps envelope.
5.   *S* picks up envelope.
6.   *S* holds envelope with one hand in front of self.
7.   *S* With other hand, *S* lifts up flap of envelope.
8.   *S* looks at folded paper.
9.   Still holding flap up, with other hand *S* reaches toward one folded paper.
10.   *S* touches paper.
11.   *S* grasps paper.
12.   *S* picks paper up.
13.   *S* carries folded paper toward envelope.
15.   *S* inserts one folded paper partially in envelope.
16.   *S* inserts one folded paper completely in envelope.
17.   *S* moves envelope toward box holding stuffed envelopes.
18.   *S* puts stuffed envelope in box holding stuffed envelopes.

SEALING ENVELOPES

Instructional Objective: Given a stack of unsealed envelopes and a moistening apparatus placed in front of *S*, *S* will moisten flap of envelope with glue on edge and seal envelope correctly, 10 out of 10 times, for 3 consecutive training days. *Note:* After *S* has completed this objective, time limitations and production rate are added.
Prerequisite Skills: Palmar grasp.
Task Analysis:
1.   *S* looks at envelopes.
2.   *S* reaches toward stack of envelopes.
3.   *S* touches stack of envelopes.
4.   *S* grasps one envelope.
5.   *S* picks up envelope.
6.   *S* places envelope in front of self with flap containing glue faceup.
7.   *S* looks at moistening apparatus.

8. *S* reaches toward moistening apparatus.
9. *S* touches moistening apparatus.
10. *S* picks up moistening apparatus.
11. *S* turns moistening apparatus with sponge tip facing down.
12. *S* places sponged tip of moistening apparatus on top edge of flap.
13. *S* moves moistening apparatus along outside edge of flap to center point.
14. *S* moves moistening apparatus along outside edge of flap to bottom of envelope.
15. *S* places moistening apparatus on desk.
16. *S* touches flap while holding envelope down with other hand.
17. *S* pushes flap down until it touches rest of envelope.
18. *S* places fingers on top edge of flap.
19. *S* moves fingers along edge of flap to center point while applying pressure.
20. *S* moves fingers along edge of flap to bottom of envelope while applying pressure.
21. *S* places sealed envelopes in box.

APPLYING PRESSURE-SENSITIVE LABELS

Instructional Objective: Given a stack of envelopes, pressure-sensitive labels, and the command "Label the envelope," *S* will correctly label the envelope, 10 out of 10 times, for 3 consecutive training days.
Prerequisite Skills: Pincer grasp and full use of both arms and hands.
Task Analysis:
1. *S* looks at envelopes.
2. *S* reaches toward stack of envelopes.
3. *S* touches stack of envelopes.
4. *S* grasps one envelope.
5. *S* picks up envelope.
6. *S* places envelope in front of self with front of envelope facing up.
7. *S* picks up sheet of labels.
8. *S* places sheet of labels in front of self.
9. *S* positions fingers on label in upper left-hand corner.
10. *S* grasps one corner of label.
11. *S* pulls label off sheet.
12. *S* moves label over envelope.
13. *S* positions label in center of envelope.
14. *S* places label on envelope.
15. *S* rubs back and forth across label.
16. *S* places labeled envelope in box.

Pretest:

1. Do not provide consequences or physical assistance during the pretest.
2. Place *S* in the training area with the materials listed above.
3. Say to *S*, "Label the envelope." Give no further verbal cues.
4. Watch *S* to determine which steps of the program he or she completes correctly.
5. Record a plus (+) for each step *S* completes correctly. Record a minus (−) for each step *S* does incorrectly or omits.
6. *S* may be able to do some of the steps in the program before training begins. If this occurs, *do not* eliminate these steps from the training sequence.

Teaching procedures:

1. *T* will place a stack of envelopes in front of *S*. On the back of each envelope *T* will draw a happy face so that the envelope will be right side up.

2. *T* says, "Watch me. I will get this envelope ready for labeling."
3. *T* proceeds through task analysis steps 1–6, giving special instructions to make sure the happy face on the back is not upside down (i.e., that envelope is not upside down).
4. *T* instructs *S*, "Now you get these envelopes ready for labeling."
5. *T* guides *S* through steps 1–6, giving verbal and tactile cues only as necessary.
6. Reinforce with praise or tangibles as appropriate. (When *S* can correctly position 5 envelopes for 3 consecutive attempts, proceed to next step.)
7. Using a magic marker, *T* marks off a rectangular area approximately 1¹/₂ times the size of the label on the front of the envelopes.
8. *T* says to S, "Watch me. I will label this envelope."
9. *T* proceeds through task analysis steps 7–16, giving special instructions that the label is to go *inside* the marked rectangle.
10. *T* instructs *S*, "Now you label these envelopes."
11. *T* guides *S* through analysis steps 7–16, giving verbal and tactile cues only as necessary.
12. Reinforce with praise or tangibles as appropriate. (When *S* can correctly label 5 envelopes for 3 consecutive attempts, proceed to next step.)
13. Repeat steps 1–16 while gradually fading out all visual cues. To do this:
    a. Fade out the happy face on the back of the envelopes by pencil-

ing in the faces more and more lightly. Then remove cue completely.

b. Fade out the rectangle by switching from magic marker to pencil. As it becomes lighter, also make it smaller so that it approximates the size of the label. Then remove cue completely.

14. This skill is considered learned when S completes all steps of the task correctly for 3 consecutive training days.

PUNCHING HOLES

Instructional Objective: Given paper and a hole puncher, S will punch holes, with 100% accuracy on 10 trials for 3 consecutive training days.
Prerequisite Skills: Palmar and pincer grasps.
Task Analysis:
1. S looks at hole puncher.
2. S grasps hole puncher.
3. S places hole puncher in front of self.
4. S positions hole puncher with opening facing dominant hand.
5. S looks at stack of papers.
6. S touches stack of papers.
7. S picks up one sheet of paper.
8. S moves sheet of paper toward hole puncher.
9. S places left side of paper in hole puncher.
10. S aligns sheet of paper in hole puncher.
11. S holds sheet of paper with palm of dominant hand.
12. S pushes down top of hole puncher with other hand.
13. S removes sheet of paper from hole puncher.
14. S places paper in box.

REMOVING STAPLES

Instructional Objective: Given staples, pieces of paper, and a staple remover, S will completely remove the staple in a 1-minute period, 10 out of 10 times, for 3 consecutive training days.
Prerequisite Skills: Pincer grasp.
Task Analysis:
1. S looks at stapled papers.
2. S touches stapled paper.
3. S picks up stapled papers.
4. S looks at staple remover.
5. S touches staple remover.
6. S picks up staple remover.

7. S turns staple remover so that it is in the proper position.
8. S aligns end of staple remover with staple.
9. S presses sides of remover together.
10. S continues until staple is free.
11. S deposits removed staple in trash can.
12. S places staple remover back on table.

Teaching Suggestions: For step 9, if problems exist in pressing sides of remover together, have S practice pincer grasp by squeezing a foam rubber ball, with S's first two fingers pressing against thumb. When learning is demonstrated, have S practice pressing staple remover (without paper).

LOADING A STAPLER

Instructional Objective: Given a stapler and a box of staples, S will completely fill the stapler in a 5-minute work period, 10 out of 10 times, for 3 consecutive training days.
Prerequisite Skills: Pincer and palmar grasps.
Task Analysis:
1. S places box of staples in front of self on work surface.
2. S places stapler in front of self on work surface.
3. S grasps stapler (from top) with preferred hand.
4. S grasps bottom portion of stapler top with other hand.
5. S pulls stapler apart.
6. S opens box of staples.
7. S picks out one block of staples.
8. S inserts block of staples in stapler.
9. S closes stapler.

SHARPENING A PENCIL

Instructional Objective: Given an unsharpened pencil, a wall-mounted pencil sharpener, and the command "Sharpen the pencil," S will sharpen the pencil to a point, with 100% accuracy for 3 consecutive training days.
Prerequisite Skills: Palmar grasp and full use of right arm.
Task Analysis:
1. S picks up pencil.
2. S walks to pencil sharpener.
3. S faces pencil sharpener.
4. S grasps pencil near eraser end.
5. S aligns pencil with appropriate hole in sharpener.
6. S pushes pencil into sharpener as far as possible.

7. S grasps crank with right hand while holding pencil with left.
8. S turns crank in a circular motion away from self.
9. S turns crank several times.
10. S removes pencil from sharpener.
11. S checks pencil to see if sharp.
12. S repeats steps 6–11 if necessary.

Teaching Suggestions:

1. *T* will place a thin strip of masking tape under the hole where the pencil is to be inserted.
2. *T* will use red magic marker to draw a circle around pencil indicating the depth to which the pencil should be inserted in the hole of the sharpener.
3. *T* says to *S*, "I will show you how to put the pencil in the sharpener."
4. *T* proceeds through task analysis steps 1–6, giving special instructions to position pencil in the correct hole (using the visual cue under the hole) and to insert pencil all the way into the hole (by making sure the red circle on the pencil is just visible).
5. *T* instructs *S*, "Now you put this pencil into the sharpener."
6. *T* guides S through steps 1–6, giving verbal and tactile cues only as necessary.
7. Reinforce with praise or tangibles.
8. When *S* can do steps 1–6 correctly for 5 consecutive attempts, proceed to next step.
9. *T* places a piece of masking tape around the body of the sharpener with arrows pointing upward, indicating direction to turn handle.

masking tape

10. *T* says to *S*, "I will show you how to sharpen this pencil."
11. *T* proceeds through steps 7–12, giving special attention to the arrows on the sharpener and indicating that the arrows show the direction for turning the handle.
12. *T* instructs *S*, "Now you sharpen the pencil."
13. *T* guides *S* through task analysis steps 7–12, giving verbal and tactile cues only as necessary.
14. Reinforce with praise or tangibles as appropriate.
15. When *S* can do steps 7–12 correctly for 5 consecutive attempts, proceed to next step.

16. Repeat steps 1–12 while gradually fading out all visual cues. To do this:
    a. Make the strip of masking tape under the correct hole thinner and thinner. Remove.
    b. Make the red circle around pencil lighter and lighter. Remove.
    c. Fade the arrows by making them smaller and lighter. Finally remove masking tape.

EMPTYING A PENCIL SHARPENER

Instructional Objective: Given a full pencil sharpener and a trash can, *S* will empty the sharpener in 2 minutes, without spilling the contents on the floor, for 3 consecutive training days.

Prerequisite Skills: Pincer or palmar grasp and full extension of the upper extremity.

Task Analysis:
1. *S* walks to pencil sharpener.
2. *S* faces pencil sharpener.
3. *S* grasps cylinder of pencil sharpener.
4. *S* turns cylinder toward self to loosen.
5. *S* removes cylinder by pulling up and out.
6. *S* holds cylinder with large opening facing up.
7. *S* walks toward trash can.
8. *S* stops at trash can.
9. *S* positions cylinder over trash can with large opening turned down.
10. *S* shakes cylinder until all shavings are removed.
11. *S* walks back to pencil sharpener.
12. *S* faces pencil sharpener.
13. *S* positions large opening of cylinder on gears of sharprner.
14. *S* pushes cylinder up until grooves of two pieces match.
15. *S* turns cylinder away from self to tighten.

Teaching Suggestions: If *S* experiences difficulty on steps 4 and 5, physically guide *S's* hand through the motions at least three or four times. Then fade physical cue to verbal prompt and then to no cue at all.

If difficulty still persists, draw an arrow on top of pencil sharpener pointing in the direction that it should be turned. As learning takes place remove cue (arrow).

If difficulty exists on steps 9 and 10, physically guide *S's* hand as he or she turns the cylinder so that the opening is facedown over the can and shake. Fade physical cue to verbal cue to no cue at all.

ALPHABETIZING BY INITIAL LETTER

Instructional Objective: Given a stack of 3 " by 5 " cards, each one containing a word and each word beginning with a different letter of the alphabet, *S* will place the cards in a file box in correct alphabetical order, with 100% accuracy for 3 consecutive training days.

Prerequisite Skills: Ability to say or recognize the letters of the alphabet in order.

Task Analysis:

1. *S* looks at stack of 3 " by 5 " cards.
2. *S* reaches toward stack of 3 " by 5 " cards.
3. *S* picks up stack of cards.
4. *S* takes one card and places right-side up on table in front of self.
5. *S* repeats step 4 with remaining cards until all cards are placed on table.
6. *S* looks for card with word beginning with A.
7. *S* reaches for A-word card.
8. *S* picks up A-word card.
9. *S* places A-word card in front of 3 " by 5 " file box.
10. *S* repeats steps 6–9 progressing through the rest of the alphabet sequentially from B to Z.
11. If *S* does not find a card with a word beginning with a specific letter, *S* proceeds to next letter of the alphabet.

Teaching Suggestions:

1. *T* uses large piece of posterboard. Using masking tape and 1¹/₂ " by 5 " pieces of construction paper, *T* makes 26 slots into which a 3 " by 5 " card can be placed. Across the top of the posterboard *T* writes the alphabet using black magic marker.

masking tape

1 ½ " by 5 " pieces of
construction paper

2. *T* says, "Watch me, I'll get these cards ready to place in alphabetical order."

3. *T* proceeds through task analysis steps 1–5, giving special instructions to place all words right-side up on table.
4. *T* says, "Now I will alphabetize these words."
5. *T* places finger on the large A at the top of the posterboard, saying, "This is the letter A. Now we must find the word that begins with this letter."
6. Keeping finger on the letter A, *T* proceeds through task analysis steps 6–8.
7. *T* places the A-word card in the first slot on the posterboard.
8. Moving in left to right progression, *T* repeats steps 5–7 above until all cards have been placed in alphabetical order on the posterboard.
9. *T* removes cards from posterboard and repeats task analysis steps 3–5.
10. *T* instructs *S*, "Now you alphabetize these cards."
11. *T* guides *S* through steps 5–8 above, giving tactile and verbal cues only as necessary.
12. *T* reinforces with praise or tangibles as appropriate.
13. When *S* can correctly alphabetize using the posterboard for 3 consecutive attempts, proceed to next step.
14. *T* says, "Now we will remove these cards from the posterboard and place them in correct alphabetical order in the file box. Watch."
15. Starting in the upper left-hand corner and proceeding from left to right, *T* proceeds through task analysis steps 8–10, giving special instructions to place each card *behind* the one preceding it in the box.
16. Replacing cards in the posterboard, *T* instructs *S*, "Now you remove these cards from the posterboard and place them in correct alphabetical order in the file box."
17. *T* reinforces with praise or tangibles as appropriate.
18. This task is considered learned when *S* can correctly perform all steps of the task analysis without assistance for 3 consecutive training days.

FILING RECORDS BY NAME

Instructional Objective: Given file drawer and file records marked by name, *S* will insert the file records in order of the first letter of the last name, with 100% accuracy for 3 consecutive training days.

Prerequisite Skills: Ability to alphabetize by first letter and pincer or palmar grasp.

Task Analysis:
1. *S* opens file drawer.
2. *S* places mixed stack of files on top of file cabinet.

3. *S* picks up top file folder.
4. *S* looks at name tape on record.
5. *S* locates first letter of last name on tape.
6. *S* locates point in the files where other folders with same letter as the first letter of the last name are filed.
7. *S* locates first letter of first name on tape of folder.
8. *S* locates correct placement in files for folder.
9. *S* spreads files at this point.
10. *S* inserts file in the space.
11. *S* repeats steps 3–10 until all folders are filed.

ANNOTATED BIBLIOGRAPHY ON VOCATIONAL PROGRAMMING FOR SEVERELY DEVELOPMENTALLY DISABLED PERSONS

Azrin, N. H., Flores, T., and Kaplan, S. J. 1975. Job-finding club: A group-assisted program for obtaining employment. Behav. Res. Ther. 13:17–27.

A matched-control research design was used to evaluate the effectiveness of a new type of job-finding program with rehabilitation clients. The program was conducted in a group and stressed techniques like mutual assistance among job seekers, a "buddy system," family support, and sharing job leads. The clients received instruction on the practices of searching want ads, role playing, telephoning, constructing a résumé, and contacting friends. It was found that 90% of the counseled job seekers had obtained employment compared to 55% of the control, noncounseled group. Furthermore, the starting salary was almost one-third higher for the counseled job seekers. Benefits of this program were seen to be both the high level of placement among the experimental group and the predicted maintenance of a continuing individual support system provided by the "buddy" with little or no additional trainer time involved.

Bates, P., Wehman, P., and Karan, O. C. 1976. Evaluation of work performance of a developmentally disabled adolescent: Use of a changing criterion design. *In* O. C. Karan, P. Wehman, A. Renzaglia, and R. Schutz
(eds.), Habilitation Practices with the Severely Developmentally Disabled,
Vol. I. University of Wisconsin Rehabilitation Research and Training Center, Madison.

A case study provides a more realistic method of evaluating client work
performance of developmentally disabled persons than the use of standardized tests. Rather than pure assessment of present functioning, this
method includes training as an essential component of the evaluation technique, with the rationale that it should be demonstrated that work behaviors can be acquired by the client in favorable settings. Suggestions made
for experimental design include multiple baseline, reversal, and changing
criterion designs. The case study reported here describes the evaluation of a
subject whose capability for placement had been questionable. A changing
criterion design was used to evaluate the subject's production rate, which
increased by more than 100%.

Becker, R. 1976. Job training placement for retarded youth: A survey. Men.
Retard. 14:7–11.

A survey of work-study coordinators was taken to assess the jobs for which
retarded youth in on-the-job training programs were being trained. Coordinators working with 1,438 retarded youths completed the survey. Hotel
and restaurant occupations made up 33.5% of the jobs, while building
maintenance operations made up 13% of the jobs. The most frequent job
placement was janitorial training, followed by dishwasher and bus boy/girl
placements. Trainees were found to be working in 185 different jobs listed
in the *Dictionary of Occupational Titles* under 14 major industries. The
jobs were primarily located at the semiskilled and unskilled levels of the
various industries. Conclusions drawn from this survey were that retarded
youth were being trained to work in a variety of occupations and that a survey of the local job market needs should be completed before initiating an
on-the-job training curriculum within a school program.

Bellamy, G. T. 1976. A review of research on work productivity. *In* G. T.
Bellamy (ed.), Habilitation of the Severely and Profoundly Retarded: Reports from the Specialized Training Program. Center on Human Development, University of Oregon, Eugene.

A review of research on the work rates of severely and profoundly retarded
adults is presented. Factors that account for the variability of work rates

among individuals are classified as person, task, or setting characteristics. Setting characteristics are extensively discussed and are broken down into instructions, consequential events, and general setting characteristics. Instructions include specifying desired performance, instructions to compete, and instructions that set performance goals. Consequential events are the positive and negative reinforcement contingencies that affect the performance of the tasks. General setting characteristics include modeling and pairing, environmental distractions, and style of supervision. It is emphasized that future research in this area should be characterized by practicality of the treatments involved, the utility of the measurement procedures, economic utility in terms of increasing rates of production, and an interest in developing competitive work behaviors and improving personal and interpersonal behaviors.

Bellamy, G. T., Inman, D., and Schwarz, R. 1977. Vocational training and production supervision: A review of habilitation techniques for the severely and profoundly retarded. *In* N. Haring and D. Bricker (eds.), Teaching the Severely and Profoundly Handicapped, Vol. III. Special Press, Columbus, Oh.

Severely and profoundly retarded adults have frequently been denied vocational opportunity because of assumed limitations. Viewing retardation as a problem of behavior deficits that can be remediated, and emphasizing how vocational skills can be taught, greatly increase vocational opportunity for the retarded. Reasons for nonvocational productivity are a lack of prerequisite skills, lack of sensitivity to changes in the environment, and inappropriate strength of work skills. Review of training literature, discussing separately acquisition and production, indicates that use of behavioral techniques can result in significant increases in appropriate vocational behavior of severely and profoundly retarded persons. The expectation for generalization of these findings to a less restrictive population of subjects and their implications for the present and future are discussed.

Bellamy, G. T., Peterson, L., and Close, D. 1975. Habilitation of the severely and profoundly retarded: Illustrations of competence. Educ. Train. Ment. Retard. 10:174–186.

Severely and profoundly retarded individuals are believed to be able to benefit from significantly greater vocational opportunities than have been traditionally made available to them. A variety of vocational tasks are described that severely and profoundly retarded individuals have been trained to complete at standard rates of production. Examples of these tasks include soldering, sorting, use of a drill press, and multistep assembly operations. The Specialized Training Program, making use of difficult tasks requiring training, was developed to demonstrate the potential vocational competence of the severely and profoundly retarded. A finding of this program is that environmental changes are a most effective means of increasing production rates. It is concluded that it is possible to design work environments that develop and maintain normal work behaviors in severely and profoundly retarded individuals.

Bellamy, G. T., and Snyder, S. 1976. The trainee performance sample: Toward the prediction of habilitation costs for severely handicapped adults. AAESPH Rev. 1:17–36.

Severely handicapped individuals have frequently not been included in vocational rehabilitation programs because they failed during evaluation procedures to demonstrate satisfactory potential for vocational skill development. Information currently available in the literature indicates that this failure is primarily a function of the evaluation tools themselves. Research presently indicates that through behavior management the severely handicapped can be taught to perform vocational tasks at standard rates. Since evaluation is seen to be an unavoidable part of the vocational rehabilitation system, the Trainee Performance Sample (TPS) was developed to predict time for vocational training. The TPS is an attempt to provide a means of measuring a severely handicapped individual's potential for practical placement in training. The TPS is a 30-item test of tasks that require specific object manipulation or assumption of a defined hand position, movement after a trainer cue involving verbal direction and either a model or physical prime, the completion of a defined discrimination, and the allowing of a second chance to respond after repetition of the trainer cue. Currently available research indicates that the test is reliable and valid on the populations tested. Further research is planned on the practicality of this test for the evaluation of the severely handicapped.

Belmore, K., and Brown, L. A. 1976. A Job Skill Inventory for Use in a Public School Vocational Training Program for Severely Handicapped Potential Workers. University of Wisconsin and Madison Public Schools, Madison.

Society has traditionally excluded severely handicapped individuals from opportunities to develop vocational skills because of the low expectations held for these individuals regarding their vocational potential. These expectations are based on the following beliefs: there are a limited number of jobs presently available, mildly handicapped workers have a poor work record, the overall general development of the severely handicapped will prevent them from retaining employment, and there will be friction between severely handicapped and nonhandicapped workers. A longitudinal system of planning the eventual vocational placement of the severely handicapped is endorsed to help overcome the resistance to employment presently experienced by the severely handicapped. The Job Skills Inventory (JSI) is presented as a means of longitudinal preparation of the severely handicapped. The JSI investigates the total function of job success, including transportation, social, emotional, health, performance, and vocational factors. Use of the JSI necessitates the identification of available job opportunities early in the training program so that long range preparation for a reachable goal can be a part of the school program. It is concluded that the JSI can be adopted to a variety of individuals and situations and provides a needed tool for use in longitudinal preparation.

Bernstein, J. 1966. Mental retardation: New prospects for employment. J. Rehabil. 32:16–17, 35–37.

As the onset of automation renders unskilled jobs obsolete, increasing skill demands have been placed upon both the nonhandicapped and the retarded worker. To provide for the possibility of a need for generalization to new jobs, training for the retarded should be appropriate to several jobs in a given job family. A need for training in job-related and academic skills has become increasingly apparent as the nature of job vacancies and employer needs is modified. The inability to read has become an increasingly significant barrier to the employment of the retarded, hindering job application training, public transportation training, and higher level work skills acquisition. Assumptions that the retarded cannot learn to read sufficiently well to function well in skill training have been found inadequate. Conceptual understanding of the operations involved in training and job performance must be present in the retarded worker to facilitate generalization to the new routines dictated by job changes.

Braunstein, W. 1975. Gainful employment: The myth and hope of rehabilitation consumers. J. Appl. Rehabil. Counsel. 8:22–27.

Workers in rehabilitation systems must be sensitive to individual systems of belief about work as well as to the self-actualization and social contact they know to be provided the individual by gainful employment. Some of these belief systems encourage dependency upon external sources rather than independent functioning, as do the current systems of monetary incentives for work. The loss or threat of loss of Supplemental Security Income, Social Security Disability Insurance, and Medicaid because of entry into the job market results in a frequent reduction of work load in order to lower the standard of income to retain benefits. The implications for an individual with high medical costs but without the skills to obtain a job that brings wages and benefits to a level provided by the above-mentioned systems are obvious. It is important, that, in order to provide for maximum integration of the handicapped into society, a method of subsidizing income through pay for work, instead of through a benefits check, be implemented. An expansion of Medicare to include the rehabilitation consumer when his or her work does not provide comparable medical coverage would be an assurance to the consumer. Tax credits for employers willing to hire the handicapped would be another possible way of providing incentives.

Brolin, D. 1972. Value of rehabilitation services and correlates of vocational success with the mentally retarded. Am. J. Ment. Defic. 76:644–651.

The efficacy of rehabilitation services for the retarded, the adequacy of present services, and the variables related to success in vocational placement were assessed. Noninstitutionalized clients, ranging in age and functioning level, who were receiving rehabilitation services were used as a sample. The type of services provided after initial evaluation was compared with the outcome of the services. Variables including age, sex, intelligence, academic level, and history of institutional living were assessed as to their importance in employability levels. It was found that rehabilitation services are valuable for the mentally retarded individual. It was recognized, however, that a large number of clients were not attaining their vocational potential even though they received adequate services in terms of output. When clients were not provided with adequate services, as would be expected, less than half reached their vocational potential.

Brolin, D. E. 1976. Vocational Preparation of Retarded Citizens. Charles E. Merrill Publishing Co., Columbus. Oh.

The book is an attempt to provide a comprehensive presentation of information pertaining to the vocational preparation of retarded persons, for use by teachers, service delivery personnel, and others interested in the vocational preparation of the retarded. The vocational model presented in the book is as follows: intake, vocational evaluation, vocational training, job placement and follow-up, and program evaluation. An in-depth discussion of each step in the model is included. Many conclusions and implications for the vocational preparation of the retarded are presented that deviate from traditional vocational programs and practice.

Brown, L., Johnson, S., Gadberry, E., and Fenrick, N. 1971. Increasing individual and assembly line production rates of retarded students. Train. School Bull. 67:206–212.

The arrangement of work setting into individual and assembly line procedures and the use of reinforcement, social only and social plus tangibles, were studied for their ability to increase the production rates of six trainable level students in an envelope-stuffing task. It was found that the students placed in independent work settings consistently exceeded the production rates of those placed in assembly line settings, regardless of the reinforcement contingencies in effect. Production rates consistently improved when tangible reinforcement was made contingent on attaining a group-specified goal. These environmental manipulations were successful in raising production rates because of contingent reinforcement.

Brown, L., and Pearce, E. 1970. Increasing the production rate of trainable retarded students in a public school simulated workshop. Educ. Train. Ment. Retard. 5:15–22.

The use of teacher praise and feedback in increasing the production rates of emotionally disturbed students in workshop tasks and the effectiveness of using these students as models for trainable retarded students were evaluated. An increase in production rate was effected using a combination of practice, peer modeling, verbal and social reinforcement, and teacher feedback on work rates. Exposure of the retarded students to the workers during reinforcement resulted in an increase in the production rates of these workers, even though they received no direct reinforcement or feedback. A second intervention phase, during which the retarded workers were exposed to the workers during reinforcement and received direct reinforcement and feedback, also resulted in average increases in production rates. Individual differences were found to be a major factor in evaluating the effectiveness of different methods.

Brown, L. F., Van Deventer, P., Perlmutter, L., Jones, S., and Sontag, E. 1972. Effects of consequences on production rates of trainable retarded and severely emotionally disturbed students in a public school workshop. Educ. Train. Ment. Retard. 7:74–81.

The effects of social praise, charting individual production rates, and providing money contingencies on the increased production rates of the retarded were demonstrated. A systematic manipulation of the use of a charting procedure, during which the workers were assisted in charting their work rates and given feedback verbally and visually on their previous performance, was found to increase production rates. Production rates of an individual worker were found to be of more use in assessing the potential worker than were standard means such as IQ scores.

Brown, L. F., Wright, E., and Hitchings, W. 1978. Guidelines for procuring work contracts for sheltered workshop clients. Career Dev. Except. Individ. 1:88–96.

This article delineates a set of guidelines to be used by small workshops in obtaining contractual employment for their clients. Covered are the areas, initial steps in work procurement, steps in contract procurement, training clients, fee negotiation, and evaluation. The authors also cite certain types of inherent problems in this type of vocational program.

Chaffin, J. 1969. Production rate as a variable in the job success or failure of educable mentally retarded adolescents. Except. Child. 35:533–538.

Production rate has been shown to be important to successful employment. The 58 individuals participating in a special education and vocational rehabilitation project were preassessed by project staff as being "probably successful" or "probably not successful" in a work setting. Ten job sites supplied by employers who agreed to keep individual work production records were manned by 10 pairs of workers; one of each pair had been assessed as being potentially unsuccessful in a work setting. Criteria for success were based on the assessment provided by the employer's estimation of success, determined by a final interview after the study. In every case, the subject judged successful by the employer had a higher production rate than the subject judged unsuccessful. In a second experimental manipulation, clients from the first study were again placed in work settings in pairs, but intervention techniques were implemented to raise the production rates of previously judged unsuccessful clients and to decrease the rates of those previously judged successful to the level of the unsuccessful. Employer judgment of the success of an employee again appeared to be significantly influenced by the production rate of the employee.

Cohen, J. S. 1962. An analysis of vocational failures of mental retardates placed in the community after a period of institutionalization. Am. J. Ment. Defic. 65:371–375.

An analysis was made of factors relating to 73 unsuccessful placements of 57 workers who had been placed on an extended community work leave from a residential unit. The reasons for the return of these clients to the residential setting include a number of incidents beyond the control of either client or placement worker (illness, inadequacy of living quarters, parental complaints, and the seasonal nature of the placements) as well as factors related to the lack of readiness of the client for placement (inappropriate adjustment to the community, sexual and behavior problems, personal disagreements with employer, poor job attitudes, inattendance, inability to profit or respond to supervision, and inappropriate use of time). Very few of the clients were returned because of lack of skill or strength; in a few cases, physical strength was not sufficient for placement in the job. The results of this survey indicate the need for training in social and independent living skills and for an intermediate situation, where minimal supervision is given while the student is participating in the social and vocational experiences of the community.

Cohen, J. S. 1963. Employer attitudes toward hiring mentally retarded individuals. Am. J. Ment. Defic. 67:705–713.

Certain characteristics of employers and potential employers of the mentally retarded were compared with their expressed attitudes toward hiring retarded persons. Most of the employers questioned had been exposed to the work of mentally retarded persons through the community placement program of a residential setting. Significant negative relationships between the years of schooling and attitudes toward hiring the mentally retarded were found. A realistic concept of mental retardation appeared to have no effect on the favorable or unfavorable outlook of the individual on hiring the mentally retarded. The acquisition of accurate information does not appear to ensure an accepting attitude in employment situations. However, exposure to a successful placement of a mentally retarded citizen significantly influences the attitudes of placements and helps avoid failure in placement.

Cooper, M., and Parker, L. 1973. Rehabilitation — A shift in focus. J. Appl. Rehabil. Counsel. 4:8–14.

A general inconsistency of rehabilitation practice is demonstrated in the failure to measure client changes during the phases of the rehabilitation process while assuming that such changes have occurred. A shift from emphasis on the services offered to an emphasis on the sequential flow of behavioral changes in a client is seen as a prerequisite to maximum benefit to the client. The present index of employment does not assess all aspects of the behavioral changes in the client. A breaking down of complex behaviors into observable and measurable components for instruction and assessment would allow for a structuring of progress and allow measurement of the client's increases in appropriate behaviors. Placement would benefit from the assessment of the client's ability in performing the components of individual jobs.

Crosson, J. 1969. A technique for programming sheltered workshop environments for training severely retarded workers. Am. J. Ment. Defic. 73:814–818.

Sheltered workshops have traditionally been the work setting available to the mentally retarded. Workshops for a variety of reasons have failed to provide work settings that result in the retarded becoming prepared for employment. Reasons for this failure include attempting to match the job to the worker and the lack of planned training to better prepare the worker with skills needed to complete assigned tasks at standard. A training program that makes use of a direct application of principles of operant training in a work-training environment is described. This mode of training can result in retarded workers learning to perform vocational tasks at acceptable standards of speed and quality. It is concluded that workshops and vocational training programs of the retarded should make use of behavioral management procedures to effectively develop work potential.

Flannagan, T. 1974. Whatever happened to job placement? Vocat. Guid. Q. 22:209–213.

Reasons for the periodic decline in interest in the placement process are reviewed. Activities that should occur in placement procedures are defined as any activity that will help a client become affixed in a satisfactory job with a maximum level of participation by the client. General "dos" and "don'ts" are considered in working toward efficient job placement, and a number of job leads are listed.

Friedenberg, W., and Martin, A. 1977. Prevocational training of the severely retarded using task analysis. Ment. Retard. 15:16–20.

A task analysis approach to training used with two severely retarded adults on a task requiring multiple, multidimensional discrimination is described. The task analysis approach to training is adapted from research information indicating that actual work tasks and precision training methods are the most effective means of evaluating the severely retarded. The results of training indicate that both students reached criterion level of performance in a short period of training; these results are attributed to the task approach to training. Production problems indicate that tangible reinforcement may be needed to retain standard levels of production for non-reinforcing tasks. Recommendations based on the results of the research are made for the use of task analysis before initiating a training program.

Fuhriman, A., and Pappas, J. 1971. Behavioral intervention strategies for employment counseling. J. Employ. Counsel. 8:117–124.

Discussion of a hypothetical illustration of the application of goal setting, contingency management, counter-conditioning procedures, and social systems intervention stresses the need for these procedures to be part of the repertoire of the employment counselor. Steps to be taken in the use of these techniques with clients include the identification of target behavior agreement with conditions and desired level of acceptable performance. Contracts in these areas may provide additional incentive to alter behavior. Intervention strategies that eliminate or suppress error-production anxiety levels or poor discrimination should be developed. The alteration of the working environment to facilitate change in behavior may be necessary.

Galvin, D. E. 1977. Job placement: An unseemly occupation? J. Appl. Rehabil. Counsel. 7:198–207.

The benefits of work to the individual's social, psychological, and economic welfare are of particular significance to the handicapped worker. However, persons with handicaps constitute one of the most underprivileged subgroups in education and employment, with only 36% of the handicapped U.S. population between ages 17 and 65 being included in the labor force. The specific expectations of clients, family members, and referral agencies of the vocational rehabilitation agency in assisting in the placement include expert guidance in choosing, preparing for, and finding rewarding and satisfying work. Specific complaints include the low incidence of placement or acceptance for clients placed in work settings with low wages, few benefits and irregular periods of employment, and the deficiencies in job development and placement skills of the rehabilitation counselors. Counselors have not been provided with the skills and support systems needed to be effective or comfortable with job placements. Recommendations for remediation of these deficiencies include the development of placement plans specifying objectives, creation of relevant activities and inservice training procedures required to implement the plans by the district office supervisors, and the possible utilization of specialists in the areas of employer relationships and maintenance, job development, and placement, who would serve as consultants and advisors for the counselor, with whom the ultimate responsibility of placement would remain.

Gold, M. W. 1972. Stimulus factors in skill training of the retarded on a complex assembly task: Acquisition, transfer, and retention. Am. J. Ment. Defic. 76:517–526.

The transfer of learning from the acquisition of a 15-piece bicycle brake assembly to a 24-piece bicycle brake task was evaluated on 64 mentally retarded individuals in a sheltered workshop. The use of color coding with the experimental group was assessed for effect upon acquisition of the task, transfer of the task to a more complex task, and retention of learning. The control group was evaluated using the parts of the training brake as they came from the factory — form only. Training for overlearning was provided to one-half the members of each of the experimental and control group, 20 times past criterion. It was found that the color-form group learned the learning task significantly faster than the form only group and that overlearning did not affect transfer. A 1-year retention study demonstrated the significant superiority of the color-form overlearning group.

Gold, M. W. 1973. Factors affecting production by the retarded: Base rate. Ment. Retard. 11:41–45.

Retarded individuals in a sheltered workshop setting were to complete a complex assembly task (14-piece bicycle brake). No external reinforcement was used in training. Mean production rates and error rates were well within accepted standards. Implications of this training are stated in comparisons to traditional beliefs regarding the training and performance of retarded individuals in vocational areas. It is stated that the completion of the task itself is a highly reinforcing factor for many retarded workers and that it is not necessary to depend on external reinforcement to increase training. It is further stated that rate of acquisition does not correlate significantly with rate of production. It is concluded that use of current evaluation tests and practices have limited meaning with the retarded and that the capabilities of the retarded to perform vocational tasks should be investigated further in light of this research.

Gold, M. W. 1973. Research on the vocational habilitation of the retarded: The present, the future. In N. R. Ellis (ed.), International Review of Research in Mental Retardation, Vol. 6. Academic Press, New York.

This paper is a comprehensive review of research information available on the vocational evaluation and training of the retarded. Research information is reviewed both in terms of its implications for teaching the retarded and in terms of societal expectations of the retarded. Traditional means of evaluating the vocational potential of retarded persons are found to be ineffective. It is recommended that evaluation of the retarded be based on their performance when exposed to well defined behavioral management techniques. Numerous demonstrations of the utility of this approach are reviewed. It is concluded that the retarded are a population who have been denied vocational services because of inaccurate expectations and weak training methods and environments. The vocational future of the retarded and their admission into the vocational rehabilitation system will depend on the methods of evaluation and training to which they are exposed.

Gold, M. W., and Barclay, C. R. 1973. The effects of verbal labels on the acquisition and retention of a complex assembly task. Train. School Bull. 70:38–42.

A procedure in which each discrimination involved in a complex assembly task was verbally labeled was implemented, with the retention of an essentially nonverbal procedure for correcting errors. The study was limited to the effects of labels as they would occur in a classroom or workshop. It was found that the use of verbal labels in training had no effect on the retention of the learned procedure, but an overall superiority of the group who had received training using verbal cues on discrimination errors was observed. The facilitation of both acquisition and retention of discriminations is effected through the use of verbal labeling of discriminations.

Gold, M. W., and Barclay, C. R. 1973. The learning of difficult visual discrimination by the moderately and severely retarded. Ment. Retard. 11:9–11.

The ability of moderately and severely retarded individuals to learn difficult visual discriminations without the use of jigs or other prosthetic devices is demonstrated through the use of easy-to-hard sequencing. A control group instructed on the original discrimination failed to learn the discrimination, while those being instructed through an easy-to-hard sequencing of discrimination learned the discrimination. Implementation of the sequencing with the control group after learning had been demonstrated by the experimental group resulted in the learning of the task by all but two members, who demonstrated the concept of a failure set by failing to learn the task.

Halpern, A. 1973. General unemployment and vocational opportunities for EMR individuals. Am. J. Ment. Defic. 78:123–127.

An examination of the data from two broadly based studies concerning the vocational adjustment of educable retarded persons yields evidence that general community unemployment does not always have adverse impact on job opportunities for retarded workers. A follow-up of the terminators from a high school work experience project and the evaluation of 43 federally funded work-study projects were involved in assessing the conditions surrounding employment. It was found that in periods of high community unemployment, new mentally retarded workers would also experience high unemployment levels, but that retarded workers currently employed showed no higher risk of losing employment than other workers. It was concluded that in situations where mentally retarded persons have received effective prevocational training and placement services, their vocational opportunities can be substantially enhanced, even under conditions of general economic hardship.

Hardy, R., and Cull, J. (eds.). 1973. Vocational Evaluation for Rehabilitation Services. Charles C Thomas Publisher, Springfield, Ill.

This book was developed for use by the professional in working with vocational evaluation procedures. Primary topic headings included in the book are as follows: an overview of evaluation, vocational evaluation and professionalism, vocational evaluation procedures, and evaluation in speciality areas. Information is provided on the expanding role of evaluation in the vocational rehabilitation process, and evaluation tools, such as work samples and the Dictionary of Occupation Titles, are discussed. It is concluded that vocational evaluation procedures and the information gained from evaluation are of significant importance in the vocational and rehabilitation process.

Huddle, D. 1967. Work performance of trainables as influenced by competition, cooperation and monetary reward. Am. J. Ment. Defic. 71:198–211.

The effects of monetary rewards and manipulation of job conditions were studied on the industrial task performance of trainable retarded workers. The division of the sample group into individual workers, competitive workers, and cooperative workers was the instrument for assessing the relative efficacy of these work conditions. It was found that the reward group performed significantly better than the group receiving no monetary reward; however no differences in the work performance of the subgroups were found significant. Anecdotal and observational records postulate a possible acceleration of work rate resulting from interclient competition which was self-initiated.

Irvin, L., and Bellamy, G. T. 1977. Manipulation of stimulus features in vocational skill training of the severely retarded: Relative efficacy. Am. J. Ment. Defic. 81:486–491.

The relative effectiveness of three methods of teaching a difficult visual discrimination task was evaluated with 51 severely retarded adults. The addition and reduction of large cue differences on the relevant form dimensions, the addition and fading of a redundant factor, such as a color dimension, and a combination of the two techniques were the three procedures assessed. A significant difference between the three interventions was seen in both the number of trials and the number of errors made before reaching criterion. The combination of cue redundancy and enlargement of relevant dimension proved to be the most effective, and the use of cue redundancy was the second most effective method.

Jens, K., and Shores, R. 1969. Behavioral graphs as reinforcers for work behavior of mentally retarded adolescents. Educ. Train. Ment. Retard. 4:21–26.

The motivational value of behavioral graphs and progress charts was investigated in the work performance of retarded adolescents on two sheltered workshop tasks. The use of an assisted self-charting of work production rates as an intervention tool was contrasted with the use of verbal prompts to begin work. Behavioral graphs were revealed to be a motivational factor in increasing the production rate of these subjects, as demonstrated by the increase and decrease in production rates upon introduction and removal of the graphing procedure.

Jones, R. J., and Azrin, N. H. 1973. An experimental application of a social reinforcement approach to the problem of job-finding. J. Appl. Behav. Anal. 6:345–353.

The employment process is commonly conceived of as matching the work requirements with the skills of the best qualified applicants. An alternative conception is proposed that social factors play a major role in the process. A survey of 90 graduate students was conducted to determine the extent to which job seekers rely on information, influence, and assistance of personal associates to locate and secure employment. It was found that two-thirds of the job leads came from friends, relatives, or acquaintances who knew of a specific opening, were themselves employed by the firm, or actively influenced the hiring process. An experimental evaluation was made of "Information Reward" advertisement procedures for motivating community residents to report unpublicized openings. It was found that the "Information Reward" procedure produced ten times as many job leads and eight times as many placements as a no-reward control advertisement. It is concluded that the employment process depends largely on factors unrelated to job skills and that more empirical research is necessary on the technology of job finding.

Karan, O. C. 1976. Contemporary views on vocational evaluation practices with the mentally retarded. *In* O. C. Karan, P. Wehman, A. Renzaglia, and R. Schutz (eds.), Habilitation Practices with the Severely Developmentally Disabled, Vol. I. University of Wisconsin, Madison.

The Rehabilitation Act of 1973 places a priority on services to the severely disabled. Problems confronted in implementing the Act include lack of guidelines for the counselor and the stress on employability as a goal. Retarded individuals are frequently denied rehabilitation services because of faulty evaluation procedures. Reasons are stated why using evaluation for the purpose of making predictions based on current behavior repertoires frequently denies services to the retarded. It is recommended that evaluation be used as an opportunity to teach needed vocational and independent living behaviors.

Karen, R. L. 1974. Behavior modification in a sheltered workshop for severely retarded students. Am. J. Ment. Defic. 79:338–347.

As a follow-up to research findings that the severely retarded can be effectively trained to perform vocational tasks through use of behavior modification techniques, a study was designed using a token economy system and environmental adjustments to the work area. A complex multistep production task was used. Use of a token system of reinforcement resulted in increases in the mean production rate and decreases in the mean error rate. Production gains did not drop significantly when the environmental modifications (screening clients from general work population) were removed. It is concluded that behavior modification techniques are effective behavior change agents for the retarded and that training staff are positively affected by the gains seen in their clients through use of behavior modification.

Keil, E. C., and Barbee, J. R. 1973. Behavior modification and training the disadvantaged job interviewee. Vocat. Guid. Q. 22:50–55.

In a personal job interview, disadvantaged clients tend to exhibit apprehension, low verbal production, and a fear of self-disclosure. It is believed that a program can be developed to train disadvantaged clients to improve their job-interviewing skills and obtain jobs more quickly and keep them longer. Videotaped pre-interviews were employed as an intervention with 30 disadvantaged adults. Counselor evaluation and self-evaluation based on these tapes resulted in the shaping of interview behaviors using role reversals and social and verbal reinforcement. Magazines were provided for control subjects' use in the interim.

McCarthy, W. 1976. Exploration of skills associated with successful functioning of retarded individuals in a sheltered workshop. Educ. Train. Ment. Retard. 11:23–31.

The tasks performed in a sheltered workshop are more repetitious, place fewer and less stringent demands on the worker, and give the worker less contact with nonhandicapped persons than do tasks found in community employment. The use of group profiles may aid in understanding the type of training necessary for more desirable community settings. On-the-spot evaluation, interviews with clients, and closed circuit television were used as alternative methods of evaluating the potential employability of retarded workers. Perceptual motor skills were found to have greater association with employability in the sheltered workshop setting than were verbal skills and were considered the more important cluster of skills in this setting. In community settings, verbal ability and production of the worker, personality, and attitudes were found to be the more important skills and attributes in employment. Training for employability might profit from an emphasis on conceptual and perceptual strengths and weakness of the clients, in general, and on self-concept and the ability to ask for help when needed.

McClure, D. P. 1972. Placement through improvement of clients' job seeking skills. J. Appl. Rehabil. Counsel. 3:188–196.

A more effective and efficient approach to assisting clients in obtaining employment is indicated in view of the probable growth of the rehabilitation client pool, the shortage of qualified personnel, and the changing concept of effective counseling. Many clients, even those having acquired marketable skills, require a great deal of counselor time during the job placement phase as a result of their lack of success in initial interviews with employers. A number of clients with this experience were involved in a 2-day intensive small group training for job-seeking skills. This intensive classroom training was designed to increase job-seeking skills and the number of placements for the intervention group, and to decrease the time required in aiding the client in obtaining employment. Training on sources of job leads, interview preparation application blanks, problem questions, and job interviews was included. It was found that the experimental group, who received this intensive training averaged 10.1 days to placement, in comparison with the 19.0 days of the control group.

McDonald, D. J. 1974. The rehabilitation counselor: A resource person to industry: A revitalized approach to selective placement. J. Appl. Rehabil. Counsel. 5:3–7.

The role of the rehabilitation counselor in selective placement situations is seen to be that of a coordinator of all placement efforts. The responsibility of making contacts with employers and of specifying the placement needs and assets of his or her client is that of the rehabilitation counselor. The presentation of the rehabilitation counselor as a resource for the employer is an important part of establishing a working relationship. The counselor may serve as a resource to an employer by making the community resources and his or her own resources available. The first step in making the employer aware of the potential of handicapped clients should include a tour and analysis of the physical plant by the counselor. Through observation and analysis, the counselor should make recommendations to the employer concerning the potential use of handicapped individuals in certain jobs and possibly the efficiency of subcontracting certain tasks to sheltered workshops.

MacMillan, D. 1977. Mental Retardation in School and Society. Little, Brown & Co., Boston.

This book is a comprehensive presentation of the societal and educational issues regarding the mentally retarded in light of the implications of PL 94-142, court decisions regarding the retarded, and the work of advocacy groups for the retarded. The presentation deemphasizes the biomedical aspects of mental retardation. It is intended for use as an introductory text for students who are interested in the psychological and educational issues regarding retardation. Primary topic areas discussed include: overview of mental retardation, causes of retardation, assessment, diagnosis and placement, characteristics of the retarded, and their education, training, and treatment. Extensive reference information is included for the topic areas. It is concluded that the pointing of services for the retarded toward a goal of normalcy is a difficult but appropriate goal to seek.

Mallik, K., and Sablowsky, R. 1970. Model for placement-job laboratory approach. J. Rehabil. 41:14–20.

With appropriate work assignments and provision of the necessary adaptive aids, the motivated severely handicapped individual is as productive as a nonhandicapped individual on the same job. A procedure that facilitates adequate adaptation and appropriate placement should enter into the analysis of the job. This must occur on site and include specification of criteria for the selection, training adaptation, and placement of clients. The functional aspects of each job must be considered, particularly in the case of employment for the physically impaired. Analysis should encompass considerations of the job site environment, including access, height of equipment, and physical strength needed in performing tasks, and alternative methods of performing tasks if necessary. Assessment of the client's level of physical and mental functioning as related to the job tasks is aided by the job analysis.

Mithaug, D., Hagmeur, L., and Haring, N. 1977. The relationship between training activities and job placement in vocational education for the severely and profoundly handicapped. AAESPH Rev. 2.

This article points out that use of a generalized training program for the severely and profoundly handicapped frequently results in the trainees being unqualified for specific job areas available to them in the community. It is recommended that long range job analysis be done before training is initiated. The results of the job analysis will provide training programs with specific information concerning jobs available to the handicapped in the community. Training will then be geared toward the potentials of the individual students and the job needs in the community. A pilot study using this approach is discussed, and a survey instrument developed from the study is included for use by others in assessing needed job skills.

Perrin, T. 1977. Job seeking skills training for adult retarded clients. J. Appl. Rehabil. Counsel. 8:181–192.

Various visual aids and group and individual exercises were implemented by instructors in a program designed to teach job-seeking skills. The benefit-cost ratio of providing such instruction was found to be sufficient to support the inclusion of such measures in rehabilitation services programs.

O'Neill, C., and Bellamy, G. T. 1978. Evaluation of a procedure for teaching saw chain assembly to a severely retarded. Ment. Retard. 16:37–41.

The relationship between learning difficult vocational tasks and defined training procedures was explored in a demonstration of the potential work behavior of the retarded. A severely retarded woman was trained in the assembly of an 11-part chain saw. Training involved the use of a parts bin, in which the parts were stored in order of assembly, and a platform upon which the client moved a wooden block to mark her place in the assembly. A combination of modeling, guidance, and reinforcement procedures was demonstrated to have produced learning of the task. It was found that the segments of the task trained last required less teaching time, suggesting generalization of learning.

Pumo, R., Sehl, R., and Cogan, R. 1966. Job readiness: Key to placement. J. Rehabil. 32:18–19.

Selection, location, and maintenance of an employment placement are of equal importance in the placement of a handicapped person in gainful employment. In 1965 the Rehabilitation Services department of Toledo Goodwill Services took a survey of the merits of their clinic. The clients, whose handicaps included mental retardation, emotional disturbance, and cerebral palsy and orthopedic impairments, were required to have completed vocational training and to have acquired at least one marketable skill. Six 1-day sessions over a 4-week period were divided into the topics of job applications, job readiness, personal cleanliness, job finding methods, and employment offices. Instructional methods included self- and client-initiated feedback, self- and peer-recording of errors, and correct performances in role plays. The final three sessions were designated job-finding sessions, and the 11 enrollees were required to make a specific number of employee contacts, keeping an accurate record of each contact. An analysis of the resulting placements yielded the gainful employment of nine clients, with the average number of employer contacts being 15.

Renzaglia, A., Wehman, P., Schutz, R., and Karan, O. C. 1976. Use of cue redundancy and positive reinforcement to accelerate production in two profoundly retarded workers. In O. C. Karan, P. Wehman, A. Renzaglia, and R. Schutz (eds.), Habilitation Practices with the Severely Developmentally Disabled, Vol. I. University of Wisconsin, Madison.

A combination of cue redundancy and positive reinforcement as employed in an effort to accelerate the production rate of two retarded workers. Cue redundancy use in production rate refers to additional cues defining the work rate necessary to meet criteria. In this study a kitchen buzzer set at fixed intervals defined the necessary work rate. Predetermined units of reinforcement were also established. Increases in production rate were demonstrated using these forms of cue redundancy and reinforcement.

Sarkees, M. D. 1979. An overview of selected evaluation systems for use in assessing the vocational attitudes of handicapped individuals. Diagnostique 1:10–13.

Vocational evaluation is described as a comprehensive process of utilizing real or simulated job samples to gather data relative to an individual's vocational aptitude and interests. The primary objective is to identify a handicapped or disadvantaged person's vocational potential. Several commercial vocational evaluation systems are discussed. Although the author recognizes many components that are involved in a high quality of vocational evaluation, work sample data and situational assessment are noted as being particularly important in obtaining pertinent vocational aptitude data.

Schilit, J., and Pace, T. J. 1978. High-risk employment and the mentally retarded student. Career Dev. Except. Individ. 1:97–103.

An investigation was made concerning the feasibility of preparing educable mentally retarded students for high risk employment in the metal processing industry. High risk employment is defined as any position that requires an age minimum and is associated with higher than average possibility of injury or death while on the job. In a simulated setting the participants were assessed in terms of time and speed of mold preparation and low amounts of wastage while operating a jolt-squeeze molder. The results suggest that educable mentally retarded students are more vocationally competent than previously perceived and that special educators have been underpreparing them for the working world.

Schroeder, S. 1972. Parametric effects of reinforcement frequency, amount of reinforcement, and required response force on sheltered workshop behavior. J. Appl. Behav. Anal. 5:431–441.

Three experimental manipulations of reinforcement contingencies were implemented in an automated sheltered workshop setting. The first demonstrated a correlation between a decrease in the reinforcement frequency on a fixed interval schedule and a substantial decrease in production rates and level of tool use. A decrease in reinforcer on a fixed ratio showed an increase in production rate and usage. The second demonstrated that a high response force requirement on a small ratio schedule of reinforcement maintains output better than a large ratio. If both the ratio and the work requirements are high, output is significantly reduced. The third experimental condition demonstrated a large decrease in production and tool usage when reinforcement ratios were increased, regardless of the schedule

of reinforcement. On a task requiring too much effort, the fading of reinforcement results in a decrease in performance.

Spooner, F., et al. 1976. Acquisition of complex assembly skills through the
use of systematic training procedures. AAESPH Rev. 1.

It is stated that work activity centers frequently fail to use controlled training procedures in teaching trainees to perform vocational tasks. As a result
the severely handicapped have limited opportunity for skill development,
and production and quality levels of work suffer. This article reviews a
study that used systematic training techniques to teach complex industrial
acquisition through use of backward chaining in a training setting removed from the regular work station, presentation of total task, and the
development of criterion levels of performance at the regular work stations
after acquisition has been reached. The five trainees involved in the study
reached criterion level of performance after training through this systematic behavior management program. It is concluded that non–profes-
sionally educated trainers can effectively use behavior management techniques to affect significant behavior in severely handicapped clients.

Starkey, P. D. 1969. Job Placement: The rehabilitation counselor's dilemma.
Rehabil. Counsel. Bull. 12:211–213.

A number of dilemmas face the rehabilitation counselor in the area of
placement. Among those discussed are the professionalism of placement
procedures, pressure for placements, the shrinking job market, and the criteria for success in rehabilitation. Where in the counseling continuum
placement belongs is questioned.

Tate, B., and Baroff, G. 1977. Training the mentally retarded in the production of a complex product: A demonstration of work potential. Except.
Child. 33:405–408.

Training on the assembly of relay panels and similar psychological apparatus was provided in a workshop for mildly and moderately retarded residents of a state institution. Steady work was provided for the residents, for
whom the entry criterion was willingness to work. The task involved 20
operations on an assembly line model, including the assembly of four telephone type relays, the connection of wire to relays, and the making and
soldering of 62 wire connections. The use of positive reinforcement, jigs,
and color coding and the introduction of a token economy resulted in acquisition of the tasks by workers.

Vocational Research Institute. (undated). VIEWS: A Vocational Evaluation System for the Mentally Retarded (brochure). Jewish Employment and Vocational Service, Philadelphia.

VIEWS is the Vocational Information and Evaluation Work Samples system designed specifically for the mentally retarded. It consists of 16 individual work samples that vary from simple sorting and assembly tasks to complex tasks requiring tool usage. The VIEWS evaluation process is a four-step procedure covering orientation, demonstration, training, and production. Norms were established on a retarded population. Evaluation is accomplished through assessment of vocational interests and observed behavior in a simulated work setting, measurement of rate of learning, quality of work, and productivity, and utilization of industrial time standards. It is concluded that use of the VIEWS evaluation system will assist service delivery staff in making training and job placements for the retarded.

Walls, R. T., Tseng, M. S., and Zarin, H. 1976. Time and money for vocational rehabilitation of clients with mild, moderate and severe mental retardation. Am. J. Ment. Defic. 80:595–601.

A national sample of mildly, moderately, and severely retarded vocational rehabilitation clients as selected for a study of the relative levels of time and money involved in the training and placement of retarded workers. Half of the sample had been closed as clients of rehabilitation services with a label of rehabilitated, meaning that they had completed several steps in the rehabilitation process and were suitably employed for a minimum of 30 days. The second half was designated nonrehabilitated, not having met their requirements. It was found that, on the average, the same amount of services was rendered to both the rehabilitated and nonrehabilitated groups in the months from acceptance to closure, including the months of training. The rehabilitated clients, however, had received more time in referral stages of placement. The largest amount of service time and money was consumed by the nonrehabilitated severely retarded group, although the severely retarded rehabilitated clients received no more services than did their counterparts among the moderately and mildly retarded.

Wehman, P. 1976. Vocational training of the severely retarded: Expectations and potential. Rehabil. Lit. 37:233–236.

Legislative acts, such as the Rehabilitation Act of 1973 and PL 93-112, have mandated that vocational services be provided to the severely handicapped. Severely retarded clients have not received assistance through vocational rehabilitation service systems, in part because of a lack of understanding of the behavioral characteristics of the severely retarded, low expectations for their work skills, and their social skill deficits. Components of an effective vocational training program for the retarded are discussed. It is stated that behaviorally oriented rehabilitation counselors are needed to work with the severely retarded, and suggestions are given concerning the development of the behaviorally oriented counselor. Conclusions are drawn concerning the vocational outlook for the severely retarded.

Wehman, P., Renzaglia, A., Schutz, R., and Karan, O. C. 1976. Stimulating productivity in two profoundly retarded workers through mixed reinforcement contingencies. *In* O. C. Karan, P. Wehman, A. Renzaglia, and R. Schutz (eds.), Habilitation Practices with the Severely Developmentally Disabled, Vol. I. University of Wisconsin Rehabilitation Research and Training Center, Madison.

Increase in workshop task production with two mentally retarded clients was demonstrated to result from the use of mixed contingencies. The concurrent use of verbal and social reinforcers, and token and edible reinforcers, accelerated work production rates on two tasks, i.e., a drapery hook packaging task and the assembly of a small drapery pulley. An experimental sheltered workshop was the setting for the study, in which the two clients displayed competing behaviors and slow motor movement. Moderate increases in the production rates of the two workers was observed; no relative effectiveness of the methods involved was postulated.

Wehman, P., Schutz, R., and Renzaglia, A., and Karan, O. C. 1976. Use of positive practice to facilitate increased work productivity and instruction following behavior in profoundly retarded adolescents. *In* O. C. Karan, P. Wehman, A. Renzaglia, and R. Schutz (eds.), Habilitation Practices with the Severely Developmentally Disabled, Vol. I. University of Wisconsin Rehabilitation and Research Training Center, Madison.

A demonstration of the successful application of positive practice with profoundly retarded adolescents in increasing the production rate of workers who display high rates of excessive competing behaviors during work periods and in reducing the noncompliant behavior of a worker who consistently refused to follow the work routine was effected by two experiments. In the first, penny and social reinforcement for appropriate work rates was administered, with positive practice and rapid physical guidance through the workshop task being contingent on not reaching the criterion work rate. An increase in production rate and simultaneous reduction in competing behaviors occurred as a result of these procedures. The second study involved the selection of four instructions frequently given throughout the work day and the use of positive practice procedures in their acquisition. An increase in instruction following on the four commands — punching the time clock, going to the bathroom, going to work and break, and starting work — was demonstrated.

3 5282 00082 5466